Math and Literature
Grades 4-6
Second Edition

Math and Literature

Grades 4–6
Second Edition

Rusty Bresser

Introduction by

Marilyn Burns

Math Solutions Publications
Sausalito, CA

Math Solutions Publications
A division of
Marilyn Burns Education Associates
150 Gate 5 Road, Suite 101
Sausalito, CA 94965
www.mathsolutions.com

Figure 17–1 on page 164: From *The $1.00 Word Riddle Book* by Marilyn
Burns. © 1990 by Math Solutions Publications.

Library of Congress Cataloging-in-Publication Data
Bresser, Rusty.
    Math and literature. Grades 4–6 / Rusty Bresser.
        p.   cm.
    Includes bibliographical references and index.
    ISBN 0-941355-68-3   (alk. paper)
    1. Mathematics—Study and teaching (Elementary)   2. Children's literature
in mathematics education.   I. Title.
    QA135.6.B737 2004
    372.7—dc22
                                    2004014370

ISBN-10: 0-941355-68-3
ISBN-13: 978-0-941355-68-1

Editor: Toby Gordon
Production: Melissa L. Inglis
Cover and interior design: Catherine Hawkes/Cat and Mouse
Composition: TechBooks
Printed in the United States of America on acid-free paper
08   07   06   ML   3   4   5

A Message from Marilyn Burns

We at Math Solutions Professional Development believe that teaching math well calls for increasing our understanding of the math we teach, seeking deeper insights into how children learn mathematics, and refining our lessons to best promote students' learning.

Math Solutions Publications shares classroom-tested lessons and teaching expertise from our faculty of Math Solutions Inservice instructors as well as from other respected math educators. Our publications are part of the nationwide effort we've made since 1984 that now includes

- more than five hundred face-to-face inservice programs each year for teachers and administrators in districts across the country;
- annually publishing professional development books, now totaling more than fifty titles and spanning the teaching of all math topics in kindergarten through grade 8;
- four series of videotapes for teachers, plus a videotape for parents, that show math lessons taught in actual classrooms;
- on-site visits to schools to help refine teaching strategies and assess student learning; and
- free online support, including grade-level lessons, book reviews, inservice information, and district feedback, all in our quarterly *Math Solutions Online Newsletter*.

For information about all of the products and services we have available, please visit our Web site at *www.mathsolutions.com*. You can also contact us to discuss math professional development needs by calling (800) 868-9092 or by sending an e-mail to *info@mathsolutions.com*.

We're always eager for your feedback and interested in learning about your particular needs. We look forward to hearing from you.

Math Solutions.
PUBLICATIONS

Contents

Contents

Acknowledgments

Special thanks to the teachers who allowed me to teach lessons in their classrooms: Dinah Brown, Palmquist Elementary School, Oceanside, California; Laura Chandler, Richland Elementary School, San Marcos, California; Pat Feist, Laurel Elementary School, Oceanside, California; Robin Gordon, Florence Elementary School, San Diego, California; Linda Lowe, Richland Elementary School, San Marcos, California; Lawrence Pallant, Laurel Elementary School, Oceanside, California; Patti Reynolds, Paloma Elementary School, San Marcos, California; Leslie Robinson, Laurel Elementary School, Oceanside, California; Danielle Ross, Park School, Mill Valley, California; Carol Schurlock, Knob Hill Elementary School, San Marcos, California; Carole Smith, Palmquist Elementary School, Oceanside, California; and John Swaim, Palmquist Elementary School, Oceanside, California.

Special thanks to those teachers who contributed their insights and expertise by sharing their classroom experiences with me: Caren Holtzman, Laurel Elementary School, Oceanside, California; Patty Montgomery, Pacifica Elementary School, Oceanside, California; Shelley Ferguson, East Lake Elementary School, Chula Vista, California; Suzanne McGrath, East Lake Elementary School, Chula Vista, California; Maryann Wickett, Paloma Elementary School, San Marcos, California; Juli Tracy, Laurel Elementary School, Oceanside, California; Pam Long, North Terrace Elementary School, Oceanside, California; and Danielle Gilligan, Palmquist Elementary School, Oceanside, California.

Thanks also to those people who helped me make this book a reality:

To Marilyn Burns, who gave me encouragement, critical feedback, and guidance. Without her, this book would not have been possible.

To Stephanie Sheffield, who gave me support and feedback during the entire writing process.

To Maryann Wickett, who was there every step of the way, listening to me and encouraging me.

To Annette Raphel, whose ideas are behind many of the activities in this book.

To Toby Gordon and Melissa Inglis, for seeing the book through production.

To my friends and family.

To my parents, for supporting me in my education.

To the people at the White Rabbit Bookstore, La Jolla, California, for their help in searching for children's books.

To Math Solutions consultants for sharing their wisdom and friendship.

To Kent Terrell, a special thanks.

Introduction

For months before publishing this resource of classroom-tested
lessons, I was surrounded by children's books. They were
stacked practically up to my ears on my desk and additional
piles were all around on the floor. It took some fancy shuffling at
times to make space for other things that needed my attention. But
I never complained. I love children's books and it was pure pleasure
to be immersed in reading them and then teaching, writing, revising,
and editing lessons that use them as springboards for teaching children mathematics.

This book is one in our new Math Solutions Publications series
for teaching mathematics using children's literature, and I'm pleased
to present the complete series:

Math and Literature, Grades K–1
Math and Literature, Grades 2–3
Math and Literature, Grades 4–6, Second Edition
Math and Literature, Grades 6–8
Math and Nonfiction, Grades K–2
Math and Nonfiction, Grades 3–5

More than ten years ago we published my book *Math and
Literature (K–3)*. My premise for that book was that children's books
can be effective vehicles for motivating children to think and reason
mathematically. I searched for books that I knew would stimulate
children's imaginations and that also could be used to teach important math concepts and skills.

After that first book's publication, my colleague Stephanie
Sheffield began sending me the titles of children's books she had discovered and descriptions of the lessons she had taught based on
them. Three years after publishing my book, we published

Stephanie's *Math and Literature (K–3), Book Two*. And the following year we published Rusty Bresser's *Math and Literature (Grades 4–6)*, a companion to the existing books.

Over the years, some of the children's books we initially included in our resources have, sadly, gone out of print. However, other wonderful titles have emerged. For this new series, we did a thorough review of our three original resources. Stephanie and I collaborated on substantially revising our two K–3 books and reorganizing them into two different books, one for grades K–1 and the other for grades 2–3. Rusty produced a second edition of his book for grades 4–6.

In response to the feedback we received from teachers, we became interested in creating a book that would offer lessons based on children's books for middle school students, and we were fortunate enough to find two wonderful teachers, Jennifer M. Bay-Williams and Sherri L. Martinie, to collaborate on this project. I'm pleased to present their book, *Math and Literature, Grades 6–8*.

The two books that round out our series use children's nonfiction as springboards for lessons. Jamee Petersen created *Math and Nonfiction, Grades K–2*, and Stephanie Sheffield built on her experience with the Math and Literature books to team with her colleague Kathleen Gallagher to write *Math and Nonfiction, Grades 3–5*. Hearing nonfiction books read aloud to them requires children to listen in a different way than usual. With nonfiction, students listen to the facts presented and assimilate that information into what they already know about that particular subject. And rather than reading from cover to cover as with fiction, it sometimes makes more sense to read only a small portion of a nonfiction book and investigate the subject matter presented in that portion. The authors of these Math and Nonfiction books are sensitive to the demands of nonfiction and how to present new information in order to make it accessible to children.

We're still fond of the lessons that were based on children's books that are now out of print, and we know that through libraries, the Internet, and used bookstores, teachers have access to some of those books. Therefore, we've made all of the older lessons that are not included in the new series of books available online at *www.mathsolutions.com*. Please visit our Web site for those lessons and for additional support for teaching math.

I'm pleased and proud to present these new books. It was a joy to work on them, and I'm convinced that you and your students will benefit from the lessons we offer.

MARILYN BURNS
2004

Annabelle Swift, Kindergartner

In *Annabelle Swift, Kindergartner* (1991), by Amy Schwartz, Annabelle faces her first day of kindergarten. Armed with (poor) advice from her older sister, she seems to say all the wrong things. After the kindergartners turn in 6¢ each for milk, they begin to count how much they have altogether. The other children give up at around 10¢, but Annabelle counts all the way to $1.08, impressing everyone in the room. The teacher appoints Annabelle milk monitor, and she goes to the school kitchen to collect the milk cartons. Using the information in the book, students figure out how many cartons of milk Annabelle's class purchased. They later work together to solve problems about buying milk for their own class.

MATERIALS

"Do any of you have a younger brother or sister?" I asked Leslie Robinson's fourth-grade class.

Many hands shot up in the air.

"Do any of you have a brother or a sister who is in kindergarten?" I asked them. This time, a few students' hands went up.

"What was it like for your brother or sister on the first day of kindergarten?" I asked.

"My brother cried," Julio said.

"My sister cried till she got there, then she didn't want to go home," added Antoinette.

"Raise your hand if you remember your first day in kindergarten," I said. Nearly all the students raised their hands, giggling and whispering to one another.

"I remember my first day in kindergarten and that was a long, long time ago. I remember that I cried, and my sister had to hold my hand," I said.

Everyone laughed.

"Today I want to share with you a book that's about a kindergartner's first day in school," I said. "Her name is Annabelle, and she has an older sister who's in third grade. But since you're in the fourth grade, let's pretend that her older sister is a fourth grader."

The class listened attentively as I read the story. The students enjoyed hearing Annabelle's older sister, Lucy, teach Annabelle all the "fancy stuff" in preparation for her first day of school. They giggled when Lucy told Annabelle to "ask lots of questions because teachers like that." They were happy for Annabelle when she showed her teacher how smart she was by counting all the children's milk money. At that point, I stopped reading for a moment to ask a question.

"How much money did Annabelle count?" I asked.

"One hundred and eight!" the students responded.

"One hundred and eight what?" I asked.

"One hundred and eight cents!" they answered.

On the board, I wrote:

108 cents

"This is one way to write the total amount of milk money. Does anyone know another way I could write it?" I asked.

"You could write one dollar and eight cents," Bethany suggested. I wrote on the board:

$1.08

"How much did each carton of milk cost?" I asked. The students remembered that each kindergartner had pulled out a nickel and a penny.

"Six cents," they chorused.

I continued reading the story. I reached the part where Annabelle's teacher, Mr. Blum, congratulates Annabelle for having counted all the money and then asks her to take the milk money to the cafeteria. I stopped reading and asked the class a question.

"If Annabelle took one dollar and eight cents to the cafeteria, and each milk cost six cents, how many milks did Annabelle bring back? How could you solve this problem?" I asked.

"You could draw a bunch of milks and put a six on top of each one. Then you could add all the sixes until you got to one dollar and eight cents. Then count the milks," Daryl suggested. I wrote on the board:

Draw milks.

"Does anyone have another idea?" I asked.

"You could guess how many kids are in Annabelle's class," Martin said. "Then divide one dollar and eight cents by that number." I recorded Martin's idea on the board:

Guess and divide to check.

"Does anyone have another idea?" I asked again. I find that if I keep asking for additional ideas, children get the notion that there are many ways to solve problems. I called on Jack.

"I think that one hundred eight times six will equal the number of milks," he said.

"That would be way too many!" Dara declared.

"I'm going to write down all your ideas," I said. "Listen, and then you can try them out later to see if they work." As the students offered suggestions, I recorded them on the board.

"You could use tally marks," Antoinette said.

"How would you use them?" I asked.

"You could circle six tallies at a time till you get to one hundred and eight," she said.

"Then what?" I pushed Antoinette to elaborate further.

"Then I guess you'd have to count the tallies . . . no, the circles," she said, suddenly uncertain. "Yes, you'd count the circles."

"Any other ideas?" I asked.

"I would count by sixes till I got to one hundred and eight," Lea offered.

"How about using a calculator?" Bethany suggested.

"How would you use it?" I asked.

"You could use it to add sixes, like Lea said," Bethany explained.

"Does anyone have another way?" I asked.

"Start at one hundred eight and subtract six at a time until you get to zero," Rolf said.

"Now I'd like you to solve the problem with any one of these methods. Just be sure to choose one that makes sense to you," I said. "Or you can use a method that's different from the ones I listed on the board. But be sure to explain your solution using words and numbers."

The final list on the board looked like this:

Draw milks.
Guess and divide to check.

Multiply.
Use tally marks.
Count by 6s.
Use a calculator.
Start at 108 and subtract.

The students went to work immediately. Most seemed to know which method they wanted to use to solve the problem and started to write. Others read the ideas I had written on the board to decide which one to use.

When I approached Martin, he was starting to divide 108 by 6.

"Explain to me why you're writing one hundred eight divided by six, Martin," I said.

"I know it's a division problem. I'm not sure why I know that, but that's what I think," he answered.

Bethany waved me over and asked me to listen to her read her solution. She had written: *I solved this problem by making tally mark in groups of six to get the sum. The number I got was 18 milks Annabelle gets because theirs 18 kids in her class, and 18 times 6 is $1.08.*

Nichelle drew pictures of milk cartons with six tally marks in each, and she then wrote the number 6 above each carton. (See Figure 1–1.)

"How did you know to draw eighteen milk cartons?" I asked her.

Figure 1–1: Nichelle multiplied 18 × 5, then went back and added the ones.

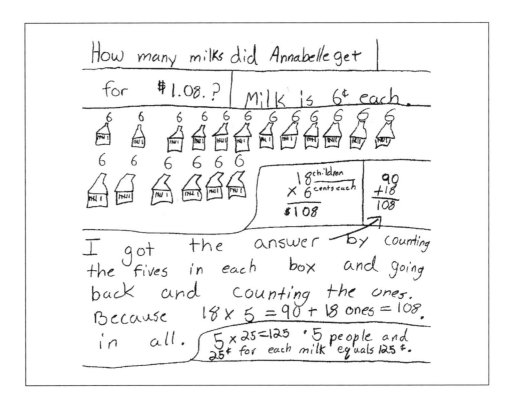

"I kept trying different numbers of milk cartons until it came to one dollar and eight cents," she explained. "What I did was count the fives in each box. Then I went back and counted the ones." She had written: *Because 18 × 5 = 90 + 18 ones = 108 in all.* When I asked Nichelle why she counted the fives first, she said, "Fives are more friendly than sixes."

When I got back to Martin's table, he was just finishing his work.

"How's it going, Martin?" I asked.

"Good! What I did was, I started with one hundred and eight and I subtracted six each time till I got to zero, and I did this eighteen times," he explained. "But I wanted to check my work, so I added eighteen six times and I got a hundred and eight, so I know I'm right."

"I have a question," Erin asked. "Is it OK if I just used words and not numbers to explain my answer?"

"It's OK if the words explain your solution and how you got it," I said. "Why don't you read your paper to me?"

Erin read: "Ten kids would have to pay sixty cents and twenty kids would have to pay a dollar twenty, but a dollar and eight cents is twelve cents less than that, which is two kids less, so that would be eighteen kids and that would be eighteen milks!"

"That makes perfect sense to me," I told her. "But I don't understand why you said you used just words and not numbers. There are lots of numbers in your explanation." I pointed out the numbers.

Erin looked at me with surprise. "But I didn't add or multiply or anything with the numbers," she said.

"How did you figure that ten kids would have to pay sixty cents?" I asked.

"I did it in my head," Erin answered.

"What did you do in your head?" I asked.

Erin responded, "I did ten times six . . . oops! I guess I did multiply, but I just didn't write it down regular." Because she hadn't done traditional arithmetic, Erin thought that she hadn't used numbers.

"Calculating in your head certainly counts for using numbers," I said. "And your explanation makes good sense to me."

Rolf ran up to me and said excitedly, "I've got the answer!" I followed him back to his seat and listened carefully as he explained.

"I got my answer by subtracting by six until I got zero, and the answer is eighteen milks Annabelle got from the lady!" Rolf exclaimed. He proudly showed me the milks he had drawn in the corner of his paper. (See Figure 1–2.)

When all of the children had finished working on the problem, I asked for their attention. "How many milks do you think Annabelle brought back from the cafeteria?" I asked.

Figure 1–2: Rolf used
repeated subtraction to solve
the milk problem.

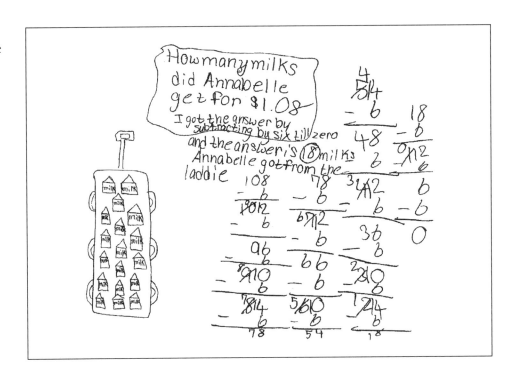

"Eighteen!" everyone responded.

"Are you sure?" I asked. This question made a few students uneasy, and I could tell by the looks on their faces that they were wondering if the answer really was eighteen.

"I want to read the rest of the book to make sure you're all correct," I said. The end of the book revealed the answer. The children applauded when I read the part where the lady in the cafeteria hands Annabelle eighteen little cartons of milk and eighteen straws.

A Second Problem

"Does anyone know how much it costs to buy a milk in our school cafeteria?" I asked after finishing the book.

"Twenty-five cents," several students volunteered.

"Figure out how much it would cost if everyone at your table bought milks today," I said. "Talk to the people at your table, and raise your hands when you have an answer."

After a few minutes, most hands were wiggling in the air. "What did you find out?" I asked.

"It would cost our table one dollar. We counted by twenty-fives. There are four people at our table, so that's a dollar," Ramon reported.

"We figured it like there was a quarter for each person. We came up with seventy-five cents for the three of us," Marcia said.

"We know that twenty-five times four is a dollar. That's how we got it," Jack said.

"Four people equals one dollar, and two more would be a dollar fifty," explained Bethany, who was seated at a table of six children.

"Who can predict what my next mathematical question will be?" I asked.

Many hands shot up. "How much would it cost for our whole class to buy milk?" Antoinette guessed.

"That's right. I want you to figure that out and explain your thinking using words and numbers. You can also draw pictures if you want," I instructed.

As the students started working, I noticed that they were all trying to count the number of people in the room. I stopped them and asked for their attention.

"What do you need to know in order to solve this problem?" I asked.

"How many students there are," Daryl said.

"I'll give you that information. One person is absent, so twenty-seven students are here today," I reported.

Antoinette made a chart for the six tables. She wrote: *I counted all the tables. Then I counted a quarter for each person and I put the money under the table number and then I added all the money together.*

Daryl got the answer by putting the number 25 on top of a drawing of each student. He then added all the numbers to get the answer.

Martin explained his thinking in writing: *I got $6.75 because I multiplied 1 × 27 × 25 = 6.75 but to get that anser I added 10 25s and got 250. Then I added 250 + 250 and got 500. Then added seven 25s and got 175. Then added 500 + 175 = 675.*

Nichelle used tally marks to solve the problem. She wrote: *If you make tallies it will be easy. But only if you count them when you're done.*

Jana kept a running total to get her answer. She made a long vertical list from 1 to 27, showing the cumulative total after each number of milks. (See Figure 1–3.)

Hart added groups of four twenty-fives to get dollars. First he recorded *25¢* too many times, but he erased the extras. He added up all the dollars and then added together the three extra twenty-fives to get $6.75. (See Figure 1–4.)

When the students were finished, they took turns sharing how they had arrived at the answer. This is an important part of the lesson, as the students hear the different ways their peers solved the problem. Hearing other solutions can reinforce for students what they already know and help them learn an easier or different way to find the solution.

When we finished our discussion, Julio raised his hand and asked, "Well, aren't we going to get milks for doing all this work?"

"If you have a quarter," I replied.

Figure 1–3: Jana kept a running tally.

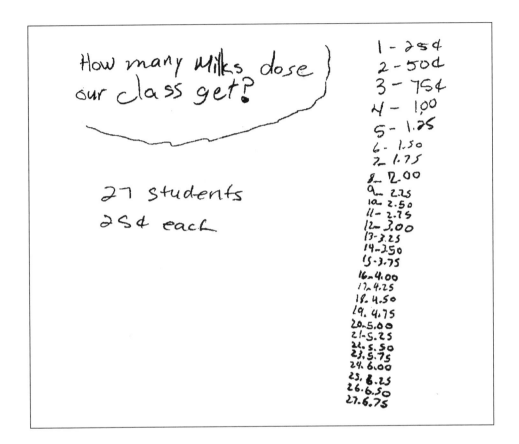

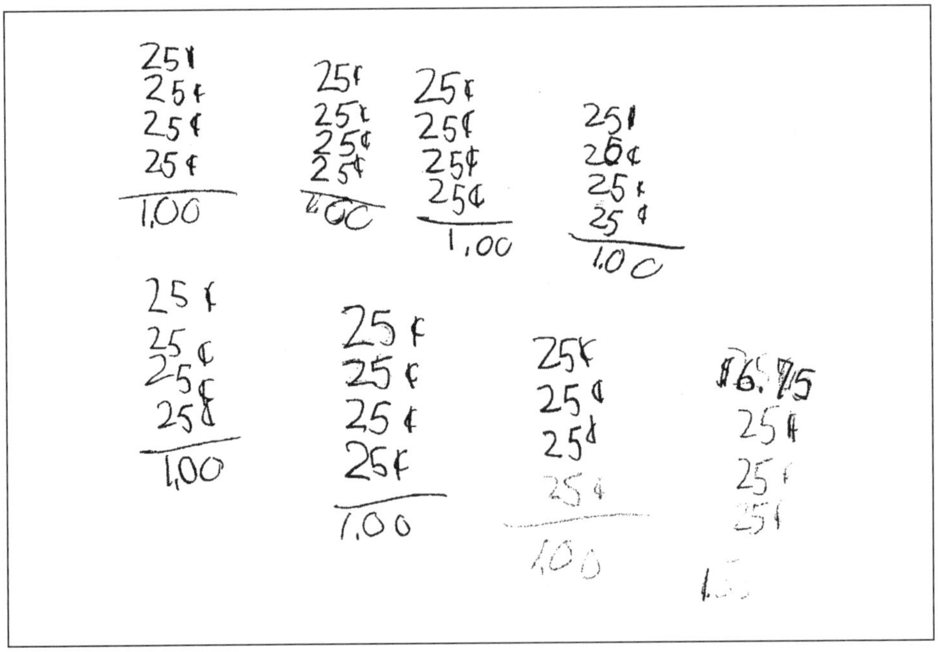

How many Milks dose our class get?

27 students
25¢ each

1 - 25¢
2 - 50¢
3 - 75¢
4 - 1.00
5 - 1.25
6 - 1.50
7 - 1.75
8 - 2.00
9 - 2.25
10 - 2.50
11 - 2.75
12 - 3.00
13 - 3.25
14 - 3.50
15 - 3.75
16 - 4.00
17 - 4.25
18 - 4.50
19 - 4.75
20 - 5.00
21 - 5.25
22 - 5.50
23 - 5.75
24 - 6.00
25 - 6.25
26 - 6.50
27 - 6.75

Figure 1–4: Hart grouped the students' money into dollars, then added to find the total for all twenty-seven students.

25¢
25¢
25¢
25¢
1.00

25¢
25¢
25¢
25¢
1.00

25¢
25¢
25¢
25¢
1.00

25¢
25¢
25¢
25¢
1.00

25¢
25¢
25¢
25¢
1.00

25¢
25¢
25¢
25¢
1.00

25¢
25¢
25¢
25¢
1.00

$6.75
25¢
25¢
25¢

Math and Literature, Grades 4–6

Presenting the Problem to a Sixth-Grade Class

I decided to try the same problem with Laura Chandler's sixth graders. However, I was interested in learning how the students would tackle the problem mentally, without using paper and pencil. Too often, students focus on paper-and-pencil computation and don't get sufficient experience and practice with thinking about numbers and reasoning in their heads.

Before reading the book, I talked with the students about what it was like to have younger brothers and sisters. Some of them loved having younger siblings, and some thought it was "a pain." Most of the students remembered what it was like being a kindergartner on the very first day of school.

The class was completely attentive as I read. When I finished reading the part where Annabelle walks to the cafeteria, I stopped.

"I have a mathematical question," I said. "How many milks did Annabelle bring back to the class? In other words, how many milks did Annabelle buy for one dollar and eight cents?" A few students raised their hands excitedly.

"Wait just a minute," I said. "I want you to solve this problem in a special way. I want you to promise me something. Please raise your right hand and repeat after me." The students all raised their hands.

"I will not use a pencil or paper to solve this problem," I said in a serious voice. The students repeated the pledge, giggling as they spoke.

"You may discuss the problem with the people at your table, but remember not to use paper or pencil," I told them.

"Can we use a calculator?" Cord asked.

"For today's problem, I want you to solve it mentally," I said. "It's important that you learn to reason with numbers in as many ways as possible, and one of those ways is to figure in your head." I said this because I think that it's valuable for students to understand the purpose of their assignments.

The students spent about five minutes sharing their ideas in small groups. When they finished their discussions, I asked for their attention.

"Would anyone like to explain how you solved the problem?" I asked.

"I counted the people in the book," Keir said, with a wry smile on his face. I couldn't tell if he was joking or if he really had counted the children in Annabelle's class when I had showed the picture from the book.

"Let's say you weren't able to see the picture and count the kids in the class. How else might you solve the problem, Keir?" I asked.

"You could count by sixes until you got to one dollar and eight cents," he replied.

"I estimated," Enzo said.

"Tell us how you estimated," I said.

"I guessed seventeen and multiplied seventeen times six and I got a hundred and two. That was too small, so I made it eighteen times six and I got a hundred and eight," he explained.

"I thought of the problem in my head like a division problem," Cord said. "For example, one dollar and eight cents divided by six cents is eighteen. All you do is think 'six goes into ten one time. And ten minus six equals four, so you bring down the eight. Then six goes into forty-eight eight times.' Your answer is eighteen."

"I multiplied six and ten," Cassie explained. "I got sixty, so I did sixty times two. From sixty times two I got one twenty. I knew that was too big, so I did one twenty minus a hundred and eight. I got twelve, and that is two milks. Now I have eighteen milks."

"Is there another way you could solve the problem?" I asked.

"You could start with one hundred eight and keep subtracting six, but that would take a long time," Charlene said.

"I kind of drew a picture of a division problem in my head," Terell offered. "It looked like a regular old division problem. I could see it in my head and I pretended to use a pencil to divide the numbers."

"I started with six times twelve as a guess and that was seventy-two, and it wasn't enough," Trina explained. "So I kept going up, like six times thirteen, six times fourteen, until I got to six times eighteen."

"Now that you've solved the problem mentally, explain in writing exactly what you did to get your answer," I instructed.

When the students finished writing their explanations, I asked them to hand in their papers. (See Figure 1–5.) "Aren't you going to finish the story?" Marcia asked.

"Do you want to hear it?" I asked.

"Yes!" they all responded. Here was a group of very sophisticated sixth graders, begging me to finish *Annabelle Swift, Kindergartner*. It made my day!

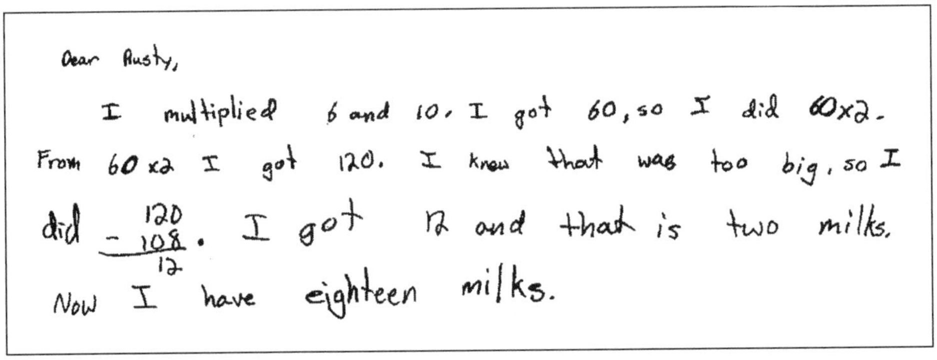

Figure 1–5: Cassie used estimation, multiplication, and subtraction to solve the milk problem.

Dear Rusty,

I multiplied 6 and 10. I got 60, so I did 60×2. From 60×2 I got 120. I knew that was too big, so I did $\frac{120}{-108}$ = 12. I got 12 and that is two milks. Now I have eighteen milks.

Anno's Magic Seeds

In *Anno's Magic Seeds,* by Mitsumasa Anno (1999), a wizard gives Jack two mysterious seeds. The wizard tells Jack that if he bakes and eats one seed, he won't be hungry for a year, and if he buries the other seed, he'll get two new seeds. Jack repeats this process for seven years, then decides to plant both seeds and find something else to eat for a year. The following year he has four seeds. He eats one and buries the other three. The story continues, with the process changing from time to time. This story leads to an activity in which students search for patterns to determine how many seeds Jack gets over ten years and then use their patterns to think about how to predict the number of seeds after longer periods of time.

MATERIALS

After I'd read just a few pages of *Anno's Magic Seeds* to Carole Smith's fourth and fifth graders, Calie had a comment. "I notice a pattern!" she exclaimed.

"Describe the pattern you notice," I said.

"Each year Jack eats one seed, plants one, and gets two magic seeds the following year," Calie explained.

"He's doing the same thing each year," Flint said.

"Does anyone else notice a pattern?" I asked.

"Eats one, plants one, gets two, eats one, plants one, gets two," Deirdre said. "It's a repeating pattern." Others nodded their agreement.

I continued with the story, reading up to the part where Jack realizes that by eating one seed and planting the other, he will continue to get two seeds over and over.

"Jack is going to do something different with the seeds this time," I told the class. "Raise your hand if you have a guess about what he might do next." Many hands shot up. I called on Jansen.

"I think he'll plant both of them," he guessed.

"He might eat both of them," Deirdre said.

"I think he might store them in case there's no food later on," Emily said.

As I read on, the students learned that Jack planted both of the seeds, hoping to get through the winter by eating something different that year.

"Raise your hand if you have a guess about what happened the following year after Jack planted both seeds," I said.

"I think he'll get four seeds," Dylan guessed.

"I think he'll forget about the seeds, and he won't have anything left," said Bernardo. "That would be sad."

After the children made their predictions, I read: "In the spring, two sprouts came up, and in the fall, four seeds were produced. In the winter, Jack baked and ate one seed and buried the other three seeds in the ground."

"How many seeds do you think Jack will get the following year?" I asked.

"Six!" students chorused.

I continued with the story, confirming that they were right and reading that in this second year, Jack eats one seed and plants the other five. The next few pages of the book describe how many seeds are eaten, how many are planted, and how many grow each subsequent year. Again, the students began to notice a pattern in the story.

"There's a different pattern happening now," Judy said. "However many seeds he plants, he then gets double that amount the following year."

"Every time he plants, he gets double that, then he eats one, then plants the rest, and gets double that, and so on," Dylan explained.

"It goes two times two minus one equals three," Jo said. "Then it goes three times two minus one equals five, and so on."

"The number of seeds is doubling each time, then Jack eats one," Maggie said.

"How is this pattern different from the first pattern?" I asked.

"The first pattern was a repeating pattern and this pattern grows," Judy said.

"At the end of the third year after Jack got the idea of burying both seeds, he gets ten seeds," I said. "How many seeds do you think Jack will have at the end of the tenth year? Talk to someone next to you and come up with an estimate." After a minute, I repeated my question and called on volunteers.

"I think he'll have eighteen seeds," Tano said.

"Why do you think that?" I asked.

"Because nine times two equals eighteen," he said.

"Why are you using the number nine?" I asked him.

"Because ten years subtract one for the one he ate times two because the number of seeds doubles," he explained.

Tano knew that the seeds doubled and that he needed to subtract one somewhere, but he had only a partial understanding of the problem at this point. I didn't correct him because I knew that he would soon have a chance to explore the problem further. Also, I was interested in hearing what others were thinking. Listening to the students' initial estimates without correcting them gave me a chance to assess their thinking.

"We calculated that he'll have sixty-eight seeds after the tenth year," Paige said. "Because after the third year, he had ten. Then he ate one and buried nine, and the seeds doubled. Then he got eighteen and he ate one, and he buried seventeen. We kept going. We're not really sure, though."

"How might you figure it out to be sure about how many seeds Jack will have at the end of the tenth year?" I asked.

"You could make a graph," Deirdre said.

"You could make a chart," Jed suggested. "I'd make a chart with columns—one column for the years, one for the seeds planted, one for the seeds he got, and one for the seeds eaten."

"You could just write it out using numbers and words," Calie said.

When all the students had shared their ideas, they began to work on the problem. Students organized themselves in various ways. Some chose to work alone, while others formed groups of two, three, or four. Each student, however, recorded on his or her own paper.

Calie solved the problem by writing sentences with numbers and words. She wrote: *1st he plants two and he gets 4 he eats 1 he gets 3. 2nd he plants three and he gets six he eats 1 he get 5. 3rd he plants 5 and he get 10 he eat 1 he gets 9.* She finished with the tenth year: *he plants 513 and he gets 1,026 he eats 1 he gets 1,025.* (See Figure 2–1.)

"How did you figure out how many seeds he gets each time?" I asked.

"I used mental math," she replied.

"Explain how you used mental math, Calie," I probed.

"I doubled each number in my head and subtracted one each time," she explained. "Like double two is four, minus one equals three. Then double three is six, minus one equals five. When I got

> Magic seeds
> [ansewer]
>
> 1st he plants two and he gets 4 he eats 1 he gets 3
> 2nd   he plants three and he   gets   six he eats 1 he gets 5
> 3rd   he plants 5 and he get 10 he eat 1 he gets 9
> 4th   he plants 9 and he gets 18 he eats 1 he gets 17
> 5th he plants 17 and he gets 34 he eats 1 he gets 33
> 6th he plants 33 and he gets 66 he eats 1 he gets 65
> 7th he plants 65 and he gets 130 he eats 1 he gets 129
> 8th he plants 129 and he gets 258 he eats 1 he gets 257
> 9th he plants 257 and he gets 514 he eats 1 he gets 513
> 10th he plants 513 and he gets 1,026 he eats 1 he gets 1,025
>
> every year he plants he get more seeds than he started with but than you have to subtract 1 because he ate one.
>
> Each year it multiples by 2 and so it gets bigger.
> Each year he eats 1 so you have 1 less than you started with.

to the big numbers, I did double thirty-three is sixty-six, minus one equals sixty-five and double five hundred thirteen is one thousand twenty-six. I knew that five hundred plus five hundred equals one thousand and double thirteen is twenty-six."

Jed made a chart to organize his figures. He wrote: *First I made a chart of all the events over the years by using multiplication & subtraction.* His chart in Figure 2–2 represents what happened to the seeds over the years.

Camilla recorded equations for each year. She wrote: *1st year—plants $2 \times 2 = 4 - 1 = 3$. 2nd year—plants $3 \times 2 = 6 - 1 = 5$.* She continued until she got to the tenth year, where she calculated that Jack would get 1,026 seeds. Camilla finished her paper by writing: *The first number is how many seeds he planted. The 2nd number is how many seeds the sprouts produced. The last is how many seed all together.*

Judy also made a chart. In vertical columns, she wrote the number of years, seeds planted, seeds produced, and seeds eaten. To explain her chart, Judy wrote: *First I made a chart with 4 colomns and 10 rows. They are titled as you can see on pg. 1. Second I*

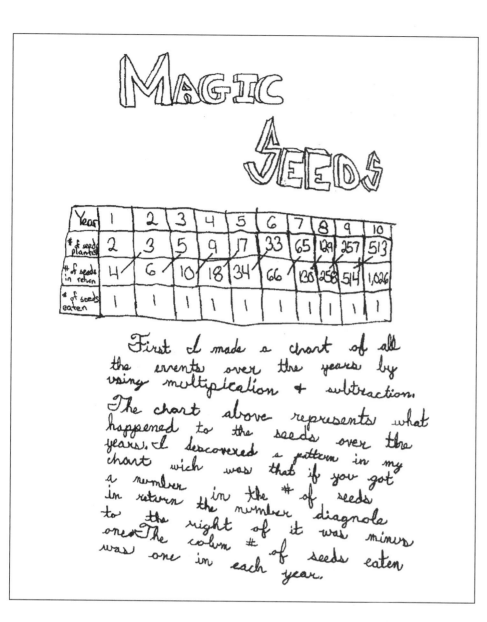

Figure 2–2: Jed drew a chart to organize his figures.

knew he had 2 seeds and ate none the first year. So, if he didn't eat any he planted 2 seeds. I wrote that in my chart. Third I multiplied on the side of my chart. I multiplied how many seeds he planted by 2. The 2 is there because you get two seeds from each plant. By doing that filled in my chart. (Judy's chart appears in Figure 2–3.)

Deirdre made a bar graph to represent the number of seeds that grew each year. Along the bottom of her graph she wrote the number of years, 1 through 10. Along the side of her graph, she wrote the number of seeds in a vertical column. She only had room enough to number the seeds from 1 to 42, so she didn't have space to show how many seeds Jack received for the years 6 through 10. She wrote: *Well this graph shows the WIDE range between the years.*

"How did you go about making the graph?" I asked her.

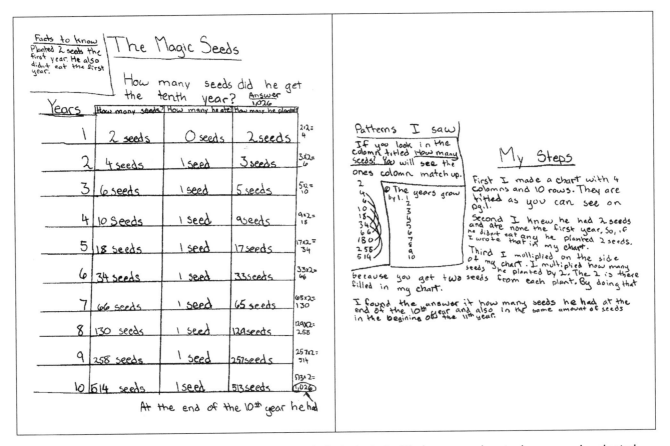

The Magic Seeds

How many seeds did he get the tenth year? Answer 1,026

Facts to know Planted 2 seeds the first year. He also didn't eat the first year.

Years	How many seeds?	How many he ate?	How many he planted?	
1	2 seeds	0 seeds	2 seeds	2×2=4
2	4 seeds	1 seed	3 seeds	3×2=6
3	6 seeds	1 seed	5 seeds	5×2=10
4	10 Seeds	1 seed	9 seeds	9×2=18
5	18 seeds	1 seed	17 seeds	17×2=34
6	34 seeds	1 seed	33 seeds	33×2=66
7	66 seeds	1 seed	65 seeds	65×2=130
8	130 seeds	1 seed	129 seeds	129×2=258
9	258 seeds	1 seed	257 seeds	257×2=514
10	514 seeds	1 seed	513 seeds	513×2=(1,026)

At the end of the 10th year he had

Patterns I saw
If you look in the colomn titled How many seeds? You will see the ones colomn match up.
2
4
6
10
18
34
66
130
258
514
ⓐ The years grow by 1. 1
2
3
4
5
6
7
8
9
10
because you get two seeds filled in my chart.

I found the answer it how many seeds he had at the end of the 10th year and also in the same amount of seeds in the begining of the 11th year.

My Steps
First I made a chart with 4 colomns and 10 rows. They are titled as you can see on pg.1.

Second I knew he had 2 seeds and ate none the first year, so, if he didnt eat any he planted 2 seeds. I wrote that in my chart.

Third I mollipied on the side of my chart. I multiplied how many seeds he planted by 2. The 2 is there from each plant. By doing that

Figure 2–3: Judy's chart showed by year how many seeds Jack started with, how many he ate, how many he planted, and the total number of seeds.

"Well, at first I tried a graph that was very confusing," she said. "It had two parts to it and probably would have taken a million years to figure out what I was doing. Well, to help me with the results, I also used a calculator to get the amounts of seeds each year. The graph really shows how much the seeds increase every year."

After about forty-five minutes, I asked the students for their attention and explained the next part of the assignment. "When you're finished with the problem, look for patterns in the numbers you've written," I said. "Can someone give an example of a pattern you noticed?"

Federico said, "The number of years goes up by one every time. The years go one, two, three, four, five, all the way to ten."

"That's one pattern," I confirmed. "Look for other patterns and describe them in words and numbers."

The class worked for another twenty minutes. I then asked volunteers to share their answers, explain how they solved the problem, and present the patterns they discovered.

"Jack always eats one seed, so there's a repeating pattern of one, one, one, one, one, and so on," Jonah said. "There's another repeating pattern, kind of. The number of seeds is always doubling, or being multiplied by two."

"I noticed that the number of seeds he plants, except for the first year, is always odd," Paige said. "And the number of plants he gets is always going to be an even number."

"Why do you think that happens?" I asked.

Paige paused a moment and then explained, "Because when he gets the seeds it's an even amount, and then he eats one seed so the number he plants will be odd."

"There's a pattern between the numbers of seeds he planted," Jo said. "He planted two seeds the first year and three the next year and the difference is one. Then he planted five seeds, and the difference between three and five is two. Then he planted nine seeds, and the difference between five and nine is four. Then he planted seventeen seeds, and the difference between nine and seventeen is eight. The difference keeps doubling."

"I saw a pattern in the numbers of seeds he got at the end of each year," said Wesley. "I put those numbers in a column, and there's a pattern with the numbers in the ones place." He read the numbers from his list: 2, 4, 6, 10, 18, 34, 66, 130, 258, 514, 1,026. "The pattern of the numbers in the ones place starts with four: four, six, zero, eight, four, six, zero, eight. It keeps going."

After the students had shared their ideas, I finished reading the story. I then said, "In the story, the author asks the reader to solve different problems than the one we solved today."

"Yeah, like when Jack gets married," Cameron said. "Jack and Alice both start eating a seed each year, so the problem changes."

"And when they have their wedding and they give seeds to their guests," added Deirdre. "The problem changes then, too."

"Does anyone have any questions about the problem we worked on today?" I asked.

"After the tenth year, Jack got one thousand twenty-six seeds," Maggie said. "I wonder if we could figure out how many seeds Jack would get after any year? Like after fifty or hundred years?"

"Does anyone have an idea how you might figure out how many seeds Jack would get after, say, fifty years?" I asked.

"We could keep doubling the numbers of seeds and subtracting one each time," Camilla suggested.

"We could use Wesley's pattern to help us," Theo said. "What was your pattern, Wesley?"

"That the answer will end in either four, six, zero, or eight," Wesley replied.

"Any other ideas?" I asked.

"The answer will be an even number," Paige said. "That's the pattern I noticed."

"We know it's going to be a huge number, if he got a thousand and twenty-six seeds after only ten years," Larissa said. "Doubling numbers makes things grow real fast."

Our discussion at the end of the lesson allowed the students to see how they could use the patterns they had found to solve larger problems. Patterns help children see order, make sense of things, and predict what will happen. This problem challenged them to make use of patterns to predict and find an outcome.

Beasts of Burden

"Beasts of Burden" is a story from *The Man Who Counted: A Collection of Mathematical Adventures*, by Malba Tahan (1993). In the story, the narrator and Beremiz, the wise mathematician, are traveling on a single camel when they encounter three fighting brothers. The brothers tell Beremiz that their father has left them thirty-five camels to divide three ways: one-half to one brother, one-third to another, and one-ninth to the last. They can't figure out how to divide the inheritance. Beremiz suggests adding his camel to the thirty-five, making thirty-six, then explains that one brother would get eighteen camels, one brother twelve, and another four. This computation leaves two camels as a remainder: One to return to the narrator, and another, which Beremiz claims for himself. The story leads to an activity in which students work with division and fractions.

MATERIALS

color tiles, 36 per group of three to four students

"Does anyone know what a beast of burden is?" Maryann Wickett asked her fifth and sixth graders.

"A horse or a donkey," Andie answered.

"Any other ideas?" she asked.

"A wild animal, I think," Adriana guessed.

"I brought a book today that I want to read to you," Maryann then said. "The book has many short stories in it, and one of them is called 'Beasts of Burden.' As I read the story, see if there are any clues that might help you understand what a beast of burden is."

Maryann's students listened with interest as she read the part where the three brothers argue and shout about how to divide the thirty-five camels that they have inherited. Maryann read the sentence that explains that the oldest brother is to receive one-half of the camels, the middle brother is to receive one-third, and the youngest, one-ninth. Maryann reviewed the information with the class.

"How many camels are there altogether?" she asked.

"Thirty-five," the class answered.

"How many camels is the oldest son supposed to get?" she asked.

"One-half!" the students answered.

"What about the middle son?" she asked.

"One-third," they said.

"And the youngest?" she asked.

"One-ninth," they responded.

Maryann wrote on the board:

35 *camels*

Oldest $\frac{1}{2}$

Middle $\frac{1}{3}$

Youngest $\frac{1}{9}$

"How many camels are half of thirty-five?" she then inquired.

After a long pause, whispers broke out across the room as the students struggled with this problem. Finally, several hands shot up.

"That would be seventeen and a half, I think," Monty offered. "But that's not a good answer because you can't have half a camel."

"Monty has a point," Maryann responded. "Talk in your groups and try to figure out some ways Beremiz can solve this problem."

A busy hum filled the classroom as the students began to share their ideas. After a few minutes, Maryann asked the students for their attention.

"How can Beremiz help the three brothers?" she asked.

"Beremiz could take one camel, and then there would be only thirty-four, and thirty-four is an even number so it can be divided into halves equally," Arleen said.

"If there were some babies in the group, they could make two babies equal one adult," Shana offered.

"Maybe instead of splitting a camel, one brother could take a whole camel and the other brother who didn't get any could have the next baby camel that was born," Edward said.

"There's one clue or detail that I didn't tell you in the beginning that might give you some other ideas," Maryann said. "This story took place many years ago, before cars. People in Iraq used camels as their method of transportation. Beremiz and his friend were both riding on the friend's camel when they met up with the three arguing brothers."

"Oh, oh, I know!" several students shouted. Maryann called on Stu.

"If Beremiz added his friend's camel to the thirty-five, that would make thirty-six, and they could divide thirty-six into halves and thirds and ninths!" Stu exclaimed.

"That's exactly what Beremiz did," Maryann said. She then continued reading the story, stopping after the part where Beremiz says to the three brothers that he is going to divide the camels fairly.

"I'd like you to work together to come up with a possible solution that Beremiz might use to divide the camels," Maryann said. "You can work with your group and share ideas, but I want each of you to write your own solution. Remember, you can use words, numbers, and pictures to explain your reasoning."

As Maryann circulated throughout the room, she observed the students and listened to their conversations. Some students reached for their calculators, while others went to get counters.

One group of four seemed stuck, with no sign of leadership from any of its members. Maryann observed the students for a few minutes, then approached them to see if they had any idea about where to start.

"What was the question I asked you to think about?" she asked.

"We're supposed to figure out how the brothers divided the camels," Shana quickly responded.

"How many camels?" Maryann asked.

"They had thirty-five," Denver said, "and Beremiz added his friend's, so that made thirty-six."

"The oldest is supposed to get half, the middle a third, and the youngest a ninth," Emilio added.

"I'll get thirty-six counters, and we can divide them into halves, thirds, and ninths," Shana said with an unsure voice.

"That makes sense," Denver said.

Feeling that the students understood the problem and had a way to begin, Maryann moved away from the group. Katrina, who was working in a different group, called Maryann over.

"Mrs. Wickett," she said, "I'm confused. We divided thirty-six by two, and that made eighteen camels for the oldest. Then we divided thirty-six into three groups and that made twelve for the middle brother. We divided thirty-six into nine groups and that made four for the youngest. But when I added it all up, it only equaled thirty-four camels, and there were thirty-six." Katrina had a perplexed look on her face.

"I know we did it right," Barrett interjected.

"Hmm, what did you expect them to add up to?" Maryann asked.

"Well, thirty-six because there are thirty-six camels," Chloe answered.

"Do your answers make sense?" Maryann asked.

"I think so," Chloe said. "I know we figured the amounts of camels the right way."

"I agree that your figuring was correct. Talk about what you think Beremiz would do in this situation," Maryann suggested. The students became involved in an animated discussion about what Beremiz might do.

After the students had had time to write their solutions, Maryann initiated a discussion. "What surprises did you run into while solving the problem?" she began.

"We expected the camels to equal thirty-six after we divided them among the brothers, but they equaled thirty-four," Natasha reported.

"Raise your hand if your group ran into this problem," Maryann instructed. Most students raised their hands.

"What did you do about it?" Maryann asked.

"We checked our work on the calculator and then used counters," Lenora said. "When it came out the same the two different ways, we decided that Beremiz should get one of the extra ones for solving the problem and his friend should get his own camel back."

"We did something like that, too, but first we thought it was a trick question," Michaela offered.

"How many camels did each brother get after Beremiz added his friend's to the group?" Maryann asked.

"The oldest got eighteen, the middle one got twelve, and the youngest got four, and there were two extras," Sean answered. Maryann quickly noted this information on the board.

"Does this seem fair?" Maryann asked. "Were the wishes of the father honored?" The students were silent.

"When there were thirty-five camels, how many camels would the oldest have gotten?" Maryann then asked.

"Seventeen and a half," several students called out.

"What about the middle brother?" Maryann asked.

Several students quickly used calculators to find out, but most of them weren't sure how to make sense of 11.666666.

"The middle brother got eleven and a little more," Jagger announced.

"And the youngest brother?" Maryann asked.

"He'd get three and some more," Katrina stated.

"That could be really messy!" Estevan said with a giggle.

Maryann added these numbers to what she had written on the board:

Oldest	*18*	$17\frac{1}{2}$
Middle	*12*	*11 and a little more*
Youngest	*4*	*3 and some more*

"Which way is better for the brothers?" Maryann asked.

"Well, they came out better with thirty-six camels, but I really don't get it," Uma said. "At the end, they lost two camels. Why did they get more when they still lost two camels?" she asked.

"Does anyone have an idea about that?" Maryann inquired.

"Maybe it has something to do with the extra parts," Sean said. None of the other students had anything to add.

Maryann then finished reading the story. Although the students were pleased to learn that Beremiz had solved the problem the same way most of them had suggested, they were still confused by the solution. Their confusion provided Maryann the opportunity to continue investigating the problem.

Figures 3–1 and 3–2 show how two students solved the camel problem.

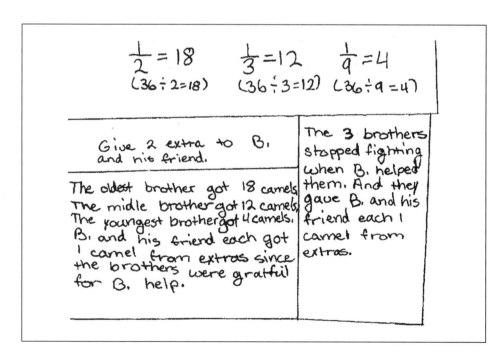

Figure 3–1: Max used division to figure out the fractional parts of thirty-six.

Figure 3–2: After solving the problem, Elise drew a spitting camel.

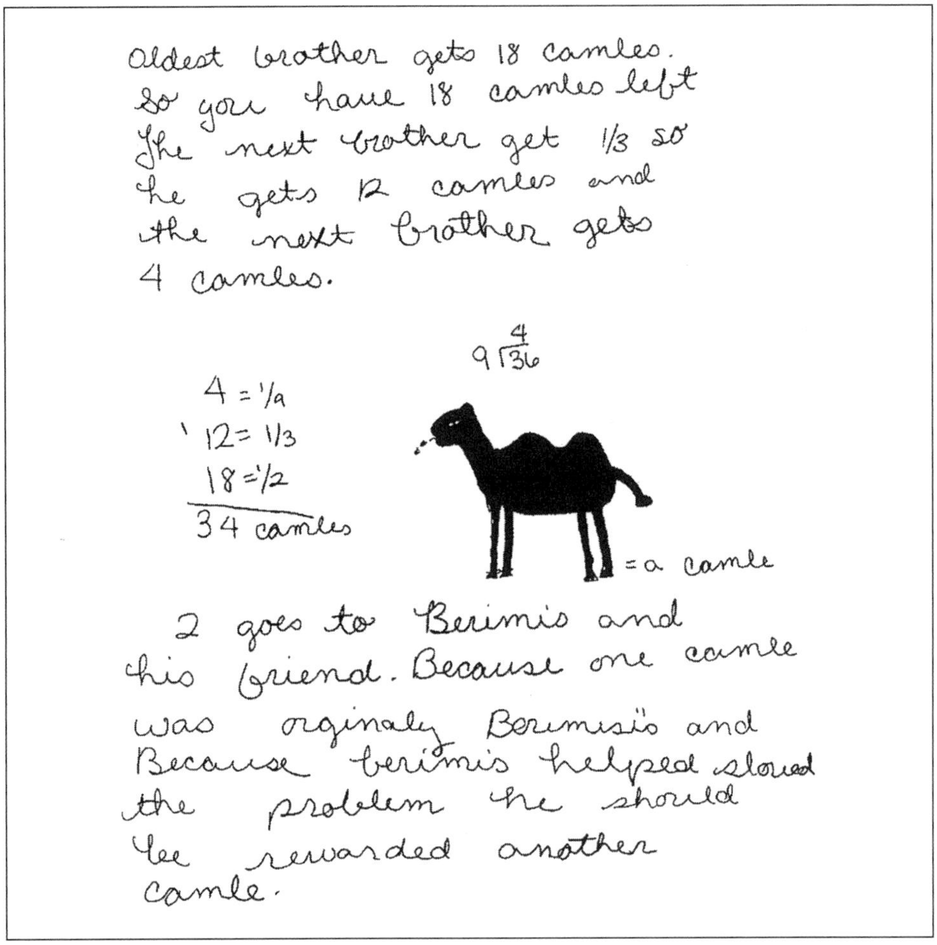

Oldest brother gets 18 camles.
So you have 18 camles left.
The next brother get 1/3 so
he gets 12 camles and
the next brother gets
4 camles.

$9\sqrt{36} \quad \frac{4}{}$

4 = 1/9
12 = 1/3
18 = 1/2
34 camles

= a camle

2 goes to Berimis and
his friend. Because one camle
was orginaly Berimisi's and
Because berimis helped sloued
the problem he should
be rewarded another
camle.

The Next Day

"Today I'd like to explore the problem of the camels a little further," Maryann said. She distributed a baggie of color tiles to each group. "Count out thirty-six for your group and return the rest to the baggie," Maryann directed. "Then use the tiles to show half of thirty-six."

The students in each group quickly counted out thirty-six tiles and divided them into two groups to show that one-half of thirty-six is eighteen. Maryann called on Chloe to explain her group's answer.

"It's eighteen," she said, "because we made two lines and they're the same. They each have eighteen."

Jagger explained how his group did it. "We took two at a time and put them in different piles," he said. "Each pile has eighteen."

"I'd like each of you to record the answer to one-half of thirty-six," Maryann said, "and explain how you got it. You can use words and pictures along with the numbers. Then do the same to figure one-third of thirty-six, and then do one-ninth of thirty-six."

As the students worked, Maryann circulated throughout the room. After the students had had time to record, she called the class back to order, asked the students to report the answers, and recorded on the board:

$$\tfrac{1}{2} \; of \; 36 = 18$$
$$\tfrac{1}{3} \; of \; 36 = 12$$
$$\tfrac{1}{9} \; of \; 36 = 4$$

"If we add up the number of camels each brother got—eighteen plus twelve plus four—we find out how many camels they got altogether," Maryann said.

"It's thirty-four," Denver said. "What happened to the two extra camels?"

"Let me try to help you understand," Maryann said. "First, let me ask you about representing the fractions differently." She wrote on the board:

$$\tfrac{1}{2} = \tfrac{18}{36}$$
$$\tfrac{1}{3} = \tfrac{12}{36}$$
$$\tfrac{1}{9} = \tfrac{4}{36}$$

"Who can explain why these sentences make sense?" Maryann asked. "Talk in your groups for a moment, and then I'll have volunteers explain."

Stu explained why one-half and eighteen–thirty-sixths are equivalent. "If you add eighteen and another eighteen, you get thirty-six, and that means that eighteen is half of thirty-six, so eighteen–thirty-sixths is just the same as one-half."

Michaela added, "It's just different numbers, but they mean the same because two is two times one and thirty-six is two times eighteen."

"What about the other two sentences?" Maryann asked.

Monty said, "It's like Michaela said. For one-third, one times three is three, and twelve times three is thirty-six. It works for the other because one times four is four, and nine times four is thirty-six." To help others understand, Maryann pointed to the fractions as he explained.

Katrina said, "When we figured out how much was one-third of thirty-six, we divided the tiles into three groups, and there were twelve in each, so that makes twelve–thirty-sixths. We did one-ninth the same way."

Riley added, "The numbers get bigger, but the amounts don't."

Although these students gave their explanations confidently, Maryann wasn't sure that everyone in the class understood why the fractions were equivalent. However, she continued, "If we add up the three fractions—eighteen–thirty-sixths, twelve–thirty-sixths, and four–thirty-sixths—we get thirty-four–thirty-sixths." Maryann wrote on the board:

$$\frac{18}{36} + \frac{12}{36} + \frac{4}{36} = \frac{34}{36}$$

"Ooooh," Max said, "that's why there are two extras."

"Yeah, there are two left over," Estevan added.

"If two are left over, what does that tell you about this set of three fractions?" Maryann questioned.

"It doesn't equal the whole group," Monty said. "The two extras means that there are leftovers, so the fractions probably don't equal up to one."

"I agree with Monty," Arleen said. "Because not all the camels were used, so the parts don't make the whole."

"What fraction would they have to add up to in order to make the whole?" Maryann asked.

Arleen, Monty, and Chloe answered in unison: "Thirty-six–thirty-sixths!" They giggled.

"I agree that eighteen–thirty-sixths, twelve–thiry-sixths, and four–thirty-sixths do not add up to one whole," Maryann confirmed. "And because these fractions are just different names for one-half, one-third, and one-ninth, then those fractions don't add up to one whole, either." Maryann wrote on the board:

$$\frac{1}{2} + \frac{1}{3} + \frac{1}{9} = less\ than\ one\ whole \left(\frac{34}{36}\right)$$

"Why didn't the father just tell the sons how many camels they would each get?" Edward asked. "Then there wouldn't be a problem."

"I know," Katrina said. "He didn't know how many camels there would be. I mean, some could have had babies or something. Then they'd still fight."

"Why do you think the father chose those particular fractions?" Maryann asked. "Do you think the father wanted to cause his children to quarrel? Do you think he realized the fractions he chose did not equal one? Why do you think he chose the fractions he did?"

"I don't think he wanted his sons to fight, so I think he didn't know the fractions wouldn't work out right and use up all the camels," Uma explained. "Maybe he didn't know how to do math and wanted better things for his sons."

"Maybe he wanted his sons to cooperate with each other," Celeste said.

"Maybe the father never learned to divide evenly," Natasha added.

"What fractions could the father have chosen to use up all thirty-six camels?" Maryann asked.

"Well, one-third plus one-third plus one-third equals one, and that would make twelve, twelve, and twelve for each brother, which is thirty-six," Jerry said. Maryann recorded on the board:

$$\tfrac{1}{3} + \tfrac{1}{3} + \tfrac{1}{3} = 1$$

"One son could get one-half, which is eighteen, one son could get one-third, which is twelve, and the last son could get six–thirty-sixths, and that equals one because there are no leftovers," Stu explained. Maryann recorded:

$$\tfrac{1}{2} + \tfrac{1}{3} + \tfrac{6}{36} = 1$$

"I have another way to write what Stu suggested," Maryann said. She wrote:

$$\tfrac{1}{2} + \tfrac{1}{3} + \tfrac{1}{6} = 1$$

"Raise your hand if this makes sense to you," Maryann said. She waited until about eight students had raised their hands. She called on Natasha to explain.

"It's like we did before," she said. "It works because in one-sixths, six is six times as big as one, and in six–thirty-sixths it's the same—thirty-six is six times as much as six."

"Would thirty-four–thirty-sixths, one–thirty-sixth, and one–thirty-sixth work?" Maryann asked the class.

"That would work and so would thirty-two–thirty-sixths, two–thirty-sixths, and two–thirty-sixths because thirty-two plus two plus two equals thirty-six and thirty-sixths–thirty-sixths makes a whole," Uma offered.

Maryann completed the sentence she began and added what Uma had suggested. The list now contained the following:

$$\tfrac{1}{3} + \tfrac{1}{3} + \tfrac{1}{3} = 1$$
$$\tfrac{1}{2} + \tfrac{1}{3} + \tfrac{6}{36} = 1$$
$$\tfrac{1}{2} + \tfrac{1}{3} + \tfrac{1}{6} = 1$$
$$\tfrac{34}{36} + \tfrac{1}{36} + \tfrac{1}{36} = 1$$
$$\tfrac{32}{36} + \tfrac{2}{36} + \tfrac{2}{36} = 1$$

Students continued to suggest other sets of three fractions with denominators of thirty-six that added to one, and Maryann recorded them. After recording about ten sentences, she posed a question.

"How many more sets of three fractions that add up to one do you think there are?" she asked.

"I think there are an infinite number of ways . . . and that's a lot!" Emilio announced.

Maryann asked the students to work in their groups to figure out and record additional sets of three fractions that would use all thirty-six camels. After ten minutes, Maryann interrupted the students and had groups report their findings. All of the groups had used fractions with denominators of thirty-six.

"Take a moment and think about the father's wishes for his sons," Maryann said. "Examine the sets of fractions on the board and decide which set of fractions he might have chosen that would have used up all thirty-six camels." After giving the students a few moments to think, Maryann called on Arleen.

"I think twenty–thirty-sixths, ten–thirty-sixths, and six–thirty-sixths because he wanted one-half for the oldest and twenty is just a little more than a half," Arleen offered. "He wanted one-third for the middle and one-ninth for the youngest, and those are close, too."

"I kind of agree with Arleen," Noel said. "I just gave the oldest one two extra, so I think twenty–thirty-sixths, twelve–thirty-sixths, and four–thirty-sixths. I think this is close to the real thing." (See Figure 3–3.)

"I think that nineteen–thirty-sixths, fourteen–thirty-sixths, and three–thirty-sixths are closer to eighteen, twelve, and four, which are the numbers they got," Andie explained. (See Figure 3–4.)

Figure 3–3: Noel estimated what the father might have given to his sons so that all thirty-six camels would be used.

Math and Literature, Grades 4–6

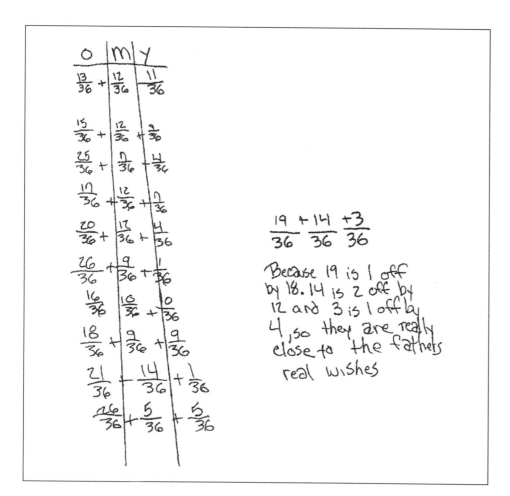

Figure 3–4: Andie chose $\frac{19}{36}$, $\frac{14}{36}$, and $\frac{3}{36}$ because the nemerators were close to the numbers of camels given to each son.

Because the students had relied only on fractions with denominators of thirty-six, Maryann suspected that they didn't fully grasp that $\frac{1}{2} + \frac{1}{3} + \frac{1}{9}$ was the same as $\frac{18}{36} + \frac{12}{36} + \frac{4}{36}$ and also didn't total 1. She felt this lack of understanding probably occurred because of their limited experience with situations involving fractions with unlike denominators. She decided to change the focus by asking the students to explore sets of three fractions that would account for all the camels when there were different numbers of camels to divide.

"I'm curious about fractions that you could use for numbers of camels other than thirty-six," Maryann said to the class. "You've found many sets of three fractions that use all thirty-six camels. What if there were only three camels? Is there a set of three fractions that would divide three camels so there weren't any extras? Or what about for any other number of camels?"

"I think you can do it for three, but I don't think you can do it for one or two because that would be parts of camels," Max explained.

"I think you can do one-third and one-third and one-third for three, and that you could use those fractions for six, but I'm not sure," Emilio said cautiously.

"How could you test your idea?" Maryann asked.

"I could use tiles," Emilio answered. "I could use six tiles and divide them into three groups. Oh, yeah, it would work; there would be two in each group."

Maryann then gave directions. "I'd like each of you to investigate possible fractions for different numbers of camels," she said. "Suppose the father wanted to be sure there wouldn't be any quarrels or leftover camels, and because he wasn't sure how many camels he'd have when he died, he decided to investigate what fractions would work for different numbers." Maryann pointed to a large chart she had prepared with the numbers from 1 to 48 listed vertically down the left side.

"Let's investigate the numbers on this chart," she continued. "Choose a number to explore, and write your initials beside it. Then investigate sets of three fractions that would divide that number of camels with no extras. When you've found at least three sets of three fractions, record them on the chart next to your number. Then we'll examine the chart and see what we can discover."

The students chose their numbers and began working. Maryann left the chart up, and the students investigated their numbers throughout the day.

The Third Day

As the students began the third day of this investigation, Maryann still had a nagging doubt about their understanding of combining fractions with unlike denominators. When recording sets of fractions on the chart, the students wrote only fractions whose denominators were the same as the number they were investigating.

Maryann quickly wrote on the board the following information:

$$\frac{1}{2} \text{ of 36 camels} = 18$$

$$\frac{1}{3} \text{ of 36 camels} = 12$$

$$\frac{1}{9} \text{ of 36 camels} = 4$$

This uses up 34 camels in all.

"What does this information tell you about the fractions one-half, one-third, and one-ninth?" Maryann asked the students. They had talked about this several times before, but Maryann knows that giving students a chance to think about the same idea several times can help them cement their understanding.

"I think that they don't use all the camels, so the fractions don't equal a whole," Edward replied. Some students still looked a little puzzled.

"What if the father had left eighteen camels?" Maryann asked. "Would these fractions use up all of the eighteen camels? Or would there be leftovers?" About half the class thought there would be leftovers and half thought all the camels would be used.

Sean explained his reasoning. "I think there would be leftovers because there were leftovers with thirty-six, and eighteen is half of thirty-six, and so I think if you are using the same fractions there would be half the leftovers," he said.

"What happens with eighteen?" Maryann said. "Take eighteen tiles for the camels and figure out how much each son would get if the oldest got one-half, the middle one got one-third, and the youngest got one-ninth. Record what you discover on your paper."

The students took only a few moments to discover that there would be one leftover camel. Maryann recorded their findings on the board:

36	18
$\frac{1}{2} = 18$	$\frac{1}{2} = 9$
$\frac{1}{3} = 12$	$\frac{1}{3} = 6$
$\frac{1}{9} = 4$	$\frac{1}{9} = 2$
Total: 34	Total: 17
Leftovers: 2	Leftovers: 1

"I see a pattern," Michaela said. Maryann asked her to explain.

"I notice that everything is half . . . or double, depending on which way you go, like nine is half of eighteen or two nineths make eighteen," Michaela said.

"I bet that you'll ask us to try nine . . . or maybe seventy-two," Laurie speculated.

"Let's see what happens with nine," Maryann said. Again, the students quickly tried this, recording the results on their papers.

"What did you find out?" Maryann asked when the students finished.

"My prediction about nine being half of eighteen was right, and there was a leftover of a half," Kennon said. As Kennon reported, Maryann recorded:

36	18	9
$\frac{1}{2} = 18$	$\frac{1}{2} = 9$	$\frac{1}{2} = 4\frac{1}{2}$
$\frac{1}{3} = 12$	$\frac{1}{3} = 6$	$\frac{1}{3} = 3$
$\frac{1}{9} = 4$	$\frac{1}{9} = 2$	$\frac{1}{9} = 1$
Total: 34	Total: 17	Total: $8\frac{1}{2}$
Leftovers: 2	Leftovers: 1	Leftovers: $\frac{1}{2}$

"So what's happening here?" Maryann asked.

"The fractions don't add up to a whole, so they can't use up all of a number," Lydia responded.

"If the father wanted to give his oldest son one-half of the camels and his middle son one-third of the camels, what fraction would he have to give his youngest son to use up all thirty-six camels? Figure out what the fraction is and explain your reasoning on your paper," Maryann told the class.

As Maryann walked around the room listening and talking with the students, her uneasiness about their understanding began to subside. Most students quickly saw that the fraction for the youngest son would have to be six–thirty-sixths, and they saw that it was the same as one-sixth.

"Let's look at the sets of three fractions you recorded on the chart," said Maryann. "What do you notice?"

"No one picked one or two because that wasn't enough camels to divide among the three brothers," Max observed. "It looks like we can't use them because there's not enough to go around."

"It seems as if the bigger the number gets, the more fractions there are, like there are more ways to make fourty-eight than eighteen," Andie added.

"I noticed you could make nine combinations with three numbers in the numerators if the lower numbers stay the same, just by switching the order of what each brother gets," Arleen shared.

"What do you notice about the numerators?" Maryann asked.

"They're mostly even numbers," Roger said.

"All the numerators were lower than the denominators and the three numerators added up to the denominators," Edward added.

Maryann posed a new question for the students.

"You saw that it's possible to use one-half, one-third, and one-sixth to divide up thirty-six camels," she said, adding those fractions to the chart next to the 36. "Could you use these fractions for any other number on the chart?"

The students were excited about this question, and they began to make predictions and test their ideas.

"I guessed seventy-two because it's two thirty-sixes. I tried it and it worked!" Elise said.

"Mrs. Wickett, Kennon thinks nine billion will work!" Chloe said, giggling.

"Ask him to explain his thinking to you," Maryann responded.

"I know that nine billion is a multiple of all three numbers [denominators] and so I'm sort of sure it would work, but I don't have the tiles to prove it!" Kennon explained.

After a few minutes, Maryann asked the students for their attention.

"Let's record all of the possible numbers that you've found," Maryann said.

"Seventy-two works—one-half is thirty-six, one-third is twenty-four, and one-sixths is twelve," Elise reported. "It's just like thirty-six, except that everything is doubled."

"I think fourty-eight works: one-half is twenty-four, one-third is sixteen, and one-sixth is eight," Celeste explained.

"And thirty works, too," Monty said, "because one-half is fifteen, one-third is ten, and one-sixth is five. Add it up and, like magic, it equals thirty!"

Maryann recorded her students' findings in a chart to encourage them to look for patterns:

Number:	72	48	30	60	6	12	96	9,000,000,000
$\frac{1}{2}$:	36	24	15	30	3	6	48	4,500,000,000
$\frac{1}{3}$:	24	16	10	20	2	4	32	3,000,000,000
$\frac{1}{6}$:	12	8	5	10	1	2	16	1,500,000,000

"Oh! I see a pattern!" Andie exclaimed. "All the numbers that are possible are even numbers and all are multiples of six . . . so I bet that any number that is a product of six will work!"

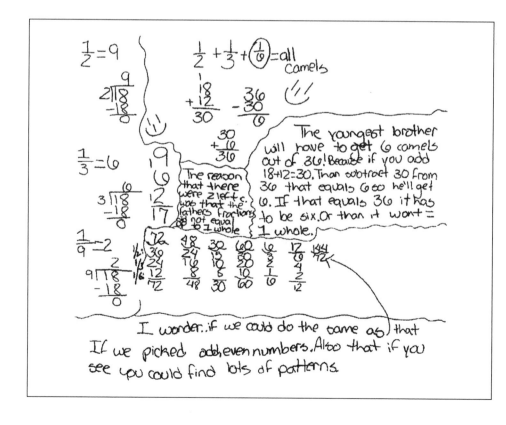

Figure 3–5: When Lenora found that 72, 48, 30, 60, 6, and 12 could be divided equally by $\frac{1}{2}$, $\frac{1}{3}$, and $\frac{1}{6}$, she wondered what patterns she could find.

"I wonder why it works with six?" Kennon asked. "I wonder if there are any numbers that aren't multiples of six that would be possible with one-half, one-third, and one-sixths?"

"I wonder if any odd numbers are multiples of six?" Uma added.

"I wonder how you would find out other fractions that equaled one whole and their possible numbers?" Edward asked.

"I am hearing all kinds of interesting, wonderful questions that you're asking as a result of this investigation," Maryann observed. "Please write on your paper at least one idea you are wondering about."

The students completed this three-day lesson by writing down their "I wonder" questions. (See Figure 3–5 on page 33.) These questions can be used to spark new investigations involving fractions.

Note: A similar problem can be found in *Stories to Solve: Folktales from Around the World*, by George Shannon (2000). In the story called "Dividing the Horses," one-half of seventeen horses has to be given to one son, one-third to another son, and one-ninth to the third son.

Counting on Frank

In *Counting on Frank*, by Rod Clement (1994), a precocious boy makes endless calculations. He figures that the average ballpoint pen can draw a line 7,000 feet long before running out of ink, that 24 Franks (Frank is his dog) can fit into his bedroom, that it would take 11 hours and 45 minutes to fill the entire bathroom with water, and much more. Witty comments and graphic illustrations accompany each unusual measurement calculation. The boy's statement that if he grew at the rate of the tree in his yard, he'd be almost 50 feet tall suggests several problems for students to solve that challenge them to reason proportionally.

MATERIALS

optional: calculators, 1 per group of three to four students

When I held up the cover of *Counting on Frank*, many of Carole Smith's fourth and fifth graders immediately recognized the funny-looking boy with the spiked hair and his pet dog, Frank. Some students said that they had heard the story before.

"It's a neat book!" Anne-Marie exclaimed.

"I remember all of those peas," Cameron chimed in.

"It seems as if many of you are familiar with the story," I said.

"We could listen to it again," Jed said.

"Yes!" others chorused.

I started reading the book and stopped on the second page to show the students the picture of the boy surrounded by twenty-four Franks in his bedroom. "The boy in the story figures that twenty-four Franks could fit in his bedroom," I said. "How many Franks do you think could fit in the classroom?"

"Are the dogs piled on top of one another?" Maggie asked.

"Although it looks as if they are in the picture, let's say we'd just fill up the floor with Franks," I answered. "Talk about this at your table and come up with an estimate."

After a minute or two, several hands went up, and I asked for the students' attention. I called on Arturo.

"I think there could be about one hundred Franks in the room," he said, "because on the other page, Frank is sitting next to his owner and it looks like he's about three feet long. So I imagined dogs that big in the room, and it seems like there would be about one hundred."

Tano had a different estimate. "I think there could be about two hundred and sixty Franks in our room because the dog looks small and dogs could snuggle up to one another," he said.

"I estimate one hundred and fifty because I think we're about twice as long as Frank, and thirty of us fit easily in the room," Calie explained.

"Calie, if we're about twice as long as Frank, and thirty of us fit in the room, what does that tell you about how many Franks fit in the room?" I asked.

"Hmmm," Calie responded. "Well, twice thirty is sixty, so maybe a little more than sixty Franks could fill up the room."

I then continued reading the story. The students laughed at the part when the boy's mother says that his dad's feet smell. They loved the picture of the boy and his family waist deep in green peas, eating dinner. Their favorite part was the picture of the house-sized toaster shooting giant pieces of toast into the air, endangering low-flying aircraft.

When I finished reading the story, I turned back to the part where the boy and Frank are standing next to a tree. The illustration shows the boy's giant feet next to a very small Frank. "I'm going to read this page to you again, and then I have a mathematical question for you to think about," I told the class. I read, "We've got a tree in our yard. It grows about six feet every year. If I had grown at the same speed, I'd now be almost fifty feet tall!"

I then said, "The boy says that he would be almost fifty feet tall if he had grown six feet every year. My question is: How old is the boy? Talk about this with your group. When you've figured it out, explain with numbers and in writing how you solved it. You may work together, but you should each record your own solution."

I paused and looked around the room. "Are there any questions?" I asked.

"Do we figure out exactly how old the boy is or about how old he is?" Larissa asked.

"I'm going to leave that decision up to you," I said.

No other students had questions, so they all got to work. After spending a few minutes talking in their groups, most students began writing. Calculators were readily available; some students chose to use them and others didn't.

The students solved the problem in a variety of ways. Some added 6s in their heads until they got close to 50. Some thought about what number they could multiply by 6 to get to 50. Some divided 50 by 6. Some students organized information into a chart to figure out the answer. Some students used a calculator to divide 50 by 6, ending up with 8.3333333 as an answer. While some didn't know what to do with the decimal point followed by the 3s, most of the students knew that 0.3333333 meant about a third. Some students translated a third of a year into months.

Jansen's first answer didn't make sense. He wrote: *I think he would be 33 years old because I ÷ 50 ÷ 6 and I got 8.3333333 and I covered up the 8 and the 53ths and I got 33, so I think he would be 33. and other thing how I got 33 is I added 25 + 8 and I got 33. and an other way how I got the answer is I added 23 + 10 and that equaled 33.*

It seemed that the ways Jansen reported to make thirty-three had nothing to do with the problem I'd posed. After listening to him read his paper, I asked questions to refocus him on the problem and nudge him to rely on reason and common sense.

"What's the mathematical question you're trying to solve?" I asked.

Jansen sat quietly for a moment, thinking. Finally, he said tentatively, "We're trying to find out how old the boy is?"

"That's right," I responded. "You said the boy is thirty-three years old. Do you think the boy in the story is thirty-three? Does he look thirty-three?"

"Not really," Jansen replied.

"How old does he look to you?" I asked.

"He looks like he's my age or maybe a little younger," he said.

"What information do you know from the book that could help you find out how old he is?" I asked.

"Well, I know that he grew six feet each year," Jansen responded. "The boy said that if he grew like the tree, he would be almost fifty feet tall. So I divided six into fifty."

"When you divided those numbers on the calculator, you got eight point three three three three three three. That number means eight and a little more. It's a number that's more than eight and less than nine; it's in between," I explained.

"Hey! Maybe he's around eight years old! That makes sense!" Jansen exclaimed.

Paige also used a calculator. She interpreted the answer in terms of months and wrote: *What we did was divided 50 ÷ 6 = the answer we came up to was 8.3333333. We think he is 8 and 4 months years old. $\frac{1}{3}$ of a year.*

Camilla, who was working with Paige, explained why 8.3333333 meant the same as 8 years and 4 months. She wrote: *We think he is 8 and 4 months. $\frac{1}{3}$ of a year 12 ÷ 3 = 4 months.*

Jo solved the problem without a calculator. She made a chart and recorded how tall the boy would be each year. She recorded that the first year he would be 6 feet, the second year 12 feet, and so on. When she got to eight years old, Jo found that the boy would be 48 feet tall. For his ninth year, she recorded that he would be 54 feet tall. Jo wrote *low* next to the 48 and *over* next to the 54.

"He has to be in between eight and nine years old," Jo told me. "He needs two more feet to be fifty feet. When he's eight, he would be forty-eight feet tall."

Jo had also recorded some questions she was wondering about: *Does he grow 6 feet in one mounth? Does he grow 1 foot every other mounth? When is his birthday?* (See Figure 4–1.)

Figure 4–1: Jo's paper showed the several false starts she made before deciding that the boy was between eight and nine years old.

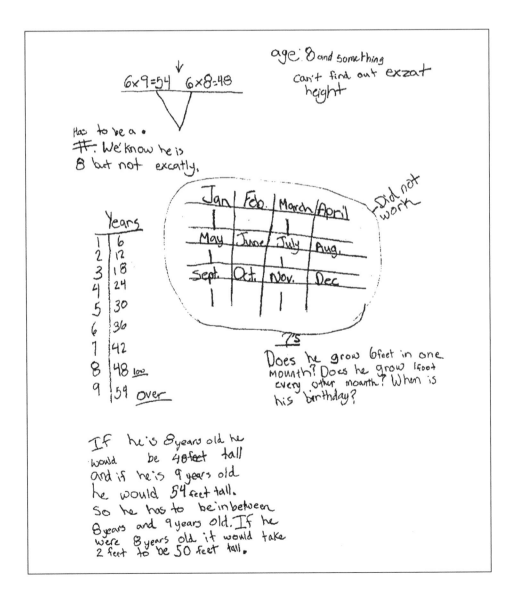

Math and Literature, Grades 4–6

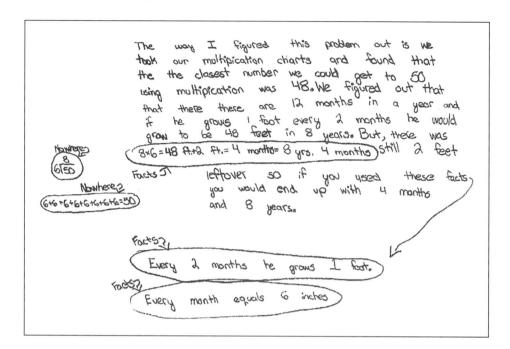

Figure 4–2: Jed's paper showed how he reasoned proportionally to find a solution.

Jed used proportional reasoning to find a solution. He wrote: *The way I figured this problem out is we took our multipication charts and found that the closest number we could get to 50 using multipication was 48. We figured out that there there are 12 months in a year and if he grows 1 foot every 2 months he would grow to be 48 feet in 8 years. But, there was still 2 feet leftover so if you used these facts you would end up with 4 months and 8 years.* (See Figure 4–2.)

Ephraim also used multiplication. He started with $6 \times 1 = 6$ feet for the first year. Then he continued with $6 \times 2 = 12$, $6 \times 3 = 18$, $6 \times 4 = 24$, $6 \times 5 = 30$, $6 \times 6 = 36$, $6 \times 7 = 42$, and $6 \times 8 = 48$. "I got up to forty-eight because it's close to fifty," he told me. "I came up with eight years."

In a class discussion, several students volunteered to share their work with the class. Everyone agreed that the boy was somewhere between eight and nine years old.

"Now that you've had the experience of figuring out how old the boy is, I have a new mathematical question for you," I said. "I'm forty years old now. If I had grown six feet each year since I was born, how tall would I be now? Talk to the person next to you and see what you come up with by figuring mentally." The students were excited about this question, and their discussions were animated.

After a few minutes, I interrupted the class. "How tall do you think I would be?" I asked.

"I think you would be two hundred and forty feet tall," Flint said. "I know this because I multiplied forty by six and it came to two hundred forty. It's kind of like the first problem we did. I solved it like Ephraim explained." Other students nodded their agreement.

I posed another problem. "Figure out how tall you'd be now if you had grown six feet each year since you were born," I instructed. "This time, record your solution and explain your thinking using numbers and words."

As I walked around the room, I overheard Judy say, "Doing the first problem really helps us solve this one!"

Anne-Marie used a chart to organize her work. She wrote the years in one vertical column, and on the other side of the table, she recorded her height for each year. She wrote: *I am 10 years old. I know I would be 60 feet tall and two months becouse I did this chart. and each year I grew 6 feet a year and I added 6 feet a year. So My tottol was 60 feet and two months.* (See Figure 4–3.)

Aubrey was interested in figuring precisely. He wrote: *I am exactly 64 feet because when 2 months = 1 foot 1 year is 6 feet, that is 60 feet in 10 years. So that means 8 months is 4 feet, so that must mean that I am 64 feet.* (See Figure 4–4.)

Jo was also concerned with being precise, and she figured out exactly how tall she would be to the month. She wrote: *I am 10 years old and I grow 6 feet every year so 10 × 6 = 60. You grow 6 inch. every mounth and it has been 8 mounths since my last birthday, so 6 × 8 = 48. 48 ÷ 12 = 4 feet. You ÷ 12 because 12 inch. in one foot. 4 feet + 60 feet = 64 feet.*

Judy decided to have fun with the fact that she was born in a leap year. She wrote: *I'm born on leap day so my birthday only*

Figure 4–3: Anne-Marie made a chart to show how she knew she would be 60 feet tall.

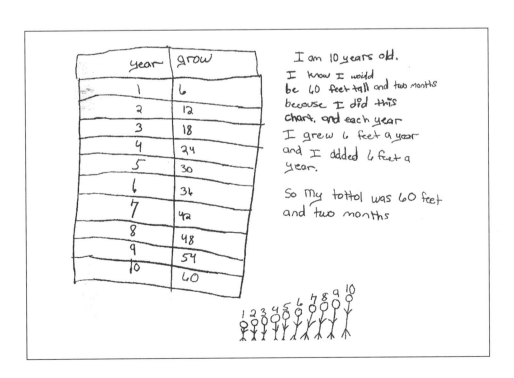

Math and Literature, Grades 4–6

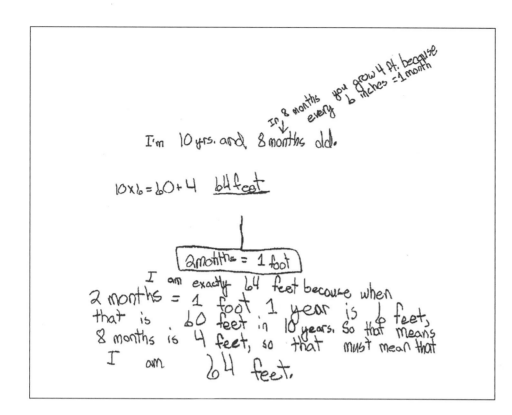

Figure 4–4: Aubrey figured out precisely how tall he would be.

comes once every four years but I have been alive 10 years a [and]
8 months. My birthdate: Feb. 29, 1984. Each year I grow 6 ft. Leap
year age: 2, 2 year, 8 months, 32 months leap year.

"How tall would you be if you counted all of the years and months?" I asked her.

"My actual age is ten years and eight months," she said. She referred to her paper and explained, "That's one hundred twenty-eight months because ten times twelve equals one hundred twenty, plus eight months is one hundred twenty-eight months. One hundred twenty-eight times six inches each month is seven hundred sixty-eight inches. And seven hundred sixty-eight inches divided by twelve is sixty-four feet tall."

Dylan added six ten times to get 60 feet. He told me, "I'm turning ten this month so I added an extra six feet."

Maggie worked with fractions to solve the problem. "I'm ten years old and seven months," she said. "I multiplied ten times six feet and got sixty feet. Then I multiplied six inches by seven months and got forty-two inches. Then I divided forty-two into twelve inches and got three and a half feet. I added that to sixty and got sixty-three and a half feet tall! That's tall!!"

When the students finished sharing their papers, Deirdre raised her hand. "If we really had grown six feet every year, I wonder who the tallest person would be and who the shortest would be?" she asked.

"Does anyone have an idea?" I asked.

"The tallest person would be the oldest!" Wesley exclaimed.

"And the shortest person?" I asked.

"The youngest!" everyone answered.

"I know who the tallest person would be. It would be you," Calie said, pointing at me and laughing.

"Here's your assignment for tomorrow," I told them. "You all know how tall you would be if you grew at a rate of six feet a year. I want you to find out what you would be as tall as. In other words, with what would you be able to see eye-to-eye?" As I was leaving, I heard Cameron ask a friend, "What in the world is sixty-six feet tall?"

Each Orange Had 8 Slices

In *Each Orange Had 8 Slices: A Counting Book*, by Paul Giganti Jr. (1999), each two-page spread shows people, animals, or objects grouped in three ways, then asks questions that require the reader to find the total number of each object in the picture. For example, the author writes, "I saw 4 trees. Each tree had 3 birds' nests. Each birds' nest had 2 spotted eggs." He then asks, "How many trees were there? How many birds' nests were there? How many spotted eggs were there in all?" The lesson based on this book gives children an opportunity to practice mental multiplication and combine story writing with mathematics.

MATERIALS

When I read *Each Orange Had 8 Slices* to John Swaim's fourth graders, they were in the middle of a unit on multiplication. Before reading the book, I explained to the students that they would write their own mathematical problems after I finished reading the book.

"As I read, pay attention to the problems that the author poses on each page," I said, "and think about how you would solve them."

After I read the first five pages, the students were eager to share their thoughts. Hands were waving in the air, and I could hear those familiar sounds that students make when they are dying to say something. I stopped reading to allow them to share their ideas.

"Who would like to tell us what kinds of things you've noticed about the book so far?" I asked.

"It's about math," Dawn said.

"You need to use times," Vivian observed.

"You're not supposed to say times," Anson said. "You're supposed to say multiplication."

"Would you agree with Vivian that you could use *multiplication* to solve the problems?" I asked. The students nodded in agreement.

"What else do you notice about the book?" I asked.

"You have to multiply three times when you solve a problem," Sheila said.

"Sheila, would you give us an example?" I asked.

"Could you turn to the page with the tricycles?" she asked.

I quickly turned back to the pages with three children riding tricycles and held it up for the class to see.

"See, there are three children and each one is riding one tricycle and each tricycle has three wheels," Sheila said. "The author asks how many kids, how many tricycles, then how many wheels in all. You could get the answer by going three times one times three. You use three numbers when you multiply."

I continued reading the story, stopping on the spread that shows four trees, three birds' nests in each tree, and two spotted eggs in each nest.

"How many trees are there?" I asked.

"Four," the class answered.

"How many birds' nests are there?" I asked.

"Twelve," they responded.

"How many spotted eggs are there in all?" I continued. "Raise your hand when you get the answer." After a few moments, several hands shot up.

"There are twenty-four spotted eggs," Colin said.

"How do you know that?" I asked.

"Because four trees multiplied by three birds' nests is twelve. Then twelve nests multiplied by two spotted eggs is twenty-four," he explained.

When I got to the last page of the book, I read the poem:

As I was going to St. Ives,
I met a man with 7 wives.
Every wife had 7 sacks.
Every sack had 7 cats.
Every cat had 7 kittens.
Kittens, cats, sacks, and wives,
How many were going to St. Ives?

The class was stunned. "Does anyone have an idea?" I asked. No one raised a hand.

"I'm going to read the last page again, and I want you to listen carefully to what the author says," I said. This time, I wrote the poem on the board and had the students read along with me. Then I asked them to discuss the problem with the people at their tables. After a minute or two, several hands were waving in the air. I asked the students for their attention, and I called on Malcolm.

"I think there were two thousand four hundred and one things going to St. Ives," he said. "I multiplied seven times seven times seven times seven and got two thousand four hundred one."

"Does anyone else have an idea to share?" I asked.

"It's a trick," Vivian said, giggling. "The author is asking how many were going to St. Ives, not how many altogether. Only one person was going to St. Ives."

Vivian's revelation received a collective groan from the class. Then the students started to laugh at the clever problem that had stumped them.

"The author asked a different question at the end of this problem," I said. "What are the questions that he asks at the end of the other problems in the book?"

"With the tricycles, he asked how many kids first. Then he asked how many tricycles. Then how many wheels in all," Cindy explained.

"So, as Sheila said earlier, the author asks three questions," I said. "The big question at the end asks about the total number of the last thing, like the wheels."

I walked to the board and made a chart with five columns. Then I handed the book to Annelise and asked her to read aloud her favorite page.

She read: "On my way to the zoo I saw three waddling ducks." In the first column, I wrote:

3 waddling ducks

Annelise continued reading: "Each duck had four baby ducks trailing behind." In the second column, I wrote:

4 baby ducks

Annelise then read: "Each duck said, 'QUACK, QUACK, QUACK.'" In the third column, I wrote:

Quack, Quack, Quack

In Column 4, I wrote the three questions:

How many waddling ducks were there?
How many baby ducks were there?
How many quacks were there in all?

"In Column Five, I want to write the multiplication sentence that tells about the story," I told them.

"It's three times four times three, and that equals thirty-six," Anastasia offered. I recorded Anastasia's idea in Column 5:

$$3 \times 4 \times 3 = 36$$

"If you were the author of your own story, what things would you include?" I asked. I called on Trudy.

"My story would go like this," she began. "I was on my way trick-or-treating, and I saw three pumpkins." I recorded *3 pumpkins* in the first column.

"Each pumpkin had one face, and each face had ten teeth," she continued. I recorded *1 face* in Column 2 and *10 teeth* in Column 3.

"What three questions should I write in Column Four?" I asked her.

"How many pumpkins? How many faces? How many teeth in all?" answered Trudy.

"And the multiplication sentence?" I asked.

"It's three times one times ten equals thirty teeth," she responded as I recorded.

"What other things could we include in our stories?" I asked.

"We could put ten trees, eight branches on each tree, and five twigs on each branch. That would be ten times eight times five," Billy suggested.

"How could we solve that problem?" I asked.

"I know," Billy said. "Ten times eight equals eighty and eighty times five is, hmmm." He was stuck.

"Can anyone think of a way we could multiply eighty times five?" I asked.

"Well, one hundred times five is five hundred," Sheila said. "And eighty is twenty less than one hundred and twenty times five is one hundred. So five hundred minus one hundred equals four hundred. The answer is four hundred."

"How about another way?" I probed.

"Well, eight times five is forty, so you just add a zero to forty and you get four hundred," Glen offered.

"Is there another way we could multiply eighty times five?" I asked.

"You could write eighty down on your paper," Vivian explained.

"Let me record what you say on the board," I said.

"OK, then write five below the zero in eighty and make a multiplication sign," Vivian continued. "Then you multiply zero times five, which is zero, and put the zero down. Then you multiply eight times five equals forty. You put the forty in front of the zero and you have four hundred."

"Now I want each of you to write your own story," I told the class. "Remember that you need to include an illustration to go along with your story. Are there any questions?"

"Can we do more than one story?" Cindy asked.

"Yes, after your first story is complete," I replied.

Some students began by discussing their story ideas with other students, some began writing immediately, and others collected colored pens or crayons. (See Figure 5–1 for one example.)

This activity gave the children an opportunity to think about multiplication in a way that made sense to them, one that was connected to things that were familiar to them. This was especially true for Macon. When I approached his desk, he was busy drawing pictures of Segas and games and bits. Macon was a Nintendo fan.

"How's it going, Macon?" I asked him.

"This is fun," he replied. "I play Nintendo all the time, and I like writing multiplication stories about the games."

"Can you explain your story to me?" I asked.

"These are ten Segas, and these are the eighteen games each Sega has," he said. "Each game has sixteen bits."

"What's a bit?" I asked, exposing my complete ignorance of video games.

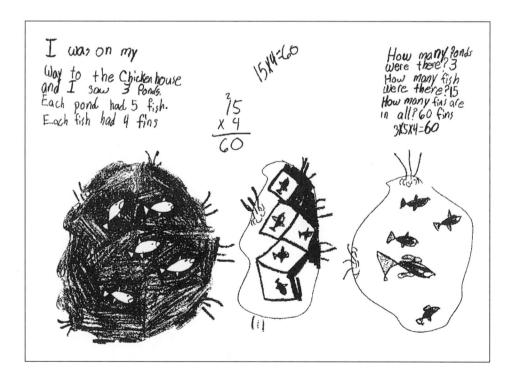

Figure 5–1: Colin connected multiplication to three ponds, which each contained five fish, which each had four fins.

"A bit is like the power each game has," Macon explained. "I multiplied ten times sixteen and got one hundred sixty. I knew it was one hundred sixty because I added a zero to sixteen for another hundred. Then I multiplied one hundred sixty times eighteen on the calculator and got two thousand eight hundred and eighty bits in all."

Aileen was drawing a large fire engine when I reached her table. "Aileen, tell me about your story," I said.

Aileen read what she had written: *On my way to the fire Station I Saw 3 fire engines on each of the fire engines I Saw 4 dalmations on each of the dalmations I Saw 7 Spots. How many firengingines did I See? 3 How many dalmations? 12 How many Spots? 84.* After multiplying three by four in her head, Aileen used the traditional algorithm for multiplying a two-digit number by a one-digit number and got the answer of eighty-four. (See Figure 5–2.)

The stories the children wrote were wonderful. The topics included ant farms, castles, ornaments on Christmas trees, salt on potato chips, and feathers on turkeys. The students enjoyed listening to one another's multiplication stories and figuring the answers. They were fascinated by how large some of the answers were, and I was impressed with the size of their imaginations! (Figure 5–3 shows another student's story.)

Figure 5–2: Aileen used the traditional algorithm for multiplying two digits by one digit in her story about fire engines, dalmations, and spots.

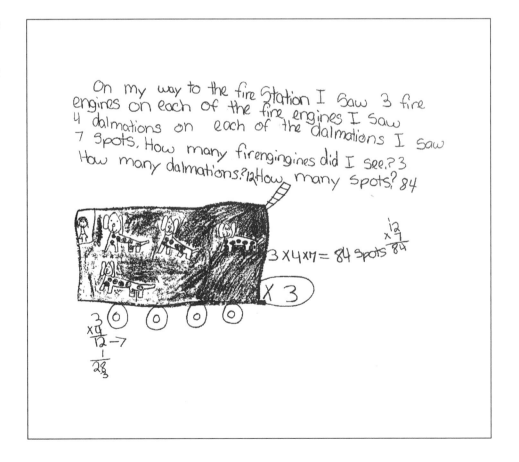

Figure 5–3: Joss's illustration helped him solve his multiplication story.

Esio Trot

Esio Trot, by Roald Dahl (2002), tells the story of two elderly people, Mr. Hoppy and Mrs. Silver, who talk to each other from their apartment balconies. Mrs. Silver loves her pet tortoise but wants it to grow larger. In hopes of winning over Mrs. Silver so she'll marry him, Mr. Hoppy gives her magic words to say to make the tortoise grow, then goes to a pet store and purchases 140 tortoises of various sizes. As time passes, he replaces the tortoises 1 by 1, each time with a tortoise that's a little larger. The ecstatic Mrs. Silver invites Mr. Hoppy over to see how her tortoise has "grown." When he asks, she agrees to marry him and they live "very happily ever after." Longer than a picture book, *Esio Trot* can be read over several days. It leads to several division problems for students to solve.

MATERIALS

optional: calculators, 1 per pair of students

The students in my fourth-grade class watched intently as I held up a picture from *Esio Trot.* The illustration, by Quentin Blake, shows Mr. Hoppy gingerly making his way through a room full of tortoises, being very careful not to step on any of them. The students listened intently as I began reading the story.

I read the book over four days, reading about ten to twelve pages each day. On the second day, I stopped on page 30 after I read the part where Mr. Hoppy buys 140 tortoises and takes them home in a basket, 10 or 15 at a time. I posed a question.

"I wonder how many trips to the pet store Mr. Hoppy would have to make if he took home fifteen tortoises each time?" I asked.

Although I saw this as a division situation, I didn't mention the word *division* when I presented the problem or tell the students that they were to divide 140 by 15. The students hadn't as yet had a great deal of experience with division, and I was curious to find out whether they would see this as a situation that called for dividing. I also was curious to see how they would figure out the answer.

"Does anyone have an idea of how to go about solving this problem?" I asked.

Sebastian raised his hand. "You could keep adding fifteen until you got to one hundred forty. Then you would know how many trips he took."

Amelia had another idea. "You could count by fifteens until you got to a hundred forty tortoises."

Miles chimed in, "I think it's a divide problem."

Annie said, "I think you can use take away if you start with one hundred forty tortoises."

After the students had shared their ideas for solving the problem, I explained to them what I wanted them to do. "First, make an estimate of how many trips you think it would take. Then solve the problem, and write about how you did it. Use words and numbers to explain your reasoning, and also use pictures, if they help describe your thinking." I finished my instructions by telling the students that they had a choice as to how they would work—in pairs, in small groups, or by themselves.

Some students decided to pair up with friends, and some chose to work alone. After the children had begun to work, I made my way around the room. I wanted to make myself available to those who needed help and to answer any of their questions about the task.

Sebastian immediately calculated in his head, then ran up to me and said, "This won't work because if he took nine trips, that would be one hundred thirty-five tortoises, and he would still have five left."

I responded, "Think about what to do with those five tortoises."

Sebastian decided that Mr. Hoppy would have to make an extra trip and that he could carry five tortoises the last time. Having solved the problem so quickly, Sebastian was ready for the other question I had in mind.

"When you finish writing about this problem," I said, "try figuring out how many trips Mr. Hoppy would have to take if he could carry only ten tortoises at a time." I left Sebastian and made my way to the next table of students.

Heidi seemed frustrated. She had begun by working alone. When she realized she was stuck, however, she began discussing the problem with Ilene, who was sitting next to her. Ilene suggested that they "imagine Mr. Hoppy carrying fifteen tortoises at a time from the pet store to his house." This seemed to help. Heidi wrote *140*, subtracted 15, and kept subtracting 15 until she reached 5. Then she had to subtract another 5 to get to zero. As Heidi subtracted, Ilene used the results of Heidi's calculations and recorded the number of tortoises left after each trip.

Amelia was busy counting by fifteens. I listened as she said aloud each number she got after adding fifteen more in her head. I was impressed at how easily Amelia added mentally. On her paper, she recorded *15, 30, 45, 60, 75,* and so on up to *135.* Then she jumped to 140. She wrote: *I counted like this to get my answer, and my answer is 10 trips.*

Alice estimated that it would take 50 trips. After discussing her estimate with a friend, she changed it to 15 trips. Then she multiplied 140 tortoises by 15 trips and got 2,100 trips!

"Does that seem reasonable?" I asked her.

Alice's number sense rescued her for the moment. "No way!" she responded.

I suggested that she talk to her partner about another way to solve the problem. When I left Alice to move on to another student, I noticed that she was still struggling to make sense of the numbers. (Alice eventually solved the problem by adding fifteens together until she got the answer.)

Miles was the only one to use the word *divide* in his writing. He wrote: *If you dieved 140 and 15 it will eqole 9.3333333 and I don't think that's the answer.* Although dividing was his initial instinct, when he did so on the calculator, he couldn't make sense of the decimal point and all those 3s! He didn't realize that he was on the right track. I encouraged Miles to set aside his calculator answer for a moment and try to look at the problem in a different way.

"What you're telling me," I said, "is that the answer you got on the calculator doesn't make sense to you. Can you think of another method to use in order to solve the problem?"

Miles ended up adding 15s until he reached 135. "The answer is nine trips after all," he told me, "but that's only one hundred thirty-five tortoises, so you need to add five more tortoises and one more trip and you get the answer."

"I could tell that ten was the answer from the number you got when you divided on the calculator," I told Miles.

"How?" he asked me.

"What was the number on the calculator?" I asked.

"It was this," Miles said, showing me the 9.3333333 on his paper.

"That's a number that's more than nine, but not as much as ten," I explained. "The decimal point after the nine and the numbers that follow it tell me that."

"That's neat," Miles said.

"Suppose you divided nine by two," I said. "What would you get?"

"On the calculator?" Miles asked.

"Try it in your head first," I answered. "Then you can see what the calculator result would be."

Miles thought for a moment. "It's four and a half," he said.

"Yes," I agreed, "and four and a half is a number that's more than four and less than five. Try dividing nine by two on the calculator."

Miles did so. "Look!" he said, excited. "It's four point five!"

I'm not sure what Miles really understood or would remember from my explanation, but I thought the digression had potential value. Much of learning happens incidentally when a need arises, and I took this opportunity to try to give Miles a new insight.

When the students finished their work, I had them meet in a circle on the rug and take turns sharing their ideas. Some of the students reported in pairs, giving details about how they worked together by giving each other ideas or taking turns recording information and counting tortoises. Others read their individual pieces, some describing how they added in their heads, some telling how they subtracted, and others reporting how they used a calculator.

Having students share their mathematical ideas both before and after the actual work time helps in two ways. Brainstorming ideas beforehand allows children to hear different ways to approach the problem. Sharing answers and strategies afterward reinforces the idea that there are many ways to solve a problem and also helps build a sense of community in the classroom.

As our meeting on the rug came to a close, I asked the children the same question I had asked Sebastian earlier. "What if Mr. Hoppy could carry only ten tortoises home at a time? How many trips would that be?" Some students were interested in tackling this problem, while others were more interested in hearing the rest of the story to find out exactly what Mr. Hoppy was going to do with 140 tortoises. I continued reading and left the problem for those who were interested to solve later.

The students loved the book. They especially enjoyed writing notes to one another in tortoise language, and some became quite adept at spelling words backward. They laughed at how gullible Mrs. Silver was and waited with anticipation to find out whether Mr. Hoppy's plan to marry Mrs. Silver would really work. They were pleased to find out that Mr. Hoppy and Mrs. Silver did marry and lived "very happily ever after." (Figures 6–1 and 6–2 show how two students worked on the tortoise problems.)

Figure 6–1: Amelia counted
by fifteens and then by tens
to figure out the number of
trips Mr. Hoppy would have
to take.

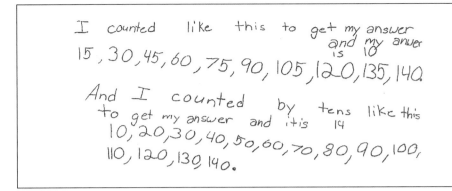

Figure 6–2: Jasper used
addition to solve the two
problems.

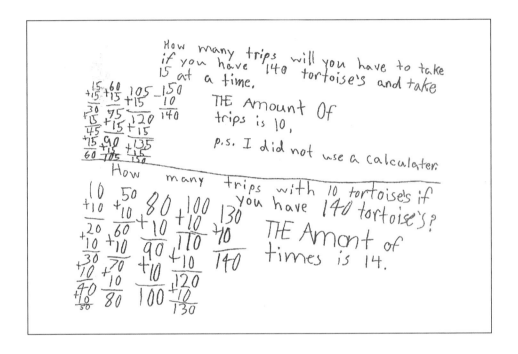

Presenting the Problem to a Fifth- and Sixth-Grade Class

The fifth and sixth graders in Patti Reynolds's class had already read *Esio Trot* and were excited to introduce me to their class pet, a red slider turtle. After discussing the differences between red sliders and tortoises, I reminded the students about Mr. Hoppy buying 140 tortoises and taking them home 10 or 15 at a time. I then posed a slightly different version of the problem I had presented to my class.

"What's the greatest number of trips Mr. Hoppy would have to make to carry the tortoises home?" I asked. "Figure this out and explain your thinking in writing. Are there any questions?"

"How many baskets does he have?" Dale asked.

"He has one basket," I replied.

"So he can take ten or fifteen. Can he take a combination, like ten one time and fifteen another time?" Liora asked.

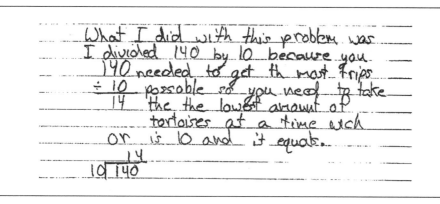

Figure 6–3: Erica divided to figure out the greatest number of trips Mr. Hoppy could take.

> What I did with this problem was I divided 140 by 10 because you 140 needed to get th most trips ÷ 10 possoble so you need to take 14 the the lowest amount of tortoises at a time wich or is 10 and it equals.
>
> 14
> 10)140

"Yes," I answered. "He takes ten or fifteen tortoises home on each trip," I answered.

"What about the size of the tortoises?" Dale asked.

"Don't worry about size. The basket is large enough to hold ten or fifteen tortoises. Just figure out the most number of trips Mr. Hoppy would have to take," I said.

After about fifteen minutes, all of the students had found an answer. (See Figure 6–3 for Erica's solution.)

"Who would like to report how you solved the problem?" I asked. I called on Sid.

"I multiplied ten times fourteen trips and got one hundred forty," Sid said. "I think Mr. Hoppy would have to take ten tortoises each time because if he took fifteen tortoises, then that would be fewer trips."

"Did anyone solve it a different way?" I asked.

"I think it will take fourteen turns because if you divide one hundred forty and ten, you get fourteen trips," Emanuel explained. He then added, "I've read that book before, and I think it's a good book."

"Did anyone solve the problem a different way?" I asked. No one raised a hand. Everyone agreed that the most trips Mr. Hoppy would have to take would be fourteen. (See Figure 6–4 for Keith's solution.)

"I have another problem for you to solve now," I told the class.

"I bet I know," Mallory said. "I bet you're going to ask us to figure out the smallest number of trips he could make."

"I think you'll ask us how much each one cost," Annie said.

"I think you'll ask us how long it took Mr. Hoppy to carry all of the tortoises," Moss guessed.

"Or something about the size of the tortoises, like their weight," Ursula said.

"All of these are interesting problems to investigate," I responded. "The problem I'd like you to work on now starts like Mallory's: Can Mr. Hoppy get the tortoises home in fewer than fourteen trips? But

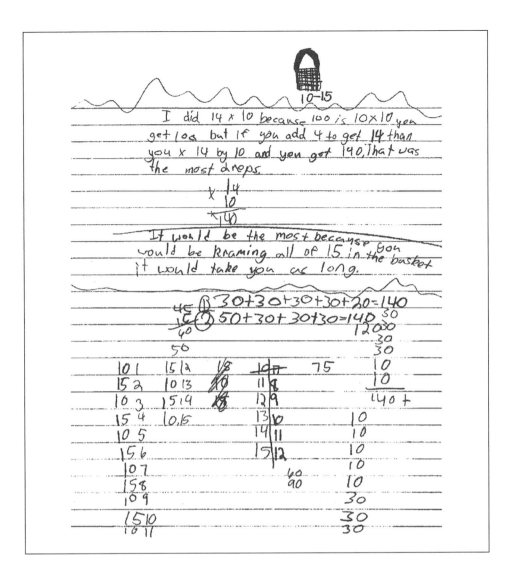

Figure 6–4: Keith used multiplication to determine that Mr. Hoppy would have to take fourteen trips.

I'd also like you to figure out how many different ways Mr. Hoppy can get the tortoises home."

"I don't get it," Mason said.

I continued, "We know that one way is for Mr. Hoppy to take ten tortoises at a time, which makes fourteen trips. But as Liora said before, he can take home ten on some trips and fifteen on others. If he still takes ten or fifteen tortoises at a time, how many different ways can he get them all home?"

As I watched the students work, I noticed that they were solving the problem in many different ways. Some were using multiplication, and others were using division or addition. Some organized their findings into charts. (See Figure 6–5.) Some were looking for patterns. After about thirty minutes, I stopped the students and asked for their attention.

"Some of you are at a point where you think you've found all of the ways Mr. Hoppy can take his tortoises home. Now I want you

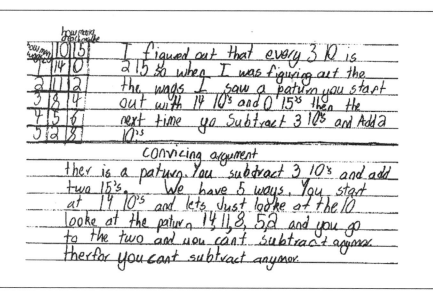

The handwritten chart and text reads:

how many of each one	10	15
how many trips	14	0
	11	2
	8	4
	5	6
	2	8

I figured out that every 3 10 is 2 15 so when I was figuring out the the ways I saw a paturn you start out with 14 10's and 0 15's then the next time yo Subtract 3 10's and Add a 10's

convicing arqument

ther is a paturn. You subtract 3 10's and add two 15's. We have 5 ways. You start at 14 10's and lets Just looke at the 10 looke at the paturn 14, 11, 8, 5, 2 and you go to the two and you cant subtract anymor therfor you cant subtract anymor.

to write a convincing argument explaining how you know you've found all the ways," I told them.

The students went back to work. I interrupted them after about fifteen minutes. "I'd like us to have a mathematical conversation about what you've discovered so far," I said. "Who would like to share your thinking about the problem?"

"There are five different ways I found," Reed said. "Mr. Hoppy can take the tortoises home in fourteen trips, thirteen trips, twelve, eleven, and ten trips. I made a chart that has two columns. One column says 'Combinations' and the other column says 'Number of Trips.' So when Mr. Hoppy takes the tortoises home in fourteen trips, he takes ten tortoises every time. When he takes them home in thirteen trips, there are eleven groups of ten tortoises and two groups of fifteen. For twelve trips, there are eight groups of ten tortoises and four groups of fifteen. For eleven trips, there are five groups of ten and six groups of fifteen tortoises. For ten trips, there are two groups of ten and eight groups of fifteen tortoises. I noticed that on the trips where I used fifteen, there was an even amount of fifteens." I had Reed reproduce his chart on the board. (See Figure 6–6.)

"How could knowing about the pattern you found about even groups of fifteen help you know you found all the ways?" I asked.

"Well, I know because odd numbers of fifteen tortoises don't work, so I can get rid of those," he explained. "Then I just have to find the greatest even number of fifteens that works for one hundred forty and add all the tens!"

Lexie looked at the problem differently. "The pattern I saw was this," she said. "If you see the times you use fifteen tortoises, it goes

Figure 6–6: Reed's chart helped him notice patterns.

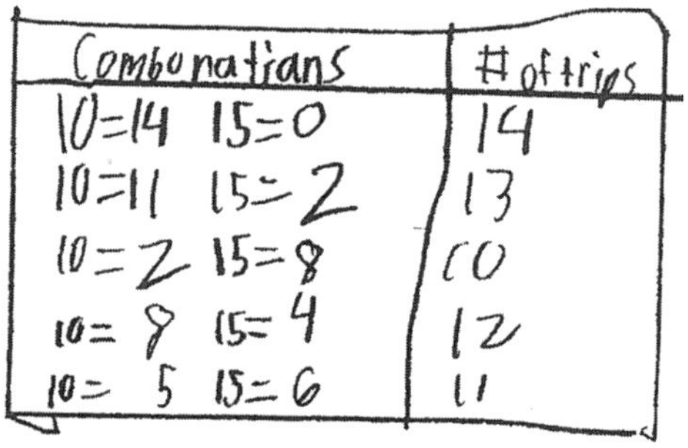

fifteen times two, fifteen times four, fifteen times six, fifteen times eight. See, the number on the right is a pattern, like two, four, six, eight. But if you go to ten you get one hundred fifty tortoises, and that's too many. The pattern is over, so that's how I know I have all the ways."

"How come Mr. Hoppy can't take fifteen tortoises three times, or five times, or seven times?" I asked.

"If you use an uneven number of fifteen tortoises you get a remainder," Erica said.

"Can you give us an example?" I asked.

"If Mr. Hoppy takes three groups of fifteen tortoises, that's forty-five tortoises," explained Amelia. "He would have to take ten groups of ten, but that makes one hundred forty-five tortoises. If he took nine groups of ten, the total would be one hundred thirty-five tortoises, with five remaining."

"I did it by adding," Moss said. "I started with the most number of trips, zero groups of fifteen plus one hundred forty. Then I did thirty plus one hundred ten, sixty plus eighty, ninety plus fifty, one hundred twenty plus twenty. I noticed the numbers on the left go up by thirty each time, like this: zero, thirty, sixty, ninety, one hundred twenty. The numbers on the right go down by thirty each time, like this: one hundred forty, one hundred ten, eighty, fifty, twenty."

"Looking at the number patterns seems to have helped some of you be sure that you have found all the ways," I said.

"I know I have all the ways because I tried all the numbers and combinations on paper and the calculator," Liora said.

"I wonder if you could change the numbers around, how many different combinations there would be?" Caitlin asked.

"Do you mean if the order were important?" I asked.

"Yes," Caitlin said. "To get one hundred forty tortoises home, Mr. Hoppy could take them in eleven trips by taking six groups of fifteen tortoises and five groups of ten. But what if he took fifteen tortoises on the first trip, ten the second, and fifteen the third? Or he could take ten tortoises on the first trip, and fifteen on the second trip, and so on. What if the order counted? How many ways would there be?"

"That would be a huge problem!" Jackson exclaimed.

After the students shared the different ways they had solved the tortoise problem, I continued reading the story. When the students found out that Mrs. Silver would marry Mr. Hoppy, they applauded. It was their way of congratulating Mr. and Mrs. Hoppy and showing their appreciation for a book they enjoyed. (Figure 6–7 shows another student's solution to the tortoise problem.)

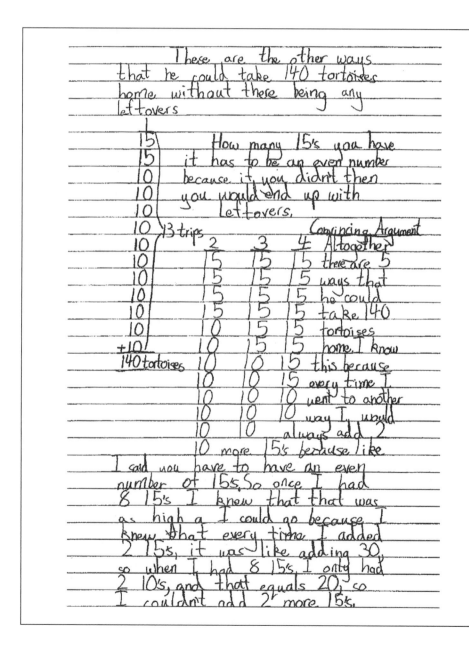

Figure 6–7: Pablo added combinations of tens and fifteens to find all the ways to carry one hundred forty tortoises.

Grandfather Tang's Story

In *Grandfather Tang's Story*, by Ann Tompert (1997), Grandfather Tang and Little Soo are sitting under a tree playing with tangram puzzles when Grandfather Tang begins telling the story of two foxes who change into different animals to outdo each other. One changes into a rabbit and the other into a dog, one changes into a squirrel and the other into a hawk, and so on. With each animal, Grandfather Tang creates a matching tangram shape. This book combines a story about friendship and competition with the fascination of tangram shapes. The book is a springboard to an activity in which students make their own tangrams, then use them to investigate geometric shapes and explore area and measurement.

MATERIALS

6-inch squares of construction paper, 1 per student

colored butcher paper, 1 large sheet

scissors, 1 pair per student

"Tangrams are ancient Chinese puzzles that adults and children still use today," I told Carol Schurlock's sixth graders to begin the lesson. "I have a book I'd like to read to you about a storyteller who tells his granddaughter a tale using pieces of the tangram puzzle."

I began reading *Grandfather Tang's Story*. Robert Andrew Parker's watercolors captured the students' attention. They listened quietly to all of the foxes's adventures and predicted what the animals would turn into as they chased after each other.

When I finished reading the story, I gave each student a 6-inch square of construction paper and a pair of scissors.

"Do we get to make tangrams?" Melanie asked.

"Yes," I answered. "We're each going to make our own set." When all of the students had the materials, I called for their attention.

"Hold up your square and fold it in half along the diagonal," I instructed. "What shape are you holding now?"

"A triangle," they responded.

"Open the triangle and cut the square in half along the diagonal," I said. I held up my square and cut it in half to show them what I meant.

"You should now have two triangles," I continued. "Put one of these triangles on your table. Take the other triangle. Fold it in half, open it up, and cut along the fold so you have two smaller triangles." I demonstrated how the students were to do this.

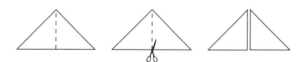

"Compare the two triangles. What do you notice about them?" I asked.

"They're exactly the same," Josiah said.

"The triangles are *congruent*," added Cecily, pleased to remember the word.

"How do you know they're congruent?" I asked.

"Because if you took one of them and laid it on top of the other, they're both the same size and shape," Cecily explained.

"What else do you notice about these triangles?" I asked. The students were flipping and rotating their triangles and talking to one another. Soon, several hands were wiggling in the air. I called on Deborah.

"They both have a square corner," she said. "It's a ninety-degree angle." Deborah held up a triangle and pointed to the 90-degree angle with her finger.

"Show me with your index finger where the ninety-degree angle is on one of your triangles," I instructed the class. Most students quickly located the 90-degree angle; a few checked with neighbors to see if they were correct.

"Mathematicians call triangles with a square corner or a ninety-degree angle right triangles," I added.

I continued with directions for cutting the tangram puzzle. "Put the two congruent triangles on your table and pick up the large triangle," I said. "Now, make two folds on the large triangle. First, fold it in half as you did with the other large triangle. Then open it up and take the top corner and fold it down until it touches the base of the triangle. Watch as I do this. You have to make two folds before you cut." I had the students follow as I demonstrated each fold and then opened the triangle and cut along the horizontal fold.

"Can someone tell us the names of these two shapes?" I asked.

"A triangle and a trapezoid," Jordan replied. "I learned about trapezoids last year." I nodded my agreement.

"Now take the trapezoid and cut it in half along the fold. That makes two trapezoids," I instructed.

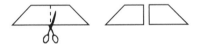

"Fold one of the trapezoids to make a square and a triangle, open it, and cut it along the fold," I then directed. This was easy for the students to do.

"Next, fold and cut the last trapezoid to make a parallelogram and a triangle," I explained. This was the most difficult step, and I had the students follow as I demonstrated, watching carefully to see that they were folding and cutting as I was.

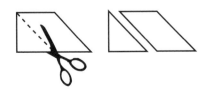

I walked around to each table, checking to see that the students had folded and cut correctly. When I got to Gunther's table, I noticed that he had cut his square into too many pieces. I handed him a new square from the extras I had in my pocket and reminded him that mistakes are a part of learning. With assistance from his neighbor, he quickly made a correct set of tangram pieces.

When everyone had a complete set of seven tangram pieces, I asked for the children's attention. "Now that each of you has your own tangram set, make a triangle on your table," I said.

"Can we use more than one tangram piece?" Joy asked.

"Yes," I replied. The students quickly made triangles, some using one piece, some two or more. I then gave instructions for the next part of the lesson.

"In the story, the foxes changed into different animals," I said. "Take the triangle you've made and change it into another triangle, then another, then another, using different pieces. Work with the people in your group and make as many different triangles as you can."

"How will we keep track of them?" Deborah asked.

"Once you've made a triangle, trace it on a piece of paper and cut it out," I explained. I pointed to a large sheet of blue butcher paper on the board. "When everyone is finished, we'll post examples of all the different triangles you found."

"When we're tracing, do we trace around each piece or just the whole triangle?" Marlon asked.

"Trace around each piece, so we can see how you made each triangle," I replied.

The students worked in their groups cooperatively, helping one another put tangram pieces together to make different triangles. I noticed that there were discussions about other shapes they encountered as they searched for triangles. A few students colored their triangles, and the idea spread throughout the class. Soon, most of them were busily coloring before they cut. After about thirty minutes, I asked for their attention.

"I'd like to have all the different triangles you found posted on the blue paper," I told them. "We'll take turns so that one group at a time posts a triangle. Choose one person from your group to do the posting. Remember that we want to post triangles that are all different."

"I have a question," Deborah said. "Are these two triangles different?" She held up two triangles that were the same size and shape, which were both made from all seven pieces, but the arrangements of the pieces were different.

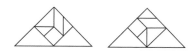

"What do you think?" I asked.

"Well, I think they're different because the pieces are in different places," Deborah answered.

"I agree," I responded. "There can be different arrangements of the same tangram pieces."

The students watched as one group after another brought a triangle up to the front of the room to post. Some students carefully held their triangles next to others on the chart to see if they were the same or different. When Frasier posted a triangle that was the same as one already posted, several hands went up.

"Frasier's is the same as the other triangle made from three pieces!" Skye exclaimed. "He used the same pieces and the same arrangement." Frasier held his triangle next to the one Skye was referring to. He studied the two triangles and realized that they were identical.

Soon the blue paper was covered with triangles made from one, two, three, four, and seven tangram pieces.

"Let's take a look at our collection of triangles," I said. "When mathematicians want to make better sense of information, they organize it. Raise your hand if you have an idea about how we could organize the triangles." I called on Lyric.

"We could make a list of the number of pieces across the board," she said. "That would be one to seven. Then we could put the triangles made from one piece under that heading, ones with two pieces under the two-piece heading, and so on."

"Does anyone else have an idea for organizing the triangles?" I asked. No one raised a hand. I quickly rearranged the triangles, following Lyric's directions.

"We don't have any triangles made with six tangram pieces," Gunther noticed.

"There are no triangles made with five pieces either," Roxanne added.

The students went back to work, searching for ways to make new triangles for the class chart.

"I think I have another triangle with seven tangram pieces," Augie said. He brought his triangle up to the chart and studied the shapes.

"Augie, yours is the same as that one," Nico said, pointing to another triangle made from seven tangram pieces. "Why don't you put your triangle next to that one and see?" Augie tested his triangle and found that it wasn't different. He quickly returned to his seat to try another idea. He soon made a triangle using five pieces. Others cheered when he posted it.

Lyric found a triangle made of three pieces that was different from the two posted. "Yes!" she said, grinning as she posted it.

"I think I've got one for six tangram pieces!" Claire shouted. Several students ran over to her desk. Running was not usually allowed in Mrs. Schurlock's class, but even she found herself rushing over to Claire's desk to see what all the excitement was about.

"Oh, she accidentally used another medium-sized triangle from someone else's set," Jarvis said, disappointed. Undaunted, Claire went right back to work.

Some students were gathered at another table, watching someone work. I peeked over their shoulders and found Jordan working feverishly to put six tangram pieces together.

"I've got it!" he exclaimed. He quickly traced and cut out his discovery and then posted it on the class chart. Melanie and Frasier also made triangles from the same six pieces that Jordan used, but theirs were different arrangements of the pieces. They posted them. Our class chart now looked like this:

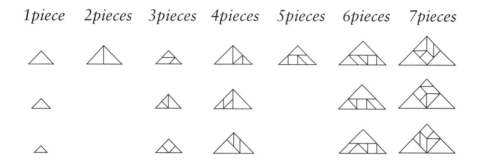

I called the class to attention. "I'd like everyone to take a look at the class chart and talk with someone next to you about what you notice," I told them. After a minute or so, several students had their hands raised. I called on Curt.

"They're all triangles," he said.

"Some are the same size but they're still different," Alexandra said. "Like those two triangles are both made from four pieces, but they have different pieces." She went up to the chart to prove it to the class.

"Well, a lot of them are congruent, really," Deborah said.

"Tell us what you mean, Deborah," I said.

"If you just look at the size and not the position of the pieces inside, then a lot of them are congruent," she explained. "Like, all of the seven-piece triangles and six-piece triangles."

"The triangles made from one tangram piece are all different sizes," added Gunther.

"Let's take a look at the triangles Gunther is talking about," I said, pointing to the three triangles made from single tangram pieces. "Because these triangles aren't the same size, they aren't congruent."

I posed another question. "Look at all the triangles. How else are they different?"

"They have different areas," Ryan said.

"Let's say that the square piece is worth one unit of area," I said. "Take one of the other tangram pieces, and figure out what its area is. Check with your neighbor." While most of the students were able to figure the area of a piece, a few checked with their neighbors for help.

"What's the area of the small triangle?" I asked.

"One-half," some of the students responded.

"That's easy," several said.

"If the square is worth one unit of area, what's the value of the parallelogram?" I asked. This was not as easy. The students talked about this in their groups for a bit, and then several hands shot up.

"I think the parallelogram is worth one unit because you can fit two small triangles on top of it," Frasier explained. "Since the small triangles are worth one-half, I added one-half plus one-half and it makes one whole."

"What about the large triangle?" I asked. I gave them time to think and then called on Lyric.

"The large triangle is worth two units," she said.

"How do you know?" I asked her.

"Because four small triangles fit on it," Lyric replied. "I know that if you add one-half plus one-half plus one-half plus one-half, it equals two."

"And the medium-sized triangle?" I asked.

"It's the same as the square," Alexandra said. "You can prove it by matching two small triangles on top of it."

"Now that you know the value of each piece, I have a problem for you to solve," I said. "I want you to choose a triangle with at least two pieces from our class chart. Use your tangram pieces to make that triangle, then trace it onto a sheet of white paper. Then figure the area of your triangle if the square is worth one unit of area. Remember to explain your thinking using words and numbers. You can work together and help one another, but each of you needs to record individually."

The students were excited about the problem. I distributed sheets of $8\frac{1}{2}$-by-11-inch white paper, and the students began tracing triangles. After a few minutes, everyone was working hard to figure the area of his or her triangle.

Raven read to me how she figured the area. She had written: *To find the area you need to add each shape and since a square equals 1 so you would measure the square with all the shapes and the small triangle equals $\frac{1}{2}$ and the medium triangle equals 1 and the large* triangle equals 2 and the other small triangle equals $\frac{1}{2}$ and then you add it all up and you get 4. $\frac{1}{2} + 1 + 2 + \frac{1}{2} = 4$.

Ryan explained in writing how he solved the problem: *I think this triangle equals 8 because you can get a hole square and put it on the triangl 6 times, but ther are four halfes left over put 2 halfes together and you get a hole then do the same with the other two and its a hole, and those two pluse the other 6 is 8.*

As the students finished, I gave them the challenge of figuring the area of their triangle when the value of the square was $\frac{1}{2}$ or $\frac{1}{4}$.

Again, Ryan explained how he figured the area of his triangle when the value of the square was $\frac{1}{4}$: *If the squar is worth $\frac{1}{4}$ than the triangle is worth two because you need $\frac{4}{4}$ in order to make a hole, and in the triangle $\frac{1}{4}$ goes into it 8 times. . . . If you have $\frac{4}{4}$ it is a hole and the other $\frac{4}{4}$ equal 1 hole than that makes 1 hole + 1 hole = 2 holes and the value is two.*

Lyric read from her paper: "If the square is one-fourth, the whole triangle is worth one. It is one because the big triangle is worth one-half plus the medium triangle, which is one-quarter, plus two-eighths, or one-quarter, from the two small triangles equals one."

When the students were finished, we worked together to record the areas of all the triangles on the class chart using the square as 1 unit of area.

"Now that you know the areas of the triangles on our chart, raise your hand if you have any questions, comments, or observations," I said.

"All the triangles made from seven pieces have the same area," Lyric said.

"That's also true for the triangles made from six pieces," Alec added.

"There are three different triangles made from four pieces," Jordan said. "Two of them have areas of four and the other one has an area of four and a half; it's a little bigger."

"It's weird that the triangle made from five pieces has the same area as two of them made from four pieces," Deborah said.

"The more pieces you use, the greater the area, except for one or two triangles," Ryan said.

"I wonder what a pentagon chart would look like?" Claire inquired. "I wonder if we could find more pentagons than triangles?"

"That would be interesting," I said. "We can investigate pentagons on another day."

This activity gave the students a chance to see mathematics in a way that integrated several topics. It not only gave them the chance to explore how geometric shapes can be put together in different ways but also linked a geometry experience to the areas of number

Figure 7–1: Marius chose a five-piece triangle and figured the areas when the square was worth $\frac{1}{4}$ and when it was worth 1.

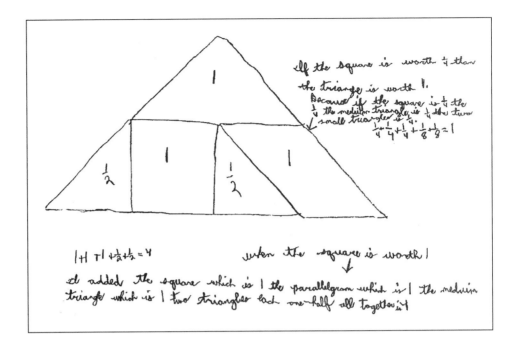

and measurement. Also, the activity gave the students the opportunity to think about fractions. (See Figure 7–1 for one student's paper.)

Is a Blue Whale the Biggest Thing There Is?

In *Is a Blue Whale the Biggest Thing There Is?* author and illustrator Robert E. Wells (1993) gives readers an incredible look at the size of things in the world around us. The book starts by introducing the largest creature on earth: the blue whale, which can grow to be 100 feet long. Then the book shows that a tower of jars, each filled with one hundred blue whales, "would look quite small balanced on top of Mount Everest!" Mount Everest is compared to Earth, Earth to the Sun, the Sun to "a red supergiant star called Antares," Antares to our galaxy, and galaxies to the universe. After reading the book, students complete activities that involve measuring, finding averages, and comparing lengths.

MATERIALS

1 ball of yarn at least 100 feet long

yardsticks and tape measures, 1 each per group of four students

3-by-3-inch sticky notes, 1 per student

"A blue whale can grow to be one hundred feet long and weigh one hundred fifty tons!" Patty Montgomery read as she showed her fourth graders a picture of a blue whale from *Is a Blue Whale the Biggest Thing There Is?*

The children were fascinated by the size comparisons throughout the book. The picture of an enormous jar of one hundred blue whales next to an elephant, a horse, and a lion drew "oohs" and "aahs." Another picture of a tiny bag of one hundred full-sized Earths orbiting around a gigantic Sun prompted exclamations of disbelief. The students were amazed that more than one million Earths would equal the size of the Sun, and that more than fifty million Suns would equal the size of Antares, "a red supergiant star."

When she finished reading the book, Patty turned back to the page showing the picture of the blue whale.

"In the book it says that blue whales can reach one hundred feet in length," Patty said. "How long do you think one hundred feet is?"

"About as long as the field outside," Amon said.

"I think it's longer than our classroom," Kira offered.

To demonstrate a length of 100 feet, Patty used a yardstick and a ball of yarn. "Since there are three feet in a yard," she said, "let's count by threes as I measure." As Patty measured the yarn 1 yard at a time, one student rolled the yarn back into a ball so it wouldn't get tangled.

When Patty had measured 4 yards and the students had counted to 12 feet, Patty asked, "Will we land on one hundred feet if we continue counting by threes?"

"No," Amika said. "We'll say ninety-nine, then one hundred two."

After the class had counted by threes to ninety-nine, Patty measured one more foot of yarn to equal 100 feet. She then cut the yarn.

"If we stretch out this hundred-foot yarn across the room, how would it compare with the length of the room?" Patty asked.

Students called out several answers. "It's longer." "It would go much farther." "It's a lot more."

"How about through this room, the next room, and onto the playground?" she asked. This time, most of the students were unsure.

Patty took the class into the hall. The students helped unravel the yarn by standing a few feet apart in a long line and holding the yarn at their waists.

"This is the length of a blue whale," Patty reminded them. "Try to keep this picture in your mind."

The students then rolled the yarn back up and returned to the classroom. Patty posed a question.

"How many fourth graders do you think it would take to equal a blue whale's length of one hundred feet?" she asked.

"Do you mean lying down end-to-end or standing next to each other?" Gideon asked.

"Lying down end-to-end," Patty replied. "Discuss this in your groups and decide on an estimate."

After a few minutes, Patty repeated the question and had the groups report their estimates. The students at Table 1 couldn't agree. They each had come up with a different estimate—forty, fifty, eighty, and one hundred.

"How tall would each student be if one hundred students equaled one hundred feet?" Patty asked to help the students think about whether their estimates were reasonable.

"Only one foot tall," Derek said.

"Is that possible?" Patty asked.

"No!" the students chorused.

Patty thanked Table 1 for giving their classmates an opportunity to think more about their estimates. Then she gave the students a minute or so to revise their estimates and again asked for their ideas. Now their estimates ranged from ten to fifty.

"What would you need to know to solve this problem?" Patty asked.

"Measure each person," Gina suggested.

"You have to know how many kids there are," Kira said.

"You have to picture how big a blue whale is and then picture how many kids would fit along it," Jill said.

"Maybe you could take the yarn outside again and have kids lie on it," Gina said.

"What if you weren't allowed to use the yarn?" Patty asked.

"Make up sizes for the children," Sawyer replied.

"What would be a reasonable size for a fourth grader?" Patty continued.

"Four feet tall?" Kira guessed.

"Do any of you think you are four feet tall?" Patty asked. Dalya raised her hand. Using the yardstick, Patty measured Dalya's height. She was just about 4 feet 2 inches tall.

"But lots of kids are taller than Dalya," Jonas said.

"What else could be a reasonable height for a fourth grader?" Patty asked.

"Maybe four feet ten inches," Jonas said. He came up to the front of the group to be measured. Jonas was a little taller than 5 feet.

"I think we should have everyone measure themselves," Kira suggested. The students seemed eager to find out how tall they were.

Patty demonstrated how to measure a student's height by measuring Amon. She used one of several tape measures she had in the room. Patty had another student hold the tape at Amon's toes, and she stretched it above his head, pinching the tape where it reached the top of his head.

"Amon is fifty-six inches tall," Patty said. "When you know your height, record it on a sticky note in two ways. First, record it in inches, as you read it on the tape measure, and then record it in feet and inches." Patty wrote on the board:

56" or 56 in.

"You can write it in inches in either of these two ways," she said. "Then also record your height on the sticky note in feet and inches. How many feet are in fifty-six inches? Talk at your tables about that."

After a few moments, Patty asked for their ideas.

"It's four feet and eight inches left over," Gina said. "We counted by twelves—twelve, twenty-four, thirty-six, forty-eight, sixty. We knew sixty was too much, so we went back to forty-eight and then counted up on our fingers to fifty-six."

"I did it a different way," Leon said. "I know that five feet is sixty inches, so I knew that fifty-six inches is four inches less, so I took away four inches from twelve inches and got eight inches. So it's four feet and eight inches."

Patty recorded on the board:

4 ft. 8 in. or 4'8"

"You can write it either way," she said.

Patty then instructed the children to work together, measure their heights, record on sticky notes, and post them on the board. When everyone was finished, the board was filled with thirty sticky notes. Patty then asked the class a question.

"Who has an idea about how we could organize the sticky notes so we can look at the information about everyone's height?" she asked. Hands flew up. Patty called on Alma.

"Put them in order from shortest to tallest," Alma said.

"If there are people with the same measurements, theirs should go in a column, one on top of the other," Amon added.

Patty quickly arranged the sticky notes. As she did so, the students commented about the range of heights and noticed which measurements occurred more than once.

"Now that you have some experience measuring yourselves, how do you think scientists figured out that the blue whale can reach one hundred feet in length?" Patty asked. "How do you think they measured a blue whale?"

"I think scuba divers measured some big ones and some little ones with underwater equipment," Danica said.

"They couldn't have measured them all because there are too many and they're hard to find," Jésus said.

"So you think they measured just a sample of whales?" Patty asked.

"Yes," several students answered.

"I think scientists measured some blue whales and then figured out how small and big they could get," Tierney said.

"If a scientist was using our measurements to report how tall a fourth grader might typically be, what might he or she say?" Patty asked.

"Between four and five feet," Danica said.

"About four and a half feet tall because that's between four and five feet. It's kind of like an average," Jill said.

"I think a scientist would say that a fourth grader can reach five feet in height," said Gina.

"Here's what I'd like you to do now," Patty said. "Figure out about how many fourth graders would need to lie end-to-end to equal the length of a blue whale that's one hundred feet long. You may use the data posted on the board to help you. Explain your thinking in words and numbers, and also include a picture, if you'd like."

The students worked on the problem until the end of the math period. Patty explained that they would continue their investigation during the following day's math period.

The Next Day

During math time the next day, the students resumed their work on the whale problem.

Amika, Danica, and Tierney added the heights of five students and arrived at a total of 21 feet 2 inches. Then they added the heights of six more students to come up with a measurement close to 100 feet. On her paper, Danica wrote: *Tierney, Amika, and I added inches and feet. We tryed to add short people and tall people. And we got 100' 5". I think it will take 20 people to equal 100 feet. But it took 21 people. I was really close.*

Alma's paper explained how her group members used the repeat function on the calculator to help them solve the problem. She wrote: *We just put 51 and we pushed the plus button and the equal button and we got for an answer 1224 inches but we where sopos to get 1200 for an answer. . . . We think 24 4th graders would equal a blue whale because 51" × 24 = 1224" and a blue whal is 1200" long.*

Amon and Quimby used multiplication. Quimby wrote: *We rownded it off to 5 feet and times did 5 feet 20 times and came up with 100 feet. I chose 5 feet because it is easyer then all of the other numbers. And some people are 5 feet tall.* (See Figure 8–1.)

Derek skip-counted by fives to one hundred. He wrote: *One girl in my class is five feet and I counted by 5s and got 100 I think it would take 20 of her to eqal 100 feet. I pick 5 becase it was esey to count by fives.*

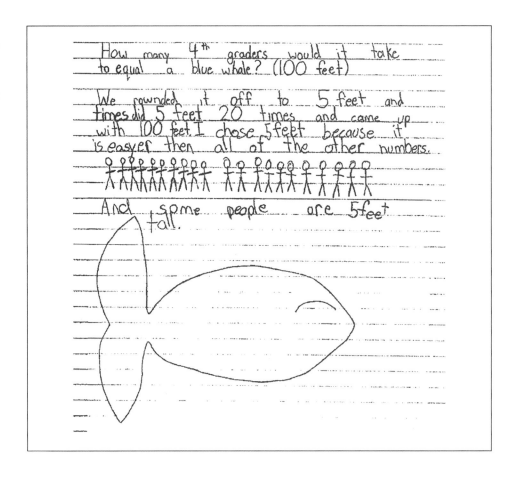

Jill solved the problem in two different ways. She wrote: *20 people that are 5 feet tall each would fit in a blue whale. I chose 5 because its easy to count by and some kids are 5 feet tall. Inches— 22 kids that are 56 inches tall would fit in a blue whale. I chose 56 because it was the mode and most people were 56 inches tall.*

Tanya and several other students chose 4 feet as the average height of a fourth grader. She wrote: *If you have 25 4th grade students that were each 4 ft. you would get 100 (the size of a blue whale). I chose 4 ft. because it is a factor of 100 and it's like counting quarters and because I realy like the number and its close to the average number in our class.*

Patty reported that this investigation was valuable for her students because it called for using several math skills, including estimating; adding; multiplying; measuring; and collecting, organizing, and using data. (See Figure 8–2 for another student's solution to this problem.)

Presenting the Problem to a Fifth- and Sixth-Grade Class

I read *Is a Blue Whale the Biggest Thing There Is?* to the fifth and sixth graders in my class. When I asked them how many of their

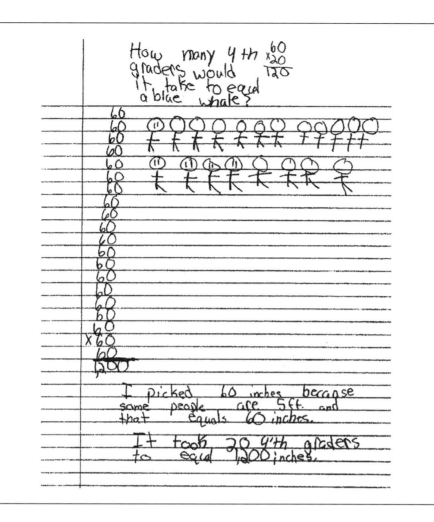

lengths would equal the length of a blue whale, their estimates covered a wide range, similar to the estimates that Patty had reported from her fourth graders.

"I'm six feet tall," I told them. "How many feet would two of my lengths equal?"

"Twelve feet," the students chorused.

"How about four of my lengths?" I continued.

"Twenty-four feet," several students responded.

"How did you figure?" I asked.

"Because six feet times four of you would equal twenty-four feet," Tamar explained. "You use multiplication."

"How many of my lengths would equal one hundred feet, or the length of a blue whale?" I asked. Having them think about the relationship between my height and 100 feet helped them revise their estimates and make them more reasonable.

I then told the students that they were going to find out how many of their heights would equal the length of a blue whale. I had attached a tape measure to the wall in the back of the classroom, and I modeled for them how to measure height. I stood with my back to the tape and asked Jacob to hold a ruler on top of my head to see how tall I was.

"Work with a partner to find your height," I then said. "Also, draw a picture of yourself next to a blue whale. Your picture should show how your height compares with the length of the whale."

Since the students hadn't had much experience drawing pictures to scale, I asked them how they might approach doing this. I had them talk among themselves for a few minutes and then report their ideas to the class. The most popular idea suggested was that since a blue whale is about 100 feet long, they could draw a whale 10 inches long and say that each inch represented 10 feet.

Beverly rounded off her height to the nearest foot. She wrote: *I am four foot ten inches so twenty of my lengths would equal a blue whale. I got my answer by rounding four foot ten inches to 5 foot, and 5 × 20 is 100', a blue whales length.* She drew a picture of herself and her friend Heather next to the whale. (See Figure 8–3.)

Brooke added and multiplied fractions to solve the problem. She wrote: *Because I'm 4 foot $\frac{1}{2}$ and $4\frac{1}{2}$ times 22 equals 99 and 99 is closer to 100. We added $4\frac{1}{2}$ 22 times: $4 \times 22 = 88$ and $\frac{1}{2} \times 22 = 11.88 + 11 = 99$.*

Bethia added fractions to find out how many of her lengths would equal the length of a blue whale. She wrote: *19 of my length would equal a blue whale. I'm 64 inches or 5 feet and 4 inches. or $5\frac{1}{3}$ feet tall.* She kept adding $5\frac{1}{3}$ until she got close to 100 feet. First she added $5\frac{1}{3}$ twelve times, which equaled 64 feet. Then she added $5\frac{1}{3}$ seven times and got $37\frac{1}{3}$ feet. Finally, she added 64 and $37\frac{1}{3}$ together and got $101\frac{1}{3}$ feet. (See Figure 8–4.)

Figure 8–3: Beverly found the answer, then drew a proportional picture of herself and her friend Heather next to a whale.

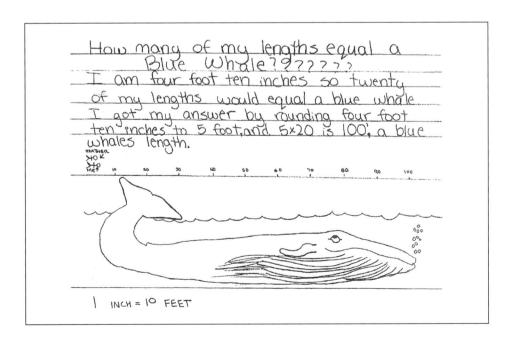

Figure 8–4: Bethia added fractions to solve the problem.

How many of my lengths would equal a blue whale.

19 of my length would equal a blue whale.

I'm 64 inches or 5 feet and 4 inches.
or 5 1/3 feet tall.

$5\frac{1}{3} + 5\frac{2}{3} + 6\frac{3}{3} + 5\frac{4}{3} + 5\frac{5}{3} + 5\frac{6}{3} + 5\frac{7}{3} + 5\frac{8}{3} + 5\frac{9}{3} + 5\frac{10}{3} + 5\frac{11}{3} + 5\frac{12}{3} = 64$
$5\frac{13}{3} + 5\frac{14}{3} + 5\frac{15}{3} + 5\frac{16}{3} + 5\frac{17}{3} + 5\frac{18}{3} + 5\frac{19}{3} = 37\frac{1}{3}$

$\begin{array}{r} 64 \\ 37\frac{1}{3} \\ \hline 101\frac{1}{3} \end{array}$

Some students measured desks and chairs and compared them with the blue whale's length. Shane and Jacob discovered in the school parking lot that about seven cars would equal the length of a blue whale.

Brittany converted the measurements to inches before tackling the problem. She wrote: *I multiplyed 100 × 12 because to see how big a blue whale can get in inches. I multiplyed 12 × 5 to see how tall I was in inches. I ÷ 1200 into 64 to see how many of me would fit the same size as a blue whale. It would take 18 Brittany's to reach the length of a blue whale.*

Some children used division to solve the problem. Elias wrote: *I am 5 feet so I divided 5 into 100 and my answer is 20. I got the answer by dividing 5 into 100.* Elias drew a blue whale using a scale in which 1 inch equaled 10 feet. He and Leon then measured the length of the classroom and drew a picture of it next to the whale.

Having my fifth and sixth graders think about the relationship between their height and the length of a blue whale proved fascinating. The measurement context motivated the students and provided an opportunity for them to apply what they knew about rounding numbers, fractions, divison, multiplication, and addition. The activity also gave the students experience with proportional reasoning and drawing pictures to scale.

Jim and the Beanstalk

In *Jim and the Beanstalk,* by Raymond Briggs (1997), Jim wakes up one day to find a great plant growing outside his window. He decides to climb up it into the clouds, where he finds a castle with an old, unhappy giant. Unlike the original *Jack and the Beanstalk* tale, in this story Jim helps the aging giant. When the giant complains about not being able to see to read, Jim measures his huge head and returns to his town to have giant eyeglasses made. Later, he measures the giant for false teeth and a wig. The proportional illustrations help students as they work to figure out the size of the giant's hand and then his height.

MATERIALS

tape measures or rulers, 1 per pair of students
3-by-3-inch sticky notes, 1 per student

Caren Holtzman showed the cover of *Jim and the Beanstalk* to her sixth graders. She asked the class, "By looking at the book's cover, do you have any predictions or questions?"

"It's going to be like *Jack and the Beanstalk,*" Patrick guessed.

"I think it will have something to do with measuring because of the picture on the cover," Martine added.

Caren began to read the book to her class. The students listened carefully as Jim went up the beanstalk to the giant's castle and back down again, each time bringing the giant something new in return for gold. First, he brought giant eyeglasses, then giant false teeth, and finally a giant wig. The students' favorite part was the illustration showing Jim carrying a giant pair of false teeth down the street, terrifying everyone in sight. The students were amused by this updated version of the story and interested in Jim's solutions to the giant's problems.

After she finished reading the book, Caren asked, "What did you think of the story?"

"It's weird," Tracy said.

"Why?" Caren asked.

"It's totally different. The giant is supposed to eat him, but he didn't," Tracy responded.

"In the other story, Jack stole from the giant," Renee said, "and in this story, Jim gives stuff to the giant."

"How big do you think the giant is?" Caren asked the class. "Do you think he could fit in our classroom?"

"He's about fifty feet tall," Otani said.

"Why do you think that?" Caren asked.

"Usually in stories the giant is fifty feet tall," he answered.

"I think he's really big because Jim is just the size of his ear," Tracy guessed.

"The giant coins look really big when Jim takes them," Renee said.

Caren showed the picture on the cover with Jim standing next to the giant's ear and then a page showing Jim next to one of the gold coins.

"So it sounds as if you're using two things to figure out the giant's size," Caren said. "You're using what you know from other stories, and you're using clues in this book. I'm going to ask you to think about the giant's hands. Could they fit in this room?"

"Both hands could fit," Carson said.

"What makes you think that?" Caren asked.

"We're the size of his ears, and his hands are about four times bigger, so they could both fit," Carson explained.

Caren held up the illustration that shows the giant sitting at his table, reading a little book. "On this page it looks as if the giant's thumb is about the size of the book," she said. "If his thumb is the size of a book, how long is his whole hand? What tools can you use to work on this problem?"

"A ruler or a measuring tape," Audrey said.

"It depends on the book," Carson added.

"Your job is to estimate the length of the giant's hand. You'll have to decide what size book to use for comparison. Then write your estimate on a sticky note and put it on the board. On lined paper, explain your thinking and tell how you got your answer. Any questions?"

"Can we work with partners?" Alejandro asked.

"Yes, you may work with a partner, but everyone needs to write a paper," Caren instructed. "One more thing: since we'll be comparing our estimates, we need to decide on a unit of measure that we'll all use."

"Inches!" the students chorused.

The students found partners and searched for books to measure and rulers to measure them with. When they settled down, Caren circulated through the classroom and visited each table, asking questions and sometimes taking notes.

Ethan wrote: *We got three rulers and we mesured the book one time and we got $10\frac{1}{4}$ then we multiplied it by three. We multiplied the book because three tumbs make a hand. The answer is $30''\frac{3}{4}$.*

Tracy and Audrey were working together. Audrey was measuring a book while Tracy was measuring her hand in thumb-lengths. When they were finished, Tracy read what she had written: *The giant's thumb is $7\frac{1}{2}$ inches and my hand is 7 inches. With my thumb next to my hand, it takes 3 of my sizes thumbs to make the size of my hand. So for the book that I am using, which is $7\frac{1}{2}$ inches, if you triple that it would be $22\frac{1}{2}$ inches. $7 \times 3 = 21 + 3$ halves is $22\frac{1}{2}$.*

"Why did you multiply the length of the book by three?" Caren inquired.

"Because if our hands equal three of our thumbs, then we think the giant's hand equals three of his thumbs," Tracy explained. "We figured that seven and a half times three equals twenty-two and a half. So the giant's hand is twenty-two and a half inches long." (See Figure 9–1.)

Carey looked at the problem in two different ways. First he considered a book, his thumb, and the length and width of his hand. Then he took visual clues from the illustration on the book's front cover. He wrote: *The book is 9 inches long. My thumbe is 2 inches.*

Figure 9–1: Tracy explained how she multiplied the size of the book by three to determine the size of the giant's hand.

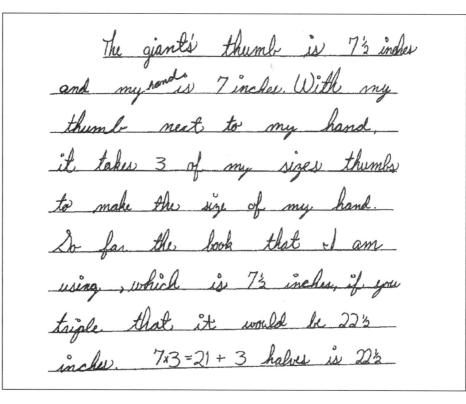

The giant's thumb is $7\frac{1}{2}$ inches and my hand is 7 inches. With my thumb next to my hand, it takes 3 of my sizes thumbs to make the size of my hand. So far the book that I am using, which is $7\frac{1}{2}$ inches, if you triple that it would be $22\frac{1}{2}$ inches. $7 \times 3 = 21 + 3$ halves is $22\frac{1}{2}$

My hand is six inches. My hand is 3× the size of my thumbe. My hand is 4 inches wide it is 2× the size of my thombe. So the with of his hard is 18 inches. By looking at the book the hand looks like it is 8 feet the kid looks like he's 4 feet long and the hand is 2× the size of the kid. (See Figure 9–2.)

"How do you know Jim is four feet tall?" Caren asked.

"Because I think that's the average height of a kid," Carey replied.

"Do you think everyone's hand measured across is two times the length of his or her thumb?" Caren asked.

"It seems like everyone at my table can go up their hand three times with their thumb. I think everyone could go across their hands two times with their thumbs, too, but I'm not sure," Carey said.

As the students completed their work, Caren reminded them to record their estimates on sticky notes and to place them on the board in the front of the room. When everyone had posted his or her estimate, Caren asked the students for their attention.

"Can someone come up here and organize these sticky notes so it's easier for us to look at the data?" she asked. Audrey volunteered and rearranged them into a horizontal line beginning with the lowest estimate and continuing to the highest.

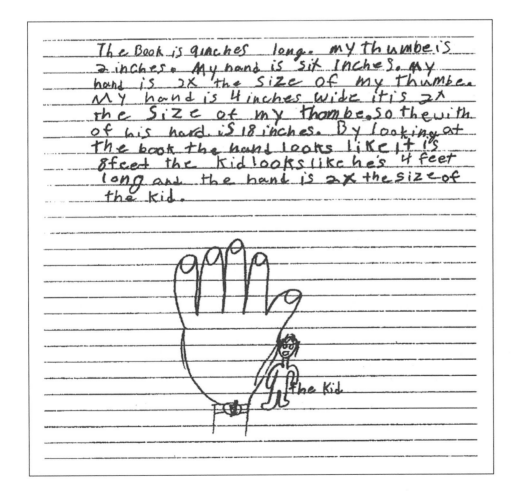

Figure 9–2: Carey drew a picture to support his contention that the giant's hand was twice the size of Jim.

Martine raised her hand. "I know something else we can do with them," she said. "Can I come up?" Caren nodded. Martine rearranged some of the sticky notes, placing identical measurements in the same columns.

"OK?" Caren asked Audrey. Audrey nodded.

Caren then said, "Raise your hand if you can make a statement about the data." She called on Annika.

"Most think it's thirty inches," she said.

"What do you call the number that appears more often than any other?" asked Caren.

"The mode," several students answered in unison.

"The range is twenty-two inches to forty-eight point seventy-five inches," Audrey said.

"It depends on the book," Carey said.

"What do you mean?" Caren asked.

"If somebody has a book that's nine inches, nine times three equals twenty-seven, but if it's ten inches, it's ten times three, and that's thirty," he explained.

"It also depends on how big your hand is, because my thumb is three times but someone else's may be four times up their hand," Janelle added.

"Let's test it," Caren instructed. "Everyone see how many thumbs long your hand is." The students quickly measured the lengths of their hands by using their thumbs. Many called out that their hands were three thumbs long. No one offered a different conclusion.

"Is it true for everyone?" Caren asked.

"Yes. If you have a bigger thumb, you have a bigger hand," Mandy said.

"Your thumb grows with your hand," Patrick said.

"I have three friends whose hands are four and a half thumbs long," Annika added.

"So we're not certain that the length of everyone's hand measures three of his or her thumbs," Caren said, "but it seems like a typical measurement."

Caren then posed another question. "What's the average of the numbers we have up here?" she asked.

"Well, thirty is the mode, and that's a kind of average," Ethan said.

"There's another way to find an average that I learned last year, but I can't remember what it's called," Tracy said. She walked up to the board and removed from the graph the sticky note that read $22\frac{1}{2}$". She then went to the other end of the graph and removed 48.75". She continued to remove the sticky notes from one end of the graph, then the other, until there was one left, which read 30".

"This is the number that's in the middle of the graph, and it's the average," said Tracy.

"Mathematicians call that kind of average the median," Caren said. "The median and the mode are the same in this case, but that's not always true."

Caren knew that her students were familiar with finding the mean as an average. She wanted them to see the benefits of looking at averages other than the mean, so she didn't pursue having them figure the mean. Too often, students think that the mean is the "real" way to determine an average.

Caren posed another question. "If the giant's hand is about thirty inches long, how tall is the giant?" Then she asked, "How might you figure this out?"

"You could find out how many hands tall you are and figure from there," said Martine.

"Measure yourself with your hand and use a calculator to multiply," suggested Dante.

"Measure yourself with your hand and multiply that by thirty," Joaquin said.

"Look at the front cover picture for clues," Carey said.

"The cover picture has a tape measure next to the giant's head," Audrey said. "The inches on the tape look like feet instead of inches. You could use that to help you."

"So you think the scale is one inch equals one foot?" Caren asked.

"Yes," Audrey replied.

Caren wrote the three strategies on the board:

Use hand data.
Use pictures from the book.
Use the giant's head measurements.

"I want each of you to commit to using a strategy for figuring the giant's height," she said. "Before starting on the problem, write your name on the board next to the strategy you plan to use." Students quickly signed up, gathered materials, and began to work.

Janelle used estimation to help her solve the problem. She wrote: *I think that the giant is 52 feet tall. Because one adult is like 5.2 [feet tall] it looks in the book it could go like 10 times up. 5.2 × 10 = 52.* (See Figure 9–3.)

Joaquin and Patrick used the data from the giant's hand to solve the problem. Joaquin wrote: *You measure your Self with your hand and then times that with thirty because the giants hand is 30 inches and it is the same as me. I did that so it came up to 9 hands so I timesed 30 × 9 = 270. So the giant is 270 inches tall. So he is 22*

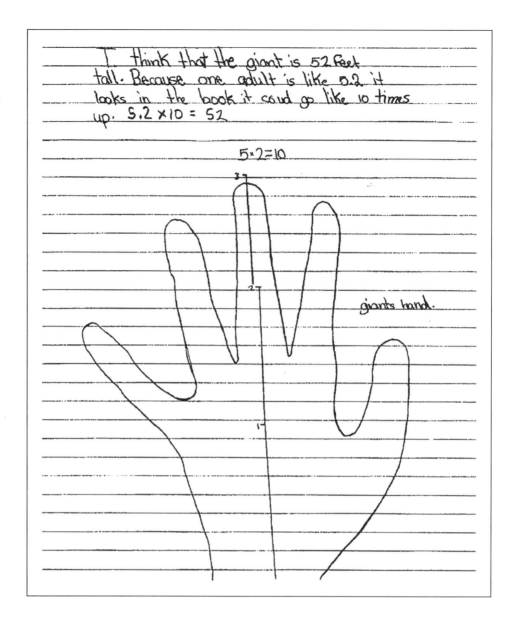

I think that the giant is 52 feet tall. Because one adult is like 5.2 it looks in the book it could go like 10 times up. 5.2 × 10 = 52

5·2=10

giants hand.

and $\frac{1}{2}$ feet tall. I know that because if you divide $12 \div$ by 270 on the calculator it will be 22.5. I divided those 2 numbers because 12" is one foot and 270 is how many inches he is.

Otani and Nigel used a picture from the book to help them determine the scale. Otani wrote: *I think the giants is 32 feet tall. What I did is measured the boy and he was 1 inch tall. I think for every inch is 4 feet. So the boy is 1 inch so he's 4 feet now the giant is 8 inchs remember that 1 inch is 4 feet, so 8 × 4 = 32. What made me work this way is the picture on page 9. A normal kid is about 4 feet, so since he is a inch, that's why every 1 inch is 4 feet.*

Annika measured the length of the giant's head on the cover page. She used a 1" = 1' scale to determine the height of the giant. She wrote: *The giants head is nine feet so we think that your head can fit on your body about 10 times. So you do 10 times 9 will be 90 feet.*

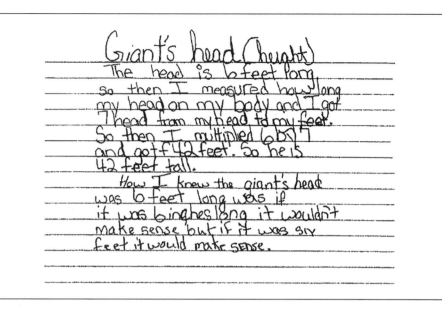

Inside the figure:

Giant's head (height)
The head is 6 feet long,
so then I measured how long
my head on my body and I got
1 head from my head to my feet.
So then I multiplied 6 by 7
and got 42 feet. So he is
42 feet tall.

How I knew the giant's head
was 6 feet long was if
it was 6 inches long it wouldn't
make sense but if it was six
feet it would make sense.

So I think that the giant is about 90 feet. Audrey also used the size of the giant's head to solve the problem, but she got a different answer (see Figure 9–4.)

After the students finished, Caren had them share their work by reading aloud what they had written. "What does this problem make you wonder about?" Caren asked.

"I'm wondering what the average height of a student in this room is," Nigel said.

"I'm still wondering if everyone's hand really is three of their thumbs tall," said Annika.

"Are we all ten of our heads tall, like Annika wrote?" Junipero asked.

"Is everyone's hand two of their thumbs wide?" Carey asked.

"When we say three thumbs equal a hand or ten heads equal your height, we're talking about body ratios," Caren told the class.

"I wonder if there are other body ratios that are the same for everybody?" asked Bonita.

Caren felt that the students' final questions could be used as springboards for further investigations into scaling and measurement.

Reflecting on the experience, Caren commented, "This was an interesting activity because it dealt with the issues of measurement, ratio, and proportion. It was open-ended enough so the students could use many different strategies. Also, the way the students justified their thinking was important. Depending on which method or reference point in the book you used, twenty-five feet tall and forty feet tall could both be correct answers."

Jumanji

In *Jumanji*, by Chris Van Allsburg (1981), Peter and Judy find a board game in a nearby park and rush home to play it. By rolling dice and moving markers on the board, they make their way from the jungle to the city of Jumanji. Each time they land on a square that mentions a wild animal, that animal suddenly appears in the living room! The same thing happens with a monsoon and a volcanic eruption. The children are frightened, but at the end of the game, everything unusual disappears, and life returns to normal. The book provides a springboard to exploring probability with dice.

MATERIALS

Roll Two Dice record sheet, 1 per student
  (see Blackline Masters)

dice, 1 pair per student

The sixth graders in Carol Schurlock's class listened with interest as I read the book *Jumanji*. The magical pastel drawings by the author fascinated the class. With the turn of each page, the students sat on the edge of their seats, anticipating the next disaster that would befall Peter and his sister, Judy, the main characters in the story.

When I got to the part that reads, "Monsoon season begins, lose one turn," I stopped to ask a question.

"Raise your hand if you know what a monsoon is." Many hands shot up. I called on Claire.

"It's like a giant storm," she said. "I think it's tropical, too. We're studying about India and China right now, and we learned about monsoons."

When I read the part when the characters in the book are visited by a herd of stampeding rhinos, Blair exclaimed, "Wow! They'll get killed if they move!"

"Why's that, Blair?" I asked.

"Rhinos have poor eyesight, but they'll charge if they notice something moving," she explained. "There are Indian rhinos, and I think they're endangered."

I continued reading until I reached the part in the story where a volcano erupts in the house. I read, "'Molten lava poured from the fireplace opening. It hit the water on the floor and the room filled with steam.' Raise your hand if you know why the room filled with steam." I called on Gunther.

"Because when something hot hits cold water, it creates steam," he said.

I continued reading. "'If you roll a twelve, you can get out of the jungle,' said Peter."

"Do you think it is likely or unlikely that Judy will roll a twelve?" I asked. "Discuss this with someone next to you." After a few minutes, I repeated the question and called on Rowena.

"I think it is unlikely because there's only one way to make a twelve and that's to roll double sixes," she said.

"I think it's unlikely because there's only one six on each dice and the rest of the sides have other numbers on them," Silas said.

"I'm not sure because I think there's an equal chance to get any number," said Gunther.

"I think it's likely because I always see doubles rolled," Nico said.

"It's unlikely because there's a one out of twelve chance to get double sixes," explained Alexandra. "Because there's six numbers on each die and six plus six equals twelve, and there's only one way to make twelve and that's six and six."

As the students conjectured, I was thinking about how difficult it is to understand probability. Also, I knew that these students had limited experience with this area of mathematics.

When I finished reading the story, I said, "Let's go back to the page where Judy is hoping to roll a twelve to get out of the jungle." I quickly turned back to the page with the illustration of Judy sitting at a table, surrounded by rising steam.

"Judy wants to roll the sum of twelve," I reminded the class. "What sum do you think she will most likely roll? Discuss this with the person next to you." When the discussion died down, I called on Lyric.

"I think that eight is most likely to be rolled because you can get eight in a few different ways, like six plus two and five plus three and four plus four," she said.

"Seven is the most likely sum because you can get it by rolling a five and a two, a four and a three, and a six and a one," Seth said.

"I think ten, but I'm not sure why," Raven added.

"Six is most likely because you can roll it a lot and, besides, it's between two and twelve," Deborah said.

"Now that you've heard some people's reasons for choosing a most likely sum, raise your hand if you think a sum of two is most likely to be rolled," I said. No one raised a hand. I continued to ask the class about the sums 3 to 12. Most students chose the sums 6, 7, and 8, a few chose 10, and two students thought that all of the sums had an equal chance of being rolled.

"We're going to do an activity called *Roll Two Dice*," I told the class. "The activity may help us find out which sums, if any, are more likely to be rolled than others."

I held up a record sheet with the numbers 2 to 12 written along the top. Each number had its own vertical column with twelve little boxes.

"Why do you suppose the record sheet has the numbers two to twelve?" I asked.

Roll Two Dice Record Sheet

2	3	4	5	6	7	8	9	10	11	12

Finish Line

"Because those are the possible sums you can get when rolling the dice," said Blair.

"Can you get a sum of thirteen?" I asked.

"No!" the students answered.

"Why not?" I asked.

"Because the numbers on the dice only go up to six," Curt responded. "The largest sum you can get is twelve, and two is the smallest."

"Here's how the game works," I began. "Each of you will receive a record sheet and a pair of dice. Roll the dice, add the numbers together, and see what sum comes up. Find that sum on your record sheet and write the addition sentence in the correct column. For example, if you rolled a two and a four, you would write 'two plus four' below the six. Keep rolling the dice and recording the addition sentences until the squares below one sum get to the finish line."

"What if we roll five and two and fill it in under the seven, and then we roll five and two again?" Alec asked. "Can we use a repeat?"

"Yes, that's OK," I replied. "Just record it again in the next space in the seven column."

I then pointed to a large sheet of white butcher paper I had taped to the board. It had the numbers 2 to 12 written vertically down the left side.

"When you finish, record your data on this class chart," I said. "Bring your record sheet up to the chart and make a tally mark for each time a sum came up. Let's say that the sum of two came up only twice. I would make two tally marks next to the two on our chart. If nine came up on the dice four times, I would make four tally marks next to the nine on our chart, and so on."

After I distributed the dice and the record sheets, the students started playing *Roll Two Dice*. As they rolled the dice, they rooted for their favorite sums.

"Seven won again!" several students exclaimed throughout the activity.

"I finally rolled a three!" someone shouted.

"Eight is winning!" Blair cried.

As the students recorded their data on the class chart, I gave additional record sheets to those who wanted to do the activity again. When all the students had finished at least one sheet, I asked for their attention.

"Raise your hand if you'd like to make an observation about the data on our chart," I said. Many hands shot up. I called on Gabrielle.

"The winner is seven," she said.

"Two and twelve have the least number of tally marks because you can only roll them one way," Skye said. "You make a twelve with six plus six and a two with one plus one."

"I see that two and twelve have about the same amount of tally marks," Silas said. "And three and eleven have about the same amount. It's the same for four and ten, five and nine, and six and eight. And seven has the most."

"So seven is the mode," Lyric said.

"Lyric, explain what you mean by *the mode*," I said.

"It's the number that occurs the most," she explained.

"Eleven only has a few tally marks because there's only one way to make it," said Skye. "You can only make eleven by rolling a six and a five."

"You could make it if you rolled a five and a six," Blair said.

"That's the same thing!" Skye countered.

"I think there are two ways, six plus five and five plus six, because the dice are different," Jarvis argued.

"You're just switching the positions of the dice, so it's the same thing," Augie responded.

"Some people think there's more than one way to make eleven and some think there's only one way," I said. "Discuss this with the people at your table so you can hear some other ideas." After about a minute, I asked for the students' attention.

"Raise your hand if you think eleven can be made only one way," I told them. About six hands went up.

"Who thinks eleven can be made in more than one way?" I asked. The rest of the students raised their hands. I decided to explain to the class why I thought the reversed addends counted as different ways. I held up one red die and one green one and pointed out that getting a 6 on the red and a 5 on the green was different from getting a 6 on the green and a 5 on the red.

"I still think it's the same thing," Augie said. A few students nodded their agreement. I wanted the students to examine their reasoning, so I asked more questions.

"How many ways are there to make seven?" I asked.

"There are six ways," Lyric said. "Three plus four, four plus three, five plus two, two plus five, six plus one, and one plus six." I wrote these addition combinations on the board.

"I think there are only three ways," Augie said. "Three plus four, five plus two, and six plus one." I circled these addition combinations as a way of showing Augie's opinion.

"What about eight?" I asked. "How many ways for eight?" I called on Jarvis.

"There are five ways: two plus six and six plus two, five plus three and three plus five, and four plus four," he said. Again, I recorded the addition combinations on the board.

"I disagree," Nico said. "There's only three ways to get an eight: four plus four, six plus two, and five plus three."

"Here's my question," I said. "If what Augie and Nico are saying is true and there are the same number of ways to make seven and eight, then why are there so many more tally marks on seven?"

"Because seven is a middle number on the graph, and you can roll it more often," Jarvis said.

"Yes, seven is in the middle, but it has more tally marks because there are more ways to make that number!" Blair exclaimed.

While most of the students in the class understood, for example, that 3 + 4 and 4 + 3 are two different possibilities, there were still some students who were not convinced. They were holding firm to their beliefs, and I knew that teaching by telling was not going to work. It often takes time and experience for students to make sense of a new idea.

"Let's go back to the question I asked you to think about earlier," I said. "When rolling the dice, what sum do you think is most likely to be rolled? I want each of you to write a convincing argument that explains and justifies your thinking."

The students' writing revealed a range of thinking about probability. I visited each table, asking the children questions and listening to their ideas.

Marius wrote: *I think when rolling 2 dice its more likely to roll a 7 because it's in the middle and there's 6 ways to roll it. Even though 6 and 8 are in the middle and have 5 ways, 7 has more numbers possible to roll and is closer to the middle than eight. Plus it is in between 6–8.* (See Figure 10–1.)

Blair wrote: *When rolling the dice, I think 8 is the number to come up most likely because you can get 8 by rolling: 2 + 6, 6 + 2, 3 + 5, 5 + 3, and 4 + 4. there are 5 ways to get an 8.*

After Blair read her paper to me, I said to her, "Blair, during our class discussion, you said that there are more tally marks next to the seven because there are more ways to make it. I'm curious to know why you're choosing eight now."

"I think eight because there's not that many more ways to make seven than eight," she answered. "They're pretty close. Seven won't always happen."

Jarvis wrote: *I think that the 7 would come up most, because where it's position is and if you look at the graph it lowers and in the middle it gets bigger than lowers and it has 6 ways to get it, 3 + 4, 4 + 3, 5 + 2, 2 + 5, 6 + 1, 1 + 6.* (See Figure 10–2.)

There were some students who realized that there were more ways to make six, seven, and eight but who held the belief that there was an equal chance that any number could be rolled. For example, Gunther wrote: *When I roll two dice I think all of the numbers have a 50 50 of geting rolled on because we can't control the way the dice rolls. The dice rolls were ever it wants and no one can make it roll were ever he/she wants. Sure other numbers have more ways to get it, but on one*

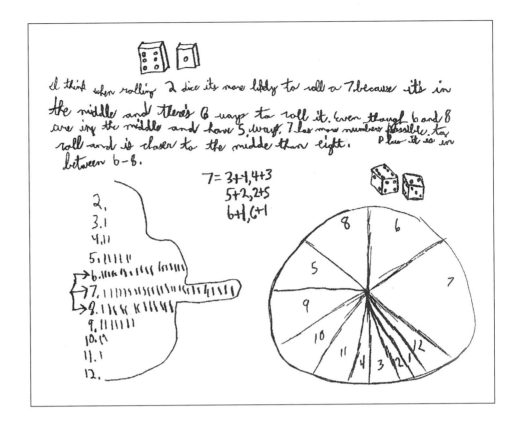

Figure 10–1: Marius reproduced the class chart and drew a pie graph to show that 7 was the most likely number to roll.

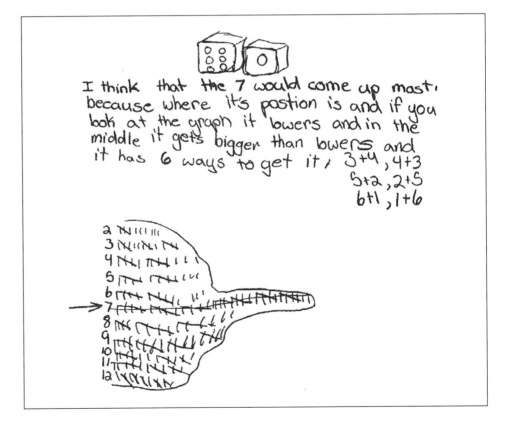

Figure 10–2: Jarvis argued that 7 would come up most on the dice.

Math and Literature, Grades 4–6

dice you can only get 1, 2, 3, 4, 5, or 6. And on the other dice you can roll the same numbers. So it's a 50 50 chance of geting any number.

After the students completed their writing, several volunteered to read aloud what they had written. This helped the other students reflect on and clarify their thinking about the mathematical situation they had just encountered. Everyone except Gunther agreed that some sums are more likely to come up than others. However, there wasn't a consensus about how many ways each sum could be made, and my goal wasn't to push everyone to agree. Some students needed further experiences and more time to think about the possible outcomes when two dice are rolled. At this time, I wanted the students to explore the idea that some events are more likely to occur than others and why that is and to have experience predicting outcomes and collecting and analyzing data.

The King's Chessboard

The King's Chessboard, by David Birch (1993), tells the story of a king who insists on giving a gift to his wise man. The man wants no gift but finally points to a chessboard and suggests that the king give him one grain of rice for the first square of the chessboard and on subsequent days double the amount of the previous day's unit until all sixty-four squares of the chessboard are covered. Not understanding how much rice would be needed, the king agrees. After thirty-one days, he realizes that he can't fulfill his agreement. The book leads into a lesson in which children use multiplication and measurement. **Note:** *The Rajah's Rice: A Mathematical Folktale from India,* by David Barry (1994), and *A Grain of Rice,* by Helena Clare Pittman (1996), offer similar stories that can also be springboards for this lesson.

MATERIALS

zip-top bags of rice, 1 per group of three to four students

plastic teaspoons, 1 per group of three to four students

measuring cups, 1 per group of three to four students

"I have a book I want to share with you called *The King's Chessboard,*" I told Patti Reynolds's fifth and sixth graders. "It's a story that's set in India a long time ago."

I began reading the story. The children enjoyed the pen and watercolor illustrations by Devis Grebu. Many students commented on the curved domes and elegant archways of old India. I stopped after I read the part where the wise man proposes rice as a reward for his good services.

"In the story, the wise man asks to receive one grain of rice on the first day, then two grains on the second day, then four, eight, sixteen, and so on," I said. I recorded on the board:

1, 2, 4, 8, 16

"There were sixty-four squares on the king's chessboard," I continued. "What's happening to the number of grains each day?"

"They're doubling," several students chorused.

"You multiply the number by two to get the next number on the chessboard, like one times two equals two, then two times two equals four, and four times two equals eight," Rachel explained.

"I want you to think about how many grains of rice will be delivered on the sixty-fourth day," I instructed. "You may discuss this with the people at your table, but I want you each to write your own answer and explain how you got it."

"Do we have to come up with an exact answer?" Jackson asked.

"No, an estimate will do," I responded. "But you'll need to explain why your answer makes sense."

It was difficult for the students to estimate. Most jotted down a guess, then proceeded to dive into the problem with their calculators in hand.

As I walked from table to table, I noticed that many students were drawing pictures of chessboards and writing the number of grains in each square. After about ten minutes, I began to hear exclamations of surprise from several groups.

"The numbers are getting huge!" Everett cried.

"The display on my calculator won't fit the numbers anymore!" exclaimed Caitlin.

One group of students was gathered around Emanuel, who had a calculator that could display larger numbers. While Emanuel pressed the buttons on his calculator, another group member read the number on the display, and a third student recorded the number on paper.

After about twenty minutes, I began a class discussion.

"Raise your hand if you'd like to report your answer and what you did," I said. I called on Meredith.

"I think there will be about five hundred billion grains of rice on the sixty-fourth day," she said. "First I drew a picture of a chessboard and then I doubled each number. On the twenty-second day, there would be two million ninety-seven thousand one hundred fifty-two grains of rice. I figured that if there was that many on the twenty-second day, the number of grains on the sixty-fourth day would be really big."

Jackson read what he had written on his paper: *I started at one and kept timesing it on the calculator and each time I times it I make a slash and I've gotten to 20 slashes and that's about $\frac{1}{3}$ of the way and I have 529,288 already. So I take the other 20 squares and that makes 40 squares so I times that by two and that makes 80. I'm going to times my answer by 80 and that's my guess and that's 42,343,040 grains of rice.*

"I think that it will be ten billion eight hundred nineteen million four hundred seventy-six thousand seven hundred thirty-six grains of rice," Lexie said, reading the number from her paper. She then

Figure 11–1: Lexie doubled the numbers to figure the grains of rice for thirty-two days, and then estimated for thirty-two more days.

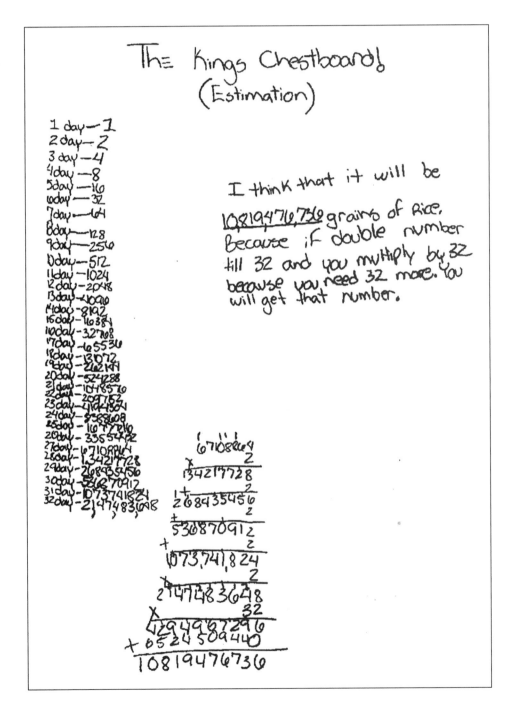

explained, "If you double the numbers up to the thirty-second square, you multiply that number by thirty-two because you need thirty-two more to get sixty-four squares." (See Figure 11–1.)

"My estimate is one hundred twenty-eight because sixty-four squares is half of that and sixty-four times two equals one hundred twenty-eight," Reed said. Although some students looked surprised when they heard Reed's estimate, they were respectful and listened to his reasoning.

Only a few students made estimates in the range of the one Reed made. Most students realized that, with doubling, the number of grains grew very fast. After their calculators became useless, many students began to multiply on paper, but some just guessed.

When all the students who were interested in sharing their results had done so, I continued with the story. The students were amazed at the amount of rice the king had to give the wise man.

"Is there a lesson to be learned in this story?" I asked. I called on Ursula.

"The lesson is, go to school!" she exclaimed. Everyone laughed.

"I think the lesson is that if you let pride get in the way, you're in for trouble," Corinne said.

A Follow-up Activity

"I have another mathematical question for you to solve," I then said. "On which square would enough rice arrive to feed everyone in the class? Talk about this with the people at your table. What do you need to know in order to solve this problem?" After a minute or so, several students raised their hands. I called on Ray.

"We need to know how many kids and adults are in our room," he said. We quickly counted that there were thirty-three people, and I wrote on the board:

33 people

"We also need to know how much rice each person will eat," Annie said. I told them that $\frac{1}{2}$ cup is a standard serving size for rice, and I wrote on the board:

$\frac{1}{2}$ *cup per person*

"Then we need to know how many grains of rice are in a half cup," Garrett said. "I think it will take a long time to count the grains in a half cup."

"Can anyone suggest an easier way to find out how many grains of rice there are in a half cup?" I asked.

"Why don't we find out how many teaspoons of rice there are in a half cup and count the grains in one teaspoon, and go from there?" Caitlin suggested. We agreed to try that method.

Several students helped me pass out a baggie of rice, a plastic teaspoon, and a measuring cup to each group.

"Work together to find out how many level teaspoons of rice are in a half cup," I instructed. The groups quickly worked this out, and students were soon flapping their hands in the air, eager to share their answers. I called on one group at a time and wrote all of their answers on the board:

Teaspoons: 26 30 33 29 30 21 33 32

"We have a range of twenty-one to thirty-three teaspoons," I observed. "Raise your hand if you can explain why we have so many different answers."

"Maybe the rice was not completely level in each teaspoon," Dale said.

"Some people were less precise than others," Annie said.

"The measuring cups are different and some are confusing to read," Moss added.

"How can we decide on one number for all of us to use to solve the problem?" I asked.

"Let's find out the average," Emanuel suggested.

"Raise your hand if you can explain a way to find the average," I said. I called on Keith.

"You add all of the numbers together and divide by eight because eight is how many numbers there are," Keith said.

The students quickly took out calculators and did what Keith suggested. They figured the average, got 29.25, and decided to use 29. I wrote *29 teaspoons* on the board. I knew that this wasn't an accurate measure of how many teaspoons are in $\frac{1}{2}$ cup (there are 24), but since all of the students' measurements would be approximate, I decided to go with this number.

"Now I want each group to figure out how many grains of rice are in a teaspoon," I instructed.

The groups worked together in a variety of ways. In two groups, the members each counted their own teaspoons of rice, then calculated the average. Two groups grouped the grains in tens to count. In some groups, everyone helped to count; in others, only one person counted while the rest kept track of the numbers. When they finished, I recorded each group's result:

170 grains
160

212
195
278
330
265
212

The students calculated the average to be 227.75 and decided to round it to 228 grains of rice in a teaspoon.

"How can we figure out how many grains of rice are in a half cup?" I asked. "Discuss this with your group." After a few minutes, I repeated the question and called on Kelsey.

"There are twenty-nine teaspoons of rice in a half cup and two hundred twenty-eight grains of rice in a teaspoon, so you multiply two hundred twenty-eight times twenty-nine," she explained.

"Is there another way?" I asked. No one raised a hand. The students quickly used their calculators to determine that in $\frac{1}{2}$ cup there would be 6,612 grains of rice.

"Because our measurements aren't really exact, our answer is an approximation. But a number like six thousand six hundred twelve seems to imply that we know exactly how many grains of rice. Raise your hand if you can think of a number we can use that is a reasonable approximation for six thousand six hundred twelve." I said. Nearly everyone's hand shot up in the air.

"I think you should round it up to seven thousand," Ursula suggested.

"Maybe sixty-six hundred," Ray said.

"Or sixty-five hundred," Corinne added.

"What number should we use?" I asked. "All of these are possible."

"I think seven thousand," Lexie said. "All of our measurements were different, and this seems easy to understand." There was unanimous agreement from the class.

"I have a question," Rachel said. "Is a half cup of cooked rice the same as a half cup of uncooked rice?"

Rachel's question was not a surprise to me. Earlier in the lesson, I had told the students that $\frac{1}{2}$ cup of rice was a standard serving. I didn't specify whether this was cooked or uncooked. I decided to wait and see if someone would inquire about this. Had Rachel not asked this important question, I would have raised it with the group.

"Rice generally expands to three times its original uncooked size," I said. "Discuss this with your group and see if this changes how we should approach our problem."

When at least one hand was raised in each group, I had students report.

"I think that you need to multiply seven thousand by three because there needs to be more rice," Noreen said.

"I disagree," Sid said. "You need to divide by three because the rice gets bigger, so you don't need as much." A flurry of comments erupted as students gave support to Noreen's or Sid's idea. I called the students to attention.

"Thumbs up if you think we should multiply by three and thumbs down if you think we should divide by three," I said. Most of the students thought that dividing was the correct operation to use. I asked them to take a few minutes in their groups to discuss this. "Try to make a convincing argument for your position," I said.

When the discussions died down, the class resolved the issue. The students agreed to divide. The students calculated that 7,000 divided by 3 was about 2,333 grains per $\frac{1}{2}$ cup.

"So, the problem is to figure out how many grains of rice it would take to feed all of us," I said. "I also want you to find out on what square there would be enough rice to feed us. You may discuss the problem with your group members, but you are each responsible for your own paper."

The class seemed to take this last question very seriously and worked quietly for more than thirty minutes. When the students were finished, I asked for their attention.

"Raise your hand if you'd like to share your answer and explain your thinking," I said. I called on volunteers to read their papers aloud.

Jackson had written: *Each person gets 2,333 grains of rice so I figured out how much rice the class needs to feed everybody by take-ing how much one person gets and times it by how many people their are in the class and that's 33 so I did this: 2,333 × 33 = 76,989. And Im going to I figur out what day they would bring about how much rice it takes to feed the class by starting at one and times by two up to the anser puting a slash each time. 131,072 grains of rice will arive on the 18 day.*

Noreen wrote: *The whole class will get 131,072 grains of rice. They will get it on the 18th day. How I got this answer is I looked at the chart we used for* The King's Chestboard.

Ray wrote: *We will need 76,989 to feed 33 people. We will reach or get that amount in the 17 day will be to little, But in the 18th it will be to much so it's $17\frac{1}{2}$ days. We will have enough rice at the 17th day at 6:00 pm.*

When students finished sharing their work, I held up another book, called *The Rajah's Rice: A Mathematical Folktale from India*, by David Barry.

"This book is very similar to *The King's Chessboard*," I told them. "At the back of the book, there's an illustration of a chessboard with sixty-four squares. In each square there is a drawing and a number explaining how many grains of rice arrive. For example, on the thirty-second square, enough rice would arrive to fill two hundred fifty-six wheelbarrows. On the sixty-fourth square, there would be a stack of rice as large as Mount Kilimanjaro!"

This elicited exclamations of surprise from the students. Esme asked, "How big is Mount Kilimanjaro?"

"I don't know," I answered.

Sid rushed to the bookshelf. He opened a book about geography to a page showing Mount Kilimanjaro compared with the other big mountains of the world.

"Mount Kilimanjaro is nineteen thousand three hundred forty feet high, and it's the fourth tallest mountain in the world!" he exclaimed. "That would be a lot of rice!"

Figures 11–2 and 11–3 show how two other students worked on this problem.

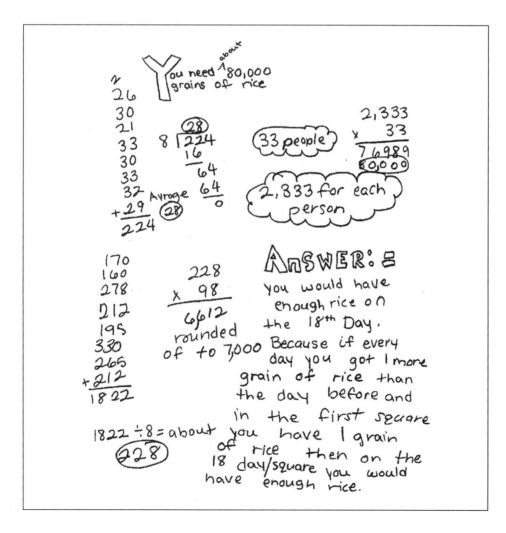

Figure 11–2: Esme explained why enough rice to feed the class would arrive on the eighteenth day.

Figure 11–3: Liv figured
that there would be enough
rice after $17\frac{1}{2}$ days.

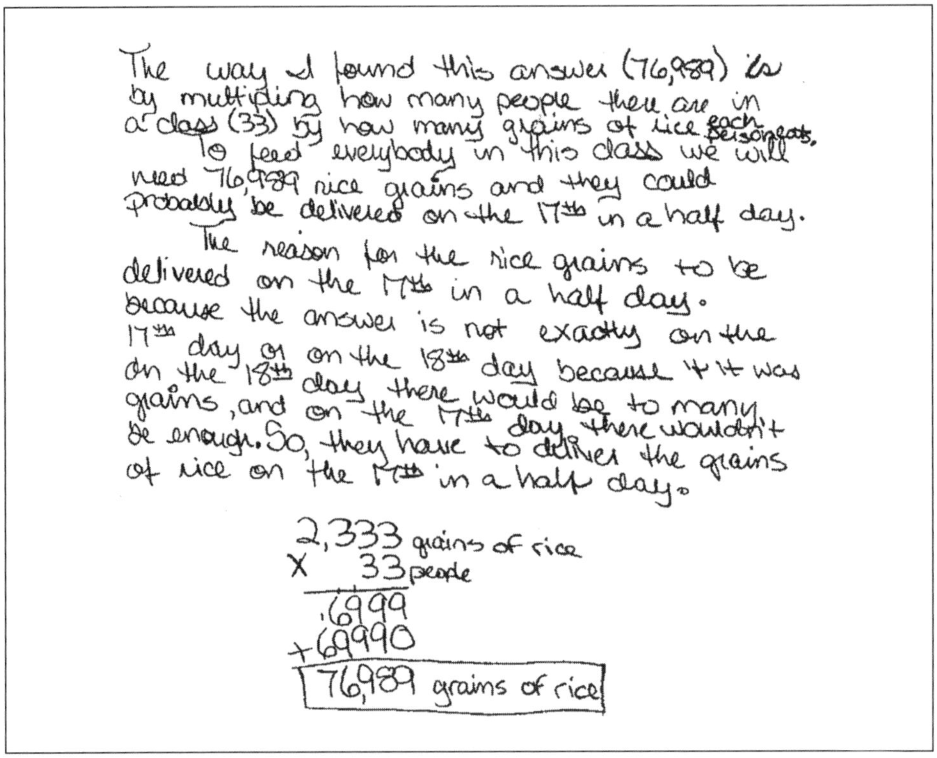

The way I found this answer (76,989) is
by multiplying how many people there are in
a class (33) by how many grains of rice each
persons eat. To feed everybody in this class we will
need 76,989 rice grains and they could
probably be delivered on the 17th in a half day.

The reason for the rice grains to be
delivered on the 17th in a half day.
because the answer is not exactly on the
17th day, or on the 18th day because if it was
on the 18th day there would be to many
grains, and on the 17th day there wouldn't
be enough. So, they have to deliver the grains
of rice on the 17th in a half day.

```
    2,333 grains of rice
  X    33 people
  ─────
    6999
 +69990
 ──────────────────
  76,989 grains of rice
```

Math and Literature, Grades 4–6

Martha Blah Blah

Martha Blah Blah, by Susan Meddaugh (1998), introduces Martha, a dog who is able to talk as the result of eating a bowl of alphabet soup every day. But one day, when Granny Flo inherits the soup company, she immediately fires thirteen of the twenty-six pasta letter makers for the sake of bigger profits. The elimination of these letters from the soup makes Martha's speech amusing but completely unintelligible. With Martha's help, however, the soup problem is resolved. After hearing the story, students are engaged in analyzing the frequency of use of the letters of the alphabet, an activity that involves them with concepts from the areas of probability and statistics. They then apply what they learn to solve a problem about the game of Boggle.

MATERIALS

adding machine tape, a 2-foot strip, with the 26 letters of the alphabet written on it in the order of their frequency of use:

e t a o n i s r h l d c u p f m w y b g v k q x j z

Note: Letters marked with a curved line have the same frequency.

Letter Frequency Record Sheet (see Blackline Masters)

Day 1

The day before reading *Martha Blah Blah* to a class of fifth graders, Marilyn Burns asked them, "Do you think that any letters of the alphabet are used more or less than other letters?" Some hands shot up, but Marilyn asked the students to turn and talk with their neighbors about her question. The room became noisy with animated talk. After a few moments, she asked the students for their attention.

"What do you think?" she asked. "Are some letters used more than others?"

"The vowels have to be used more," Kaisha said. "There are only five of them."

"We think Ss would be used a lot because of making things plural," Alexandra added.

"We don't think that you would use X, Y, or Z very much," Michael said.

"I think A is used a lot," Cara said. "My first name has two As and my last name has three."

"We think that Q wouldn't be used much," Andy said.

Marilyn then opened a book that was resting on the chalkboard tray and copied the first sentence onto the board: *Throughout human history, people have been measuring all kinds of things.*

She said, "I wonder which letters are used more in this sentence? Let me show you a way to find out." Marilyn listed on the board the letters of the alphabet in two columns, from A to M and then N to Z. Then she made tally marks, saying the letters in the sentence out loud.

a	‖‖	n	‖‖‖
b	‖	o	‖‖‖
c		p	‖‖
d	‖	q	
e	‖‖‖ ‖	r	‖‖‖
f	‖	s	‖‖‖
g	‖‖	t	‖‖‖
h	‖‖‖ ‖	u	‖‖‖
i	‖‖‖	v	‖
j		w	
k	‖	x	
l	‖‖‖	y	‖
m	‖‖	z	

"Wow, I didn't think there would be so many Hs," Travon said.

"Me, either," Natanya added. "Hs have the same number of tallies as Es, and they're the most."

"All of the vowels got used, like we thought they would," Kaisha said.

"Making tally marks like this helps us see how often each letter in the sentence was used," Marilyn said. "This way of collecting data is called a frequency distribution." Marilyn stopped to write *data* and *frequency distribution* on the board. Then she asked, "Who knows what I mean by *data?*"

"It's information," Scott said.

"That's right," Marilyn responded. "And the frequency distribution makes it easy to see the data about the frequency of the letters in the sentence I chose. What does *frequency* mean?"

"It's like how much something happens," Elissa said.

"Another way to show the information about my sentence," Marilyn said, "is to write the letters starting with the ones that were used most and keep going in order down to those that weren't used at all."

"You would have to write E and H first," Keely said.

"Then N and O tie," De'anna added.

"And then comes A, I, S, T, and U," Hassan said.

"I don't get what you're doing," Arthur complained.

"Arthur, which letter has the most tally marks?" Marilyn asked.

"It's a tie between E and H," he said.

"And which got used almost as much?" Marilyn asked.

"Oh, I get it," Arthur said. "It's like which came in first, then second, like that." Marilyn nodded, and with the students' help, she wrote the letters in order of their frequency, adding a curved line underneath those that appeared the same number of times.

eh no aistu glr mp bdfkvy cjqwxz

"So is it right?" Ebony wanted to know.

"Do you mean does this tell how often the letters are always used?" Marilyn asked. Ebony nodded. "I don't trust this information because we only analyzed one sentence," Marilyn explained. "When we look at such a small sample, we really can't rely on the information we get from the data." Marilyn stopped to write *sample* on the board. "Thinking about data and making predictions is important to two areas of mathematics—probability and statistics." Marilyn added these words to the others she had written on the board.

"To draw a more reliable conclusion from data, we need a larger sample," Marilyn said. "Tomorrow we're going to do a whole-class investigation that will help us learn more about which letters of the alphabet are used more and less than others. To prepare for the lesson, for homework I'd like you each to collect data about the letters in three sentences, the way I did for this one sentence on the board."

Marilyn showed the children the Letter Frequency worksheet (see Blackline Masters) they would use for the assignment with lines at the top for them to copy three sentences and then a list of the letters of the alphabet for them to use for their tally marks.

```
                Letter Frequency Record Sheet

        _____
        _____
        _____
        _____
        _____
        _____
        _____


        a
        b
        c
        d
        e
        f
        g
        h
        i
        j
        k
        l
        m
        n
        o
        p
        q
        r
        s
        t
        u
        v
        w
        x
        y
        z
```

"Do we make up sentences?" James asked.

"No," Marilyn said, "copy three sentences from your independent reading book."

"Do we list the letters at the end the way you did?" Alexandra asked.

"No, you don't have to do that. Tomorrow, we'll compile our information and then, after we have all of our data, we'll write the letters in order. Also, I have information about the actual order of the frequency of the letters, and we'll compare our data with the data I have."

Day 2

Before class began, Marilyn again listed on the board the letters of the alphabet in two columns, fairly far apart so that she had space to record data for each letter from each of the table groups in the class. She also had available the letters in order of their use on a piece of adding machine tape, as described in the Materials section. Then she asked the fifth graders to gather on the rug with their homework papers. First they spent a few moments talking about their results. For most of the students, the letter E had come up most often, but several had other results—A, I, O, or T. The students also reported about letters that didn't come up at all, and these included J, Q, V, X, and Z for most and additional letters for others. (See Figures 12–1 and 12–2.)

Marilyn then showed the children the cover of *Martha Blah Blah*. A few of them were familiar with the book but were happy to hear it again. "After I read the book," Marilyn said, "I'll ask you why I thought it relates to the investigation we're going to do."

Marilyn read the story aloud. The students were amused to learn that Martha, a dog, could talk because she ate a bowl of alphabet

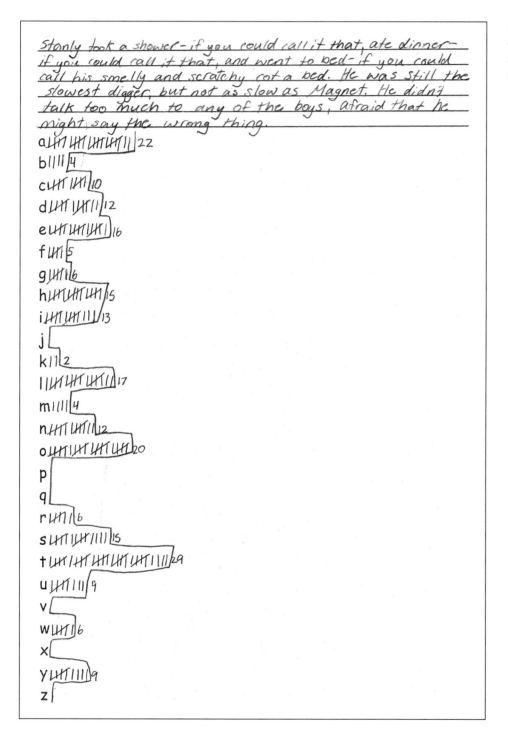

Figure 12–1: The letter T came up more often than any other in Alexandra's sample.

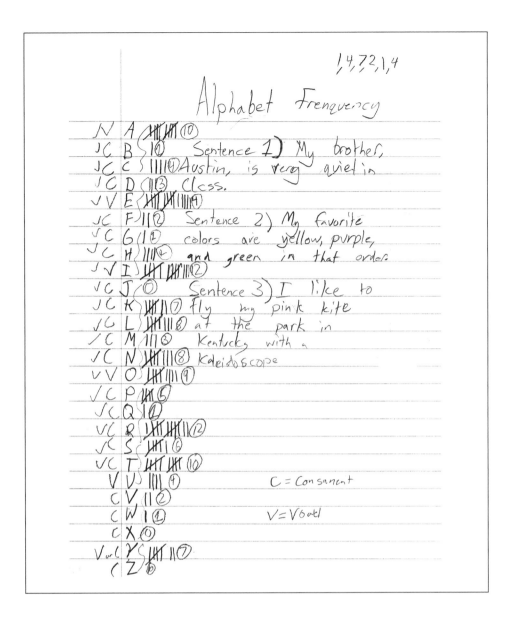

Figure 12–2: For her sample, Kaisha also noted which letters were vowels and which were consonants.

soup every day. They giggled when Martha asked, "Isn't it time for my dinner?" Some of the students gasped when the new owner of Granny's Soup Company, Granny Flo, fired half of the alphabeticians who made the pasta letters. Consequently, Martha lost her ability to speak clearly because she could no longer say half of the letters, and the children laughed out loud when Marilyn read what Martha was now saying—"Goo oup o," "Ohigiwog," and "Wogo wogo go go." They all seemed relieved when Granny Flo hired back the alphabeticians and Martha could talk again.

When Marilyn finished the story, several students had ideas about the relationship between the book and the homework assignment they did. "Granny shouldn't have said adios to A," Scott said. "You really need As."

"She could have gotten rid of J and Q and Martha might have been all right," Raul added.

"Or X and Z," Mara added.

Marilyn then explained how they would use the data from their individual frequency distributions to analyze which letters Granny Flo could have gotten rid of and done the least damage to Martha's ability to talk. "At your table groups, your job is to combine all of the information from your papers onto one list. Talk first about how you'll accomplish this, and please try to do this in no more than ten minutes."

The students returned to their desks and got to work. The groups worked in different ways. At one table, Keely, who had recorded the number of tally marks for each letter on her homework paper, suggested that she pass her paper around so that the others could add their totals. "Then we can add them up," she said. This worked well.

At another table, Scott listed the letters on a sheet of binder paper. Then the students took turns reporting their totals for A. Scott wrote the numbers down and then they figured the total. They went on to B and continued this way through the alphabet.

In a third group, with six students, five had calculators. They went around the group for each letter, with each member calling out the total. Those with calculators figured the table's total, and the sixth student, Andy, recorded the result. If they got different results on the calculators, they did the letter again.

One table with four students also went around their group with each reporting a number for the letter while they all kept a running total. If they didn't agree, they did it again. Gabiel, who was confident with numbers, said, "It was easier without a calculator." Mara rolled her eyes.

One group had difficulty settling on a system. Hassan was trying to direct them in one way while James was trying to direct them in another. The other four weren't participating. They were all getting frustrated. With some suggestions and prodding, they were finally able to complete the task.

After each table entered its totals for the letters in the chart on the board, the students used calculators to find the class total for each letter. Then, together, they identified the letters in order of their usage, and Marilyn wrote them in a horizontal row on the board, spacing them as she had spaced the letters she had written on the adding machine tape.

"Is that right now?" Ebony asked.

"Let's see," Marilyn said, unrolling the adding machine tape and taping it above what she had written.

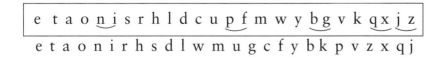

etaonisrhldcup f mwy bg v k qx j z

etaonirhsdlwmugcfybkpvzxqj

"What do you notice?" Marilyn asked.

"We're really close!" De'anna said. "The first six are exactly the same."

"But we didn't have any two letters come up the same amount," Michael said.

"The next five letters are almost the same," Raul said, "just in different order."

"And the last four letters are almost exact," Giselle said.

"I think it's weird that we had no Js at all," George said. "There are so many words with Js—*jam, jelly, jump*." Others joined in with other words, some of which were proper names—*James, Jason, joy, jar, jet*. But they soon ran out of ideas.

"Where did you get your list?" Andy asked. "Who would care about doing this?"

Marilyn responded, "Actually, I found the list a long time ago and it was information from the United States Army. Talk to your neighbor about why our army would care about this information." After a few moments, many had figured out that it could have been for figuring out codes, and Marilyn confirmed their idea.

"Also," Marilyn added, "when Samuel Morse invented the Morse code, he thought about how to make the letters that occurred most often the easiest."

"I know!" Travon said, excited to share his knowledge about the Morse code. "It's only one dot for E and one dash for T."

"It could be important for playing hangman," Elissa said.

Gissele jumped up. "I just thought about Scrabble," she said. "The E is only worth one point and there are lots of them. But there's only one J and one Q, and they're worth maybe eight or ten points, I can't remember. I bet they used this information."

Marilyn then wrote on the board as the students watched:

This is odd.
Do you know why?
Can you try to find out?

"What's odd?" Scott asked.

"It's a puzzle," Marilyn said. "See if you can figure out why what I wrote is unusual." The room got quiet as the students thought. No one had an idea.

"It's about the letters I used in the three sentences I wrote," Marilyn said.

"There's no E!" Travon blurted out.

Several students groaned when Marilyn confirmed Travon's discovery, and with this, she ended the class.

An Extension

A few days later, Marilyn posed a problem for the students that required them to apply the information they had learned from their investigation of the frequency of usage of the letters in the alphabet. The students were all familiar with Boggle, a game in the classroom that was available for the children to play during free time. Marilyn gathered the students on the rug and showed them the game. She asked for a volunteer to explain how to play.

"You shake up the box and then get the cubes into the slots," Elissa said. "Then you start the timer. You have to make as many words as you can with letters that touch."

"The letters have to be next to each other or diagonal," Andy added.

"How many cubes are there?" Marilyn asked.

"Sixteen," several students answered.

"And how many letters are there on each cube?" Marilyn asked. "How many faces does each cube have?"

"Six," they chorused.

"So with sixteen cubes," Marilyn said, "how many letters are there in all? How would you solve that problem?"

"You multiply sixteen times six," Cara said.

"Let's try to do that in our heads," Marilyn said. "Talk with your neighbor and then raise a hand if you're willing to share your strategy." The students were used to being asked to calculate in their heads and were comfortable with different strategies. After a few moments, some hands were up. Marilyn waited until more students volunteered. Then she called on Keely.

Keely said, "Ten times six is sixty, and six times six is thirty-six. So you have to add sixty and thirty-six, and that's ninety-six." Marilyn recorded on the board:

$$16 \times 6$$
$$10 \times 6 = 60$$
$$6 \times 6 = 36$$
$$60 + 36 = 96$$

Mara used a different strategy, first multiplying sixteen by two and then multiplying the result, thirty-two, by three. To do the last multiplication, she multiplied thirty-two by two to get sixty-four, and then added on thirty-two to get ninety-six. Marilyn recorded:

$$16 \times 2 = 32$$
$$32 \times 3 =$$
$$32 \times 2 = 64$$
$$64 + 32 = 96$$

Raul raised his hand to describe another method. He remembered that if you double one factor in a multiplication problem and halve the other, the product stays the same. He explained, "So I changed the sixteen to eight and the six to twelve. And I know that eight times twelve is ninety-six." Marilyn recorded:

$$16 \div 2 = 8$$
$$6 \times 2 = 12$$
$$12 \times 8 = 96$$

Natanya said, "I did it the regular way, but in my head." She told Marilyn what to write. "Put a sixteen and then six under it and draw a line. Then you go six times six is thirty-six. So you put down the six and write the three up over the one. Then six times one is six, plus three is nine." Marilyn recorded:

$$\overset{3}{16} \\ \underline{\times 6} \\ 96$$

Marilyn then presented the problem for the students. She said, "Pretend that Parker Brothers, the manufacturer of the Boggle game, is hiring you to figure out which letters to put on the ninety-six faces of the cubes. Your problem is to decide which letters you would use and how many of each. Once you figure that out, then you write a memo to the president of Parker Brothers to present your recommendation and explain your reasoning." Marilyn wrote on the board a suggestion for how the students might organize their memos:

Memo

TO: *President of Parker Brothers*
FROM: ⎯⎯⎯⎯⎯⎯⎯
             ⎯⎯⎯⎯⎯⎯⎯

RE: *Letters for the 96 faces on the Boggle cubes*
CC: *Ms. Burns*
             Ms. Ross

"That's just like sending an email," Gabriel commented.

"Yes, it is," Marilyn responded. "Or you might want to present your ideas in a letter." Marilyn wrote another suggestion on the board:

Dear President of Parker Brothers,

Marilyn added, "To make your decisions, be sure to think about the results of our investigation of the frequency of letters."

Gissele had a question. "In the game, Q and U are together on the cube. Can we do that?"

"Why do you think they're together?" Marilyn asked.

"Because you never use the Q without the U," Hassan answered.

"Then it seems to make sense to put them together," Marilyn answered.

"But can we use U separately?" Mara wanted to know.

"That would be fine," Marilyn answered.

"Should we try to make it a hard game?" Scott asked.

"Think about what Parker Brothers would like," Marilyn said. "They would like the game to be as popular as possible, so you should choose letters that make a really good game."

"Can we work with a partner?" Alexandra asked.

Danielle, the classroom teacher, responded, "You'll each work with your table partner. But you each should write your own memo."

Marilyn added, "While you're working, I'll look at the cubes in the actual game of Boggle and tally how many times each letter is used."

Before dismissing the students from the rug, Marilyn reviewed the instructions once more. She wrote on the board:

1. *Choose letters for the 96 faces.*

2. *Write a memo about your choices.*

Students approached the problem in different ways. Most listed the letters of the alphabet to get organized. Some used tally marks and others used numbers. A few pairs wrote a *1* or made one tally mark next to each number, then began to increase the number of times some of the letters should be used, keeping track as they worked their way to a total of ninety-six.

Keely reported that she and Andy first gave each letter three tally marks, except for Q, for a total of seventy-eight marks. Then they had eighteen more to use, and they put these next to the letters with the highest frequencies. "Then we took some tally marks away from some letters and moved them to other letters," Keely explained. "And we finally did a QU, too," she added.

Alexandra and Michael decided that half of the letters should be vowels, but Scott and Elissa, sitting across from them, thought that there shouldn't be that many. "Maybe just a third," Scott said.

Gabriel and Mara argued about whether there should be four or six Es and finally compromised on using five Es. Other pairs used different numbers of Es—ten, eight, six, and other amounts—but everyone used E either more times than other letters or the same number of times as T, A, and O.

The students didn't finish the assignment by the end of the period, so they continued working the next day. Then they gathered on the rug for a follow-up discussion. Marilyn asked several questions. First she asked them to report how many Es they had used, and she organized the information on the board into a graph.

How many Es?

```
1
2
3
4  XX
5
6  XXX
7  X
8  XXXXX
9  X
10 X
11
12
```

Marilyn discussed with the children the mode (eight), median (also eight), and mean (just more than seven). This was good review for the students because they had learned about these ideas a few months before.

Then she asked them to figure out what fraction of the letters they used were vowels. Finally, she asked them to figure out if they used more or less than one-third of their ninety-six letters for vowels. Many of the students were confused until Ebony explained matter-of-factly, "One-third of ninety-six is thirty-two. That should help you figure."

Finally, Marilyn wrote the order of the letters as used in the actual game of Boggle underneath the adding machine tape strip she had posted previously. Below each letter in the Boggle order, she wrote the number of times it appeared on the sixteen cubes.

Army list

| e t a o n i s r h l d c u p f m w y b g v k q x j z |

Boggle list

```
e t o a n i s r h l d y u p f m w c b g v k q u x j z
11 9 9 6 6 6 6 5 5 4 3 3 3 2 2 2 2 2 2 2 1 1 1 1 1 1
```

Math and Literature, Grades 4–6

Figure 12-3 contains two pages of a handwritten letter.

Left margin tally marks:

Letter	Tally
A	Ж II
B	III
C	III
D	III
E	Ж IIII
F	III
G	III
H	IIII
I	ИI
J	III
K	III
L	III
M	ИI
N	III
O	Ж
P	III
Q	I
R	Ж
S	IIII
T	Ж I
U	Ж
V	II
W	III
X	I
Y	II
Z	I

Dear President of Parker Brothers,

I have some ideas that could make the game of Boggle more fun and less frustrating. I think there should be more e's on the cubes because we discovered that "e" was used the most in many common words. Using the army's frequency distrubution for codes in World War 1 and one of our own, we found that the letter "e" was used the most. We thought "e" should be on exactly 8 sides of the Boggle cubes. We made a frequency distrubution by bringing sentences together and counting how many times each letter was used.

Secondly, we placed "q" with "u" because it would be easier to make words. We thought "q" should used once because on the army's distrubution "q" was third to last, and on our distrubution it was second to last. "Q" is in quite a few words, but most of them aren't 4 letters.

Thirdly, I think you should try our committee's frequeny distrubution because we tried and tested many things. We made these tally marks based on how many times each letter was used in at least 48 sentences. If you haven't tried as many mathmatical theorys as we did, it might be good to trie our idea. We started by giving each letter 1 tally mark. Then, we gave more tally marks to the more popular letters. I hope you frie our idea soon.

Figure 12-3: Adam included the specific recommendations for each letter in the left margin of his letter.

Memo

Dear Ms. President of Parker Brothers,

I have some good changes to make Boggle hard but not frustrating here are my ideas. I think we shold use T and E 6 times on a block, because they are the most used latters. I know this because we used the armys Alphabat phreqwinsy and it showd that E and T are used the most. We gave v, w, x, y and z 2 and 3 because they are not used very often. I Figured this out using the armys freqwinsy but we tried it to by chosing 3 sentinsis and telly marking how much they are used and we got almost the same as the army the first 4 were the same and so were most others. but you still can not trust ars because we did not do every word in the world. You can see how much of a latter we used on the 96 faces of the cubes on page 2. We got our ansers by charts, saples Data and freqcency distribution. We corracted every thing using the armys

freqcency the armys freqcency is ETAOMISRHLDCUPfmwy bgVkqxJz and our freqcency is ETAOinrhsdllwnuqcfy bkb PvZxji as you can see some latters are the same but not all of them. Below is how much I want a latter used. I hope you will take some of my Ideas Thank you for Reading this.

A 5	M 3	Y 3
B 4	N 4	Z 3
C 3	O 5	
D 3	P 4	
E 6	Q 3	
F 3	R 5	
G 3	S 4	
H 4	T 6	
I 5	U 3	
J 3	V 2	
K 3	W 3	
L 4	X 2	

Figure 12-4: Michael presented his ideas for making the game hard but not frustrating.

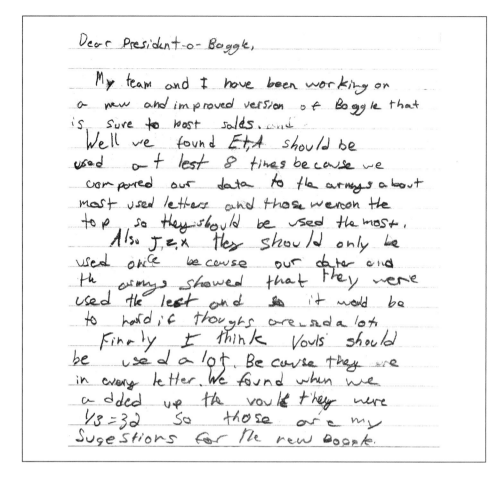

Dear President-o-Boggle,

My team and I have been working on a new and improved version of Boggle that is sure to host solds. and Well we found E,t,A should be used at lest 8 times because we compared our data to the armys about most used letters and those weron the top so they should be used the most.

Also J,z,x they should only be used once because our data and the armys showed that they were used the lest ond so it would be to hard if thoughs are used a lot

Finely I think Vouls should be used a lot. Because they are in every letter. We found when we added up the vould they were 1/3=32 So those are my Sugestions for the new Boggle.

The students talked about the similarities and differences in the two arrangements and compared them with their own recommendations. Marilyn then used the few minutes remaining in the class to have some of the students read their memos to the class. (See Figures 12–3 through 12–5.)

The lesson was a rich experience that engaged the students with calculating; using ideas from the areas of probability and statistics; revisiting the ideas of mode, median, and mean; and writing, accomplishing another link between math and language arts.

Marvelous Math

Marvelous Math is a collection of poems about mathematics. Lee Bennett Hopkins (2001) has selected poems from a variety of poets that provide a playful look at the ways in which mathematics is part of our daily lives. In the book there are poems that span the topics and tools in mathematics: numbers, operations, fractions, decimals, percents, counting, measurement, time, money, and calculators. The mostly humorous poems combine with Karen Barbour's colorful artwork to help the reader see mathematics in a whole new way. After hearing the poems, students choose a topic in mathematics and write their own math poems.

MATERIALS

Day 1

Tapping Students' Prior Knowledge About Poetry

"What do you know about poetry?" I asked Robin Gordon's fourth graders. "I want you each to think about this question for a minute without talking. Then I want you to share your thoughts with a partner." The room was quiet as the students, who were assembled on the rug at the front of the room, engaged in the first part of their "think-pair-share." I find it effective to give students some individual think time after I ask them a question. This usually gives them more to talk about with their partners or the class.

After less than a minute, I gave the signal to share with their partners, then I pulled the group back together and called on Rebecca.

"They rhyme," she said. I wrote the word *Poetry* on the board, drew a circle around the word, and then drew a line extending from the circle and wrote the word *rhyme*. This was the beginning of our "knowledge web" about poetry.

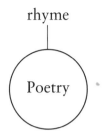

"Poems can show emotions, like you're excited or sad," Brooke reported. I wrote *show emotions—excited, sad, happy* on our knowledge web and continued to add to the web as students shared ideas.

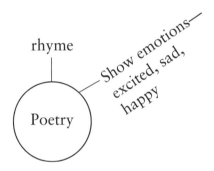

Dan added, "Sometimes they're long and sometimes they're short."

"You can write poems to your friend or girlfriend," Jalin said. The children giggled.

"That's important," I said. "Having an audience for your writing is motivating; it gives a purpose to the writing. Other ideas about poetry?"

Jackie said, "Sometimes poems are funny."

"Sometimes they don't have to rhyme," Rain added.

"That's interesting," I commented. "I'm going to read some poems to you in a minute and I want you to listen and see if the poems rhyme or not. Rebecca mentioned rhyming, and Rain said that poems don't have to rhyme."

Hernando exclaimed, "Sometimes in poetry you can break the rules! Like you don't have to use periods or capitals."

Abelardo added, "Sometimes poems can be true."

"What do we call a story or poem that is factual, or true?" I asked the class.

"Nonfiction!" they chorused.

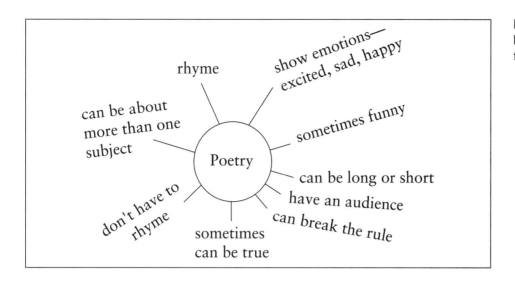

Figure 13–1: Our knowledge web for poetry.

"And when stories or poems are made up, or not based on fact?" I asked.

"Fiction!" they responded.

"I think poems can be about more than one subject," Melinda mused. "And they can be silly."

When the students were finished sharing their ideas, our knowledge web about poetry looked like the web in Figure 13–1.

Reading the Poems in Marvelous Math

"Wow, you know a lot about poetry! I'm very impressed," I exclaimed. "Now I'm going to read some poems from a book called *Marvelous Math*. Let's listen carefully and try to notice what makes each poem interesting, because later on we're going to write some poems of our own."

I read the first poem in the book, titled "Marvelous Math," by Rebecca Kai Dotlich. Each line of the poem is a question that can be answered using mathematics: The speed of a taxi? The size of an attic? How many seconds in an hour? How many miles to Istanbul? How old is the oldest dinosaur?

When I finished reading the poem, I addressed the class. "Did you notice that there were lots of questions in that poem? So if you want, you can use questions in the poems that you'll be writing tomorrow."

Next, I read a poem by Betsy Franco. Before reading it, I told the students that I wasn't going to tell them the title of the poem. I directed them to listen carefully as I read and try to think of a good title for the poem. I told them that they would eventually be creating titles for their own math poems.

When I finished reading the poem, I asked for volunteers to share their titles. Their suggestions included: "Math Is Not Just Adding and Subtracting," "Magic Math," "Mathematicians," and "Math Is

Everywhere." After students shared their ideas, I revealed the actual title: "Math Makes Me Feel Safe."

I then read another poem by Rebecca Kai Doltlich. This one is very short—only three lines—and is titled "Calculator." As with the previous poem I read, I didn't reveal the title until the end, after students came up with their own titles. The students liked this exercise because it was a sort of guessing game. It was beneficial to their learning, because it got students thinking about titles and helped them focus on the main idea of the poems.

The next poem I read was titled "SOS," written by Beverly McLoughland. It's a funny poem about long division and has several pairs of rhyming words: *pain-brain, engineer-ear, mess-SOS.* To focus on the rhyming, I paused during parts of the poem to let the students fill in each rhyming word. For example, I read:

> *Sammy's head is pounding—*
> *Sammy's in pain—*
> *A long division's got*
> *Stuck in his _____.*

Students chanted, "Brain!"

I selected two more poems to read aloud to the class before finishing up the lesson—"Fractions," by Lee Bennett Hopkins, and "Time Passes," by Ilo Orleans. When I finished, it was time for math class to end. Students were excited to begin writing their own poems, but they would have to wait for the following day.

Day 2

Writing Our Own Math Poems

I called Robin's students to the rug to begin the process of writing math poems. Since her students had been studying about geometry for about a week, I decided to focus their poetry writing on that topic. Had they been studying fractions or measurement, the poems might have had a different focus.

"Yesterday we began math class by making a knowledge web about poetry," I began. "Before we begin writing poems today, we're first going to make a knowledge web about geometry."

As they'd done the day before, students quietly thought about geometry, then shared their thinking with their partners. After a couple of minutes, I pulled them together so that I could create a knowledge web from their ideas. When we were finished, the web looked like the one in Figure 13–2.

When we finished the knowledge web about geometry, I modeled for the students the first step in writing their math poems.

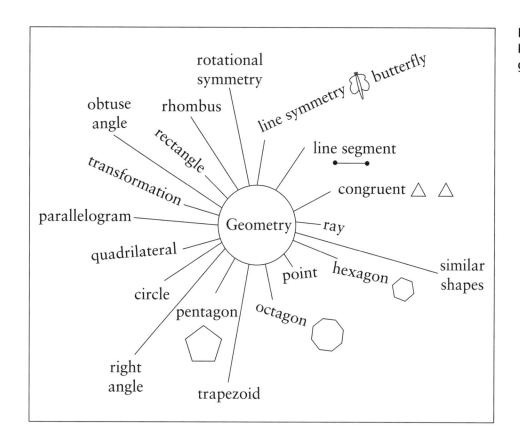

Figure 13–2: Our knowledge web for geometry.

"In a few minutes, you'll be writing your own math poems," I said. "The first thing you'll do is choose a shape or a geometry idea and make a knowledge web about it, just like we've done with poetry and geometry. You'll then use the ideas from your knowledge web to help you write your poem. Let's do one together so you can see what I mean."

Because I knew that most students would probably be familiar with the shape, I decided to use a square for the model. I drew a square on the board and wrote the word next to it and drew a circle around the word and drawing. Rather than do a think-pair-share, I decided to immediately take students' ideas about a square in order to save time. Figure 13–3 shows what our web about a square looked like.

After we finished our web about the square, I gave students directions for writing their poems. "Here's what you're going to do when you get back to your table," I said. "First you're going to choose a shape or a geometry idea, like we did with the square. Then you're going to take a piece of paper and make a knowledge web about the thing you chose. Then you're going to take another piece of paper and start writing your poem."

"What kind of poem should we write?" Dana asked.

"I'm not going to tell you how to write your poem," I responded. "Think about the math poems we read yesterday. Some had rhyming words, some didn't. Some used questions. Some were very short and

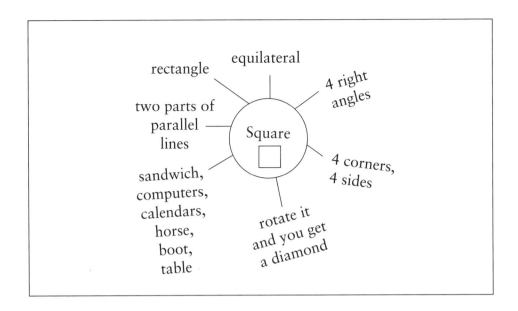

Figure 13–3: Our knowledge web for a square.

other poems were long. Some were funny. I want you to experiment with your poems."

I asked the students to think of a geometry idea or shape and raise their hands when they were ready. As students gave me their poem ideas, I handed them each two sheets of paper—one for the web and one for the poem—and dismissed them to their seats.

Making the knowledge webs came fairly easy to most students. I think the extensive modeling we did as a group helped. I gave the students about fifteen minutes to work on their webs, then I asked for their attention.

"I notice that many of you are nearly finished with your webs," I began. "Before you start writing your poems, let's write one together to give you an idea about how you might proceed."

I directed their attention back to the knowledge web that we created for the square. Taking one student's idea at a time, we wrote this poem together:

Square

4 right angles
4 sides
It's a perfect rectangle,
Do you know that?
Rotate and you have a rhombus!

Sharing the Math Poems

After the students had been working for about twenty minutes on their poems, I asked for volunteers to share their writing. I told the class that poets often have poetry readings and that we were going

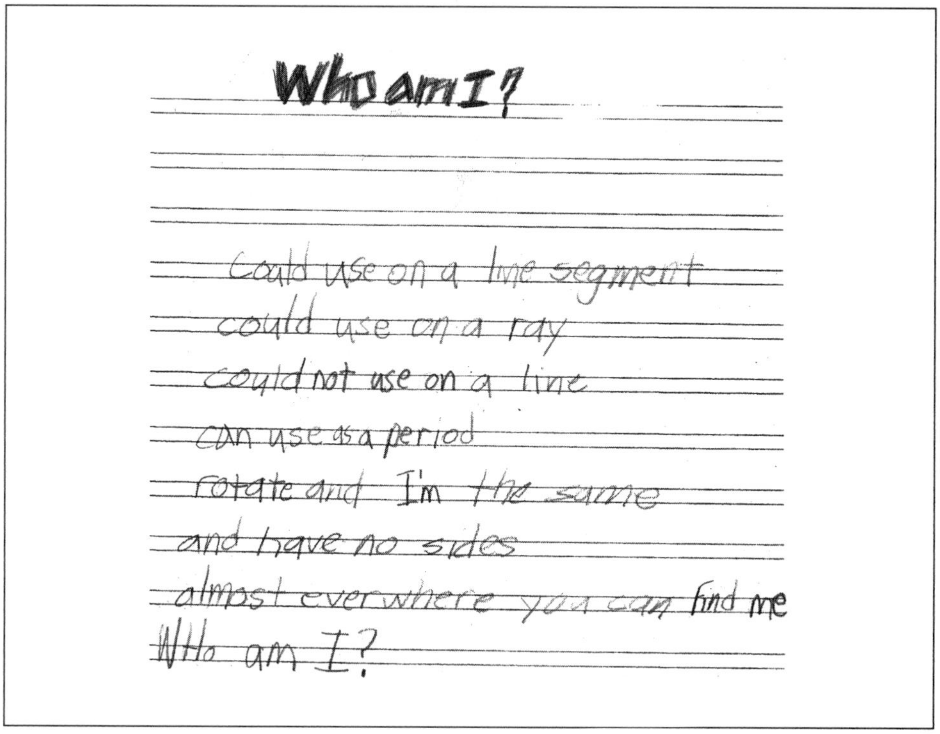

Who am I?

Could use on a line segment
could use on a ray
could not use on a line
can use as a period
rotate and I'm the same
and have no sides
almost everwhere you can find me
Who am I?

Figure 13–4: Edgardo wrote a poem about a point.

to have our own poetry reading. The students thought this was a neat idea.

Edgardo went first. His poem—titled "Who Am I?"—was a riddle about a point. (See Figure 13–4.)

Who Am I?

Could use on a line segment
could use on a ray
could not use on a line
can use as a period
Rotate and I'm the same
and have no sides
almost everywhere you can find me
Who am I?

The class applause made Edgardo smile. He was obviously happy with his poem and his classmates' response. I was impressed with the supportive atmosphere in the room. The students continued to applaud after each reading.

Brook went next. Her poem rhymed and was a little silly. It made her peers laugh. (See Figure 13–5.)

Acute

It's an acute angle. Don't you
see? When I look at one I think

of a fox that's wild and free!
Some are big and some small. The other
day I saw one at the mall!

Following are some of the other poems that volunteers read. (See Figures 13–6 through 13–8.)

Figure 13–5: Brook created a poem about an acute angle.

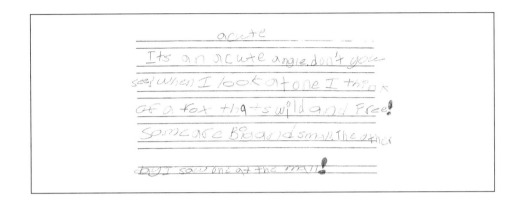

Figure 13–6: Dan wrote a poem about a trapezoid.

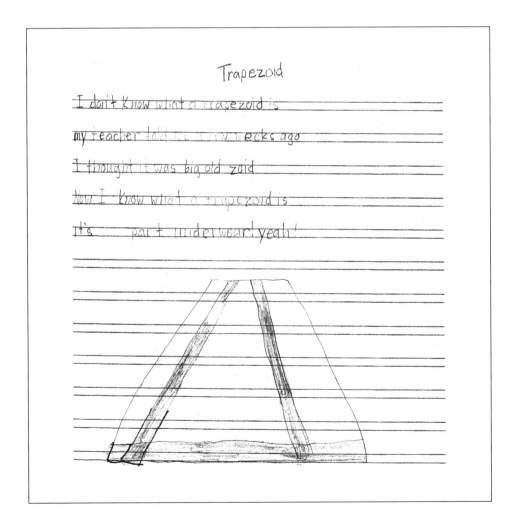

Math and Literature, Grades 4–6

Trapezoid

I don't know what a trapezoid is
My teacher told me a few weeks
*   ago*
I thought it was a big old zoid
Now I know what a trapezoid is
It's part underwear! Yeah!

Congruent

I'm not congruent to anybody
No, sorry
I'm not congruent to anybody
Nope, not me
People are similar in their own
*   special way*
But no one is exactly congruent
At least that's what I say
The thing that's congruent about us
Is very special
But what is not congruent is

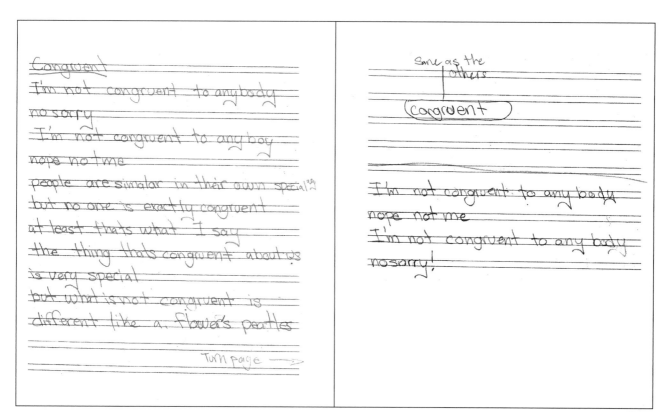

Figure 13–7: A poem by Adi, called "Congruent."

Figure 13–8: A poem by Julie about similar triangles.

different like a flower's petals
I'm not congruent to anybody
nope, not me
I'm not congruent to anybody
no, sorry

Similar Triangles

Look what I found!
Two triangles I see.
I see that they're both the same
color and the same shape.
There, the shapes have three
sides.
But when I look closely,
they are different sizes!

Our poetry reading lasted about ten minutes. Robin planned to continue having students share their poems throughout the week. I was very impressed with the students' poems; they were fun, silly, creative, and very descriptive. Writing math poems proved to be a very effective way of helping Robin's students think about the important ideas in geometry.

Math Curse

Jon Scieszka and Lane Smith's *Math Curse* (1995) is the story of a girl who thinks her teacher has put a spell on her, a math curse. Everything she looks at or thinks about becomes a math problem: How many minutes in an hour? How many kids got on the bus? How many fingers are in the class? What is another way to say one-half? How many M&Ms would it take to measure the length of the Mississippi River? The girl becomes a "raving math lunatic" and wonders if the curse will last a whole year (which only makes her think about how many minutes that would be!). Finally, she finds a way to break the math curse, only to be frightened the next day when her science teacher says, "You know, you can think of almost everything as a science experiment. . . ." This hilarious story helps students realize that math is all around us. The book can also be used as a springboard for writing math story problems.

MATERIALS

Introducing Story Problems Through *Math Curse*

"Who knows what a curse is?" I asked Robin Gordon's fourth graders.

"It's like a spell," Jackie said. "It's like when a witch casts a spell on you."

"Curses are bad," Melinda chimed in.

David added, "I think a curse is like when you have voodoo dolls and you stick a pin in one to make something bad happen to someone."

I held up the book *Math Curse* and asked if the students had heard or read it before. Several had and seemed excited to hear it again.

"This is a story of a girl who thinks her teacher has put a math curse on her," I told the class. "The book is full of math story problems. As I'm reading the book, I'll occasionally stop to ask you to solve some of the problems. Then, when I'm finished reading, you'll have a chance to write your own story problems."

I began reading the story. *Math Curse* is a very funny book with imaginative and colorful artwork. The students laughed throughout the reading, enjoying the authors' sense of humor. When I got to the page where the girl in the story is eating her cereal and milk and wondering how many inches in a foot and how many feet in a yard, I stopped to ask a question.

"Does anyone know how many inches there are in a foot? Think for a second, then we'll say the answer together."

After students said "twelve inches" in a choral voice, I held up a ruler, showing the inches and confirming their answer. I then asked the class to think about how many feet there are in a yard. After a few seconds, I held up a yardstick and pointed to the end of the stick and read aloud, "Thirty-six inches."

I then said, "If there are thirty-six inches in a yard, and there are twelve inches in a foot, how many feet are there in a yard?" Students thought for a minute, then I directed them to talk with their partners before I elicited ideas from the whole group.

"I think there are three feet in a yard," Brook volunteered. "It's because thirty-six divided by twelve is three."

"Other ideas?" I asked.

"I just knew it," Dan said. "We learned it in third grade."

"I went twelve, twenty-four, thirty-six," Nina explained.

"So you skip-counted by twelves," I said, putting a name to Nina's strategy.

I continued reading *Math Curse*. When I was finished with the book, the students applauded, expressing their delight with the story.

"There were lots of story problems in *Math Curse*," I said. "Before we begin writing our own math story problems, let's go back to one of the problems in the book and solve it."

I leafed through the book until I found the page where the girl in the story says, "We sit in 4 rows with 6 desks in each row. What if Mrs. Fibonacci rearranges the desks to make 6 rows? 8 rows? 3 rows? 2 rows?" I read this part of the page to the students.

"I'm going to model writing a math story problem based on the information I just read to you from *Math Curse*," I told the class. I directed the students to read my story silently as I wrote it on the board:

> *There are 24 kids in my class.*
> *If there are 8 rows,*
> *How many students sit in each row?*

"Think about how to solve this problem for a few seconds, then turn to your partner and take turns explaining your thinking," I told the students. "Remember, take turns sharing your ideas, maintain good eye contact, and listen carefully and respectfully." These are the rules I use for partner talk. I find it effective to review partner talk protocol at least once during a lesson.

After a few minutes, I asked for the students' attention and called on Jalen.

"It's three," he said.

"Three what?" I probed, attempting to help Jalen be more specific with his communication.

"Three kids in each row," he responded. "Because eight times three equals twenty-four."

"I'm going to draw a picture of what Jalen described," I told the class. I then quickly drew an 8-by-3 array on the board:

$$
\begin{matrix}
\bullet & \bullet & \bullet \\
\bullet & \bullet & \bullet \\
\bullet & \bullet & \bullet \\
\bullet & \bullet & \bullet \\
\bullet & \bullet & \bullet \\
\bullet & \bullet & \bullet \\
\bullet & \bullet & \bullet \\
\bullet & \bullet & \bullet \\
\end{matrix}
$$

"Does this look like eight rows with three students in each row?" I asked the class. Students nodded their heads in agreement. Making visual representations often helps students understand numbers and operations.

Amber added, "I also think it's three 'cause twenty-four divided by eight is three."

"So you can think about the problem using multiplication and division," I summarized. I wrote $24 \div 8 = 3$ on the board and asked, "Amber, what does the twenty-four mean in your equation?"

"It's the twenty-four students in the class," she answered. "And the eight is the number of rows."

"And the three is the three students in each row," Melinda chimed in.

"Any other ideas?" I asked.

"You can count by threes," Dan offered.

I thought for a moment about what Dan had said. Then I asked him, "What made you start with counting by threes? I'm asking because I don't see a three in the problem."

"I really solved it doing eight times what number is twenty-four," he confessed. "But I checked my answer by doing three plus three eight times."

"Oh, so you can use addition to check your multiplication?" I asked. Dan nodded in agreement.

Next, I asked the students to think of a math story problem to share. I gave them specific directions: "Be sure that your problem ends with a question that we have to answer to find the solution."

After giving the class some think time, I called on Charles and he presented his problem:

> *I get up at 6:15 . . . take 2 minutes to brush my teeth, 3 minutes to get dressed, 10 minutes to eat my breakfast. What time was it when I was finished?*

As Charles told his story, I quickly wrote it on the board, modeling for the students.

"Does that work?" I asked the class. "Remember, after you write your story, you have to solve it to check if it makes sense. Notice that Charles's story ends with a question mark. Your story should also end in a question."

Manuel went next. His example also involved time. I wrote his story on the board, then encouraged students to think of stories with different topics. Andrea shared a story with an unknown initial quantity:

> *I had some candies. I ate 5. I have 10 left. How many candies did I start with?*

Hernando's story caused some confusion and was a good example of how difficult it can be for children to write math story problems. Following is the story that Hernando dictated:

> *I have 5 ninjas. They each have 5 blades. 50 bad ninjas came. How many ninjas escaped?*

"That doesn't make sense," Rebecca said. "How can we figure out how many escaped?"

"Writing stories is tricky," I told the class. "Hernando, what could you add to your story that would help? It seems like some of the ninjas escaped, but what happened to the others?"

Hernando quickly solved the dilemma. "Each blade killed five bad ninjas," he said.

I added his words to the story, which now read:

I have 5 ninjas. They each have 5 blades. 50 bad ninjas came. Each blade killed 5 bad ninjas. How many ninjas escaped?

I reread Hernando's story, then I asked students to think about an answer.

"It's fifty take away five," Rain said.

"Why do you think that?" I asked her.

"There are fifty bad ninjas and five are killed," she explained.

I thought about Rain's response. She had not taken into account the fact that each blade killed five bad ninjas. She was subtracting but not realizing that she also needed to use multiplication. I didn't jump in to correct her; instead, I continued to ask for more ideas from the class.

"You can do five ninjas times five blades, which is twenty-five," Cesar explained. "If they tried to kill fifty, twenty-five escaped."

This was getting interesting. Cesar was using multiplication (five ninjas times five blades each), but he hadn't gone far enough. I called on Nina next.

"I can add on to what Cesar said," she began. "If each blade killed five bad ninjas and each ninja has five blades, each ninja killed twenty-five bad ninjas. But there's five ninjas, so you do twenty-five times five to get the answer."

"So what's twenty-five times five?" I asked. Nina stared back at me, looking a little stumped by my question. Instead of giving her the answer, I helped her out by asking another question.

"What's twenty-five times four?" I asked. Nina knew the answer to 25×4 immediately, then quickly figured 25×5.

"Sounds like there aren't enough bad ninjas for the problem to work," I observed. "Hernando, could you add some bad ninjas to your problem so that it can work?" He smiled.

I then gave the students directions for writing their story problems. I told them that they'd each be getting two pieces of paper. One paper was for their rough draft and one was for their final draft. Once they completed their rough draft and found the answer to their story problem, they had to check their story out with a neighbor and the teacher before writing their final draft.

After Marco volunteered to clarify for the class what my directions were, I asked for questions.

"Do you have to make it hard or easy to solve?" Melinda asked.

"Make it challenging but not too difficult," I responded. "Remember, you have to solve the problem first."

"Can it be a multiplication or division story?" Henry asked.

"That would be fine; you choose what math to include," I said.

Writing Our Own Story Problems

I dismissed the students, handing two sheets of paper to each as they walked back to their seats. I gave them about five minutes to quietly discuss their ideas at their tables before directing them to focus their attention on writing their stories.

As I circulated, helping students and reading their stories, I was amazed at the range of topics. These fourth graders' stories were about things that interested them: candy bars, hamsters, books, concerts, ogres, ballet dancing, friends, dogs, flowers, dragons, popcorn, cars, and ninjas, to name a few! Letting students choose their own topics for writing has long been valued by educators as an effective way to motivate reluctant writers. Allowing students to write their own math story problems not only motivates students to write but can also yield a rich range of problem types not usually found in math textbooks. Following are some of the math story problems Robin's students wrote. The first one, by Mark, involves time. The result, or answer, is unknown. (See Figure 14–1.)

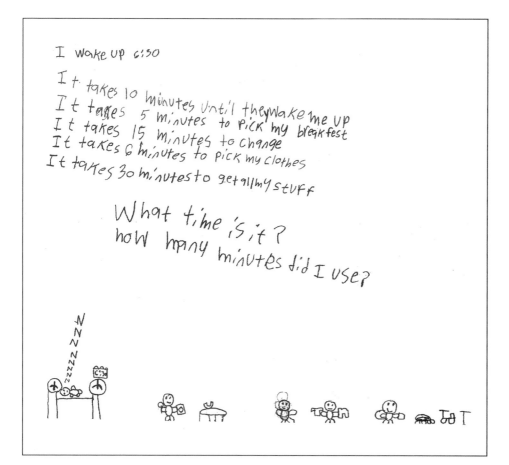

Figure 14–1: Mark wrote a story about his morning routine.

I wake up at 6:30.
It takes 10 minutes until they wake me up.
It takes 5 minutes to pick my breakfast.
It takes 15 minutes to change.
It takes 6 minutes to pick my clothes.
It takes 30 minutes to get all my stuff.
What time is it [now]?
How many minutes did I use?

Tiara solved her story using repeated subtraction (See Figure 14–2.):

Figure 14–2: Tiara wrote a story about reading.

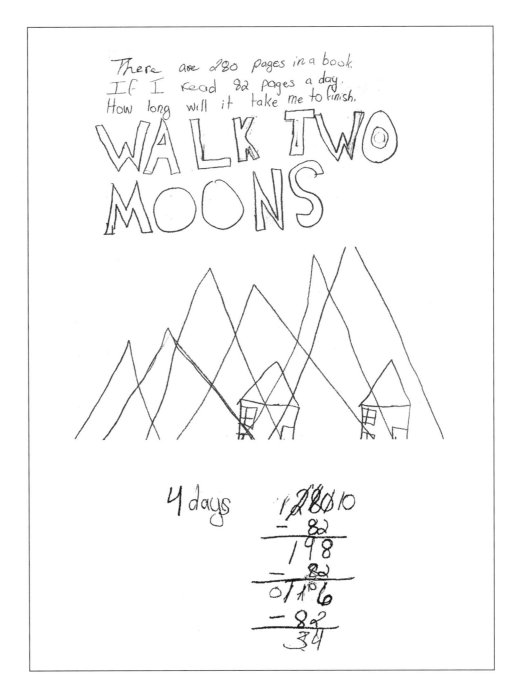

There are 280 pages in a book.
If I read 82 pages a day.
How long will it take me to finish?

Alonzo's story about an ogre, which he misspelled as *oger*, began with an unknown quantity that needed to be figured out. (I talked with Alonzo about the correct spelling of *ogre*. Dealing with spelling in the context of children's own writing is effective for helping them learn.) (See Figure 14–3.)

The Oger Problem

There was an oger who ate eyeballs. He ate 20 eyeballs now he has 5 left. How much did he start with?

Jalen's story included an unknown change (See Figure 14–4.):

There are 6 chinese dragons flying in the sky. Some mor came, now there are 12. How many dragons came to make 12?

Figure 14–3: Alonzo's story was about a hungry ogre.

Figure 14–4: Jalen's story was about Chinese dragons.

Figure 14–5: Aldive's story problem could require using several operations to find the solution.

Aldive's story involved an unknown initial quantity. Solutions to his problem could require using several operations (See Figure 14–5.):

There were some dogs—
Each dog had two bones.
Five dogs escaped.
He got 4 new dogs.
Now he has 19 dogs.
How many dogs did he use to have and how many bones did they have total?

Solving Henry's story problem could involve using more than one operation; for example, it can be solved with multiplication and subtraction:

If I had 50 dollars and I bought 6 candy bars
that cost $1.00 for 2 candy bars. Then I bought
2 more candy bars. How much money would I
have left?

Observing the Students

Most students were able to write story problems that made sense, were interesting, and were appropriate for fourth grade. There were, however, a few students who needed some help. Chris, for example, needed just one number in his story to make it clear and understandable. Following is his original story:

There were 100 good ninjas and bad ninjas.
120 ninjas died in all. How much are there now?

When figuring the answer, Chris did $200 - 120 = 80$. I noticed this and gave him some feedback.

"I really like your story, Chris," I began. "But there's one thing I'm not clear about. I see that you wrote two hundred minus one hundred twenty equals eighty. To me that means that there are one hundred good ninjas and one hundred bad ninjas. Is that correct?" Chris nodded in agreement.

"To make this clear to the reader of your problem, what do you need to add to your story?" I asked. Chris thought for a minute, then responded.

"Oh!" he exclaimed. "I need to write that there were one hundred good ninjas and one hundred bad ones!"

Figure 14–6: Monica, an English language learner, needed to edit her story for clarification.

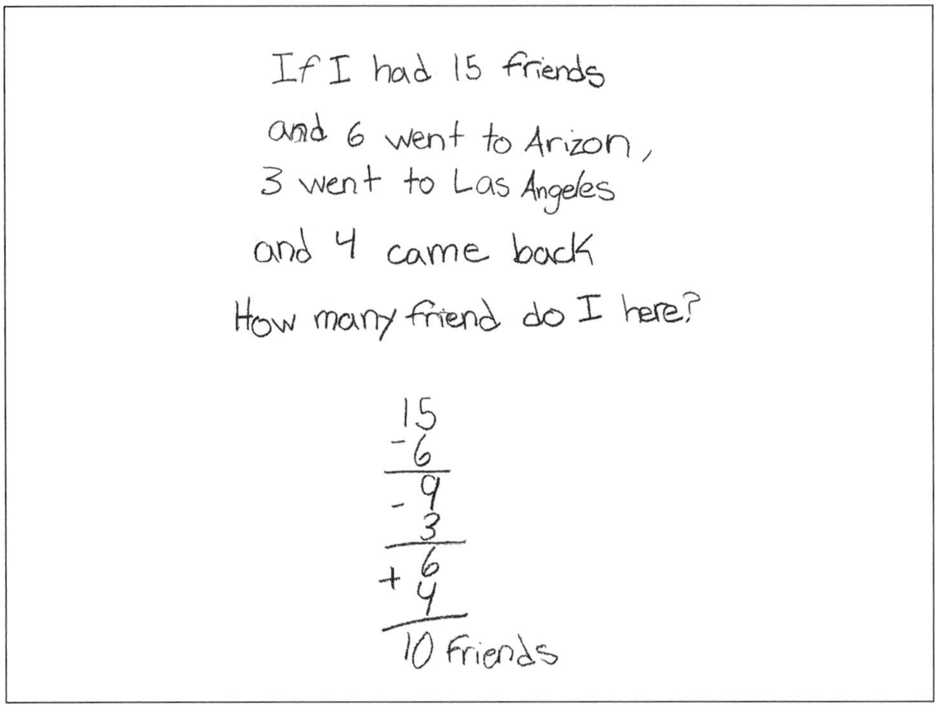
If I had 15 friends
and 6 went to Arizon,
3 went to Las Angeles
and 4 came back
How many friend do I here?

15
-6
9
-3
6
+4
10 friends

Writing math story problems can pose some difficulties for English language learners. Monica, whose first language was Spanish, wrote this story (See Figure 14–6.):

> *If I had 15 friends and 6 went to Arizon, 3 went to Las Angeles and 4 came back. How many friends do I here?*

"Monica, you have a good story here. Please read it back to me," I asked.

Monica read her story aloud but did not seem to recognize any problems with it, so I asked her a clarifying question.

"I'm a little confused," I said to her. "What do you mean by 'How many friends do I here'?"

"Oh! I mean how many friends do I have!" she exclaimed.

"How many friends do you have now?" I asked, trying to further clarify. She nodded her agreement.

Dan's answer to his problem didn't really match his story (See Figure 14–7.):

> *There are people at the pet store.*
> *There are 100 pets.*
> *Each of the persons wants 2 pets.*
> *How many pets did each person get?*

After he read his story to me, I asked Dan a question. "I like that your story has some unknown information in the beginning; you

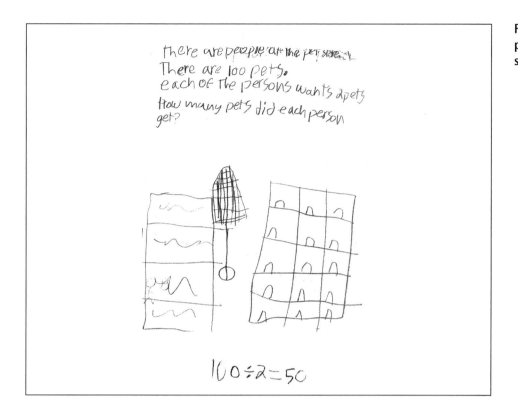

there are people at the pet store.
There are 100 pets.
each of the persons wants 2 pets
How many pets did each person get?

100÷2=50

don't tell us how many people are in the pet store. But your answer to the problem is one hundred divided by two equals fifty. I'm a little confused. What does the one hundred stand for?"

Dan thought for a minute, then responded, "The one hundred stands for the one hundred pets, and the two means each person got two pets."

"So each person wanted two pets and he got two pets?" I asked. Dan nodded his agreement.

"Then what about the fifty? What does that mean?" I asked him.

Dan stopped to think, and then said, "The number of people in the store?"

"So what's the question you want to ask—how many pets did each person get, or how many people in the store?"

"People in the store?" he responded hesitantly.

"So there are some people at the pet store and there are one hundred pets and each person gets two pets, so your question is How many people are in the store?" I asked, attempting to summarize and clarify.

"Yeah, that's right!" Dan exclaimed, finally realizing what he wanted to say in his story.

Extending the Lesson

On subsequent days, Robin used the story problems in different ways. On a few mornings, she posed a story problem for the class

Math Curse   139

to solve as a warm-up to math class. On another day, she put the story problems in a box and when students were finished with their regular assignment, they could choose a story to read and solve.

Robin and I agreed that having students write their own stories was motivating and gave them experience creating and solving a variety of problem types using all four operations. And reading *Math Curse* seemed to be a perfect springboard for introducing story problems.

A Million Fish . . .
More or Less

Strange things happen on the Bayou Clapateaux, as Hugh Thomas learns in *A Million Fish . . . More or Less*, by Patricia C. McKissack (1996). He catches three small fish—and then a million more. But before he can get all those fish home, Hugh meets an alligator, which demands a half share; raccoon bandits, which take half of the remaining share; and a hungry cat, which takes more than its share. Hugh arrives home with just enough fish for dinner—three small ones. The story leads to a discussion of large numbers and an activity in which children assign numbers to various objects and events.

MATERIALS

I read *A Million Fish . . . More or Less* to Dinah Brown's fourth graders near the beginning of the school year. The class had been investigating large numbers, and Dinah's goal was for her students to improve their number sense.

"Have any of you ever exaggerated when you told someone about something?" I asked before showing the class the book. Whispers broke out across the room, mixed with a few giggles.

"I remember one time that I told my friends that my dad got a Cadillac, and I said that it was a hundred feet long!" Grant said.

"That would be pretty long for a car," I said. "Was that how long it really was?"

"No," Grant said. "It really was only about, say, fifteen feet long, but I wanted to impress my friends."

"Has anyone else exaggerated before?" I asked.

"One time I went fishing with my dad, and I caught a fish, and I told my mom that it weighed over a hundred pounds," Ned said. "It really only weighed about a couple of pounds."

"I have a story I want to read to you about a boy who catches a million fish—more or less," I told them. "The setting of the story is a swamp. Raise your hand if you know what a swamp is." Lots of hands went up.

"It's a place that's really muddy," Tama offered.

"I think weird animals live in them, like alligators and stuff like that," Nadine guessed.

"It's a place where there's water, like a river or a lake," Anton said.

"You seem to know a lot about swamps," I commented. "This story is about Hugh Thomas, a boy who goes fishing in a river near a swamp."

I began to read the book. The children's imaginations were captured by both the story and Dena Schutzer's beautiful illustrations. They laughed when I read the part in the book where the two swampers, Elder Abbajon and Papa-Daddy, tell Hugh Thomas a whopper of a story about a turkey: "Take the time back in '03, me and the Elder here caught a wild turkey weighed five hundred pounds!"

The children snickered in disbelief when Papa-Daddy, lowering his voice to a whisper, told the story of the lantern: "As we was marchin' that gobbler home, I spied a lantern that'd been left by Spanish conquistadores back in the year 15 and 42. And it was still burning!"

"Could a turkey really weigh five hundred pounds?" I asked.

"No!" the class chorused.

"Could a lantern really burn for three hundred and fifty years?" I asked. (The correct length of time is 361 years, but the characters in the book say 350.)

"No!" the students answered back.

I continued to read the story, stopping at the part where Hugh Thomas meets Atoo, "the grand-père of all the alligators," in the swamp. At this point in the story, Hugh Thomas has his million fish loaded on his little red wagon.

Atoo slithers onto the bank and, blocking Hugh Thomas's way, demands some of the catch. The boy decides not to tangle with Atoo, and throws about half of his catch back into the bayou.

"If Hugh Thomas really had a million fish, and threw half of them back for Atoo, how many fish would Hugh Thomas be left with?" I asked. "Talk with the people in your group and try to figure this out."

After a few minutes, I asked the students for their attention and repeated the question.

"I think Hugh Thomas would have five thousand fish left," Jillian said.

"I think it would be fifty thousand fish left," Colette said.

"He would have half a million," Drew said.

"I think he would have five hundred thousand fish when he left Atoo," Tama added.

Most of the children weren't sure how many fish were half of a million. I decided that taking halves of powers of ten might help them think about the question. I began by writing the number *10* on the board.

"What's half of ten?" I asked.

"Five," they responded. I recorded a *5* next to the 10.

Then I wrote *100* under the 10. "What's half of one hundred?" I asked.

"Fifty," they answered. I recorded *50* next to the 100.

Then I wrote *1,000* under the 100 and asked the students, "Do you know what half of one thousand is?"

"Five hundred," they answered.

"So all of these were pretty easy for you," I said. "But what if someone weren't sure about your answers? How could you prove, for example, that five hundred is half of one thousand?" Many students raised their hands. I called on Drew.

"It's simple," he said. "Just add five hundred and five hundred, and you get one thousand, so it's half."

"I know another way," Lizette said. "You can go two times five hundred is one thousand."

I then wrote *10,000* under the 1,000. "Let's read this together," I said. After the students read the number aloud, I asked them to figure out half of ten thousand. I called on Amber.

"It's five thousand. All the answers have fives and zeros," she observed.

"And there's one more zero each time," Matthias added.

Next I wrote *100,000*. "Who can read this number?" I asked. About half of the students raised their hands.

"Let's say it together," I said. I had the students read the number twice so those who weren't sure the first time could join in the second time.

"What's half of one hundred thousand?" I asked. Again, about half of the students raised their hands. I called on Ned.

"Half of one hundred thousand is fifty thousand," he said.

"How did you figure?" I asked.

"I just kept going," Ned answered. "It had to be a five with four zeros."

"How else could you explain that fifty thousand is half of one hundred thousand?" I asked. I waited a few moments until about eight students had raised their hands. I called on Simone.

"I know fifty is half of one hundred. So it makes sense that fifty *thousand* is half of one hundred *thousand*," Simone explained.

Ernest raised his hand. "It's right," he said. "I did it on the calculator, and I got the same thing."

"Now for the big one," I told the class. I wrote *1,000,000* on the board.

"This is the number of fish Hugh Thomas said he had before he gave Atoo half of his catch," I said.

Some of the students murmured, "One million."

"Can you use the pattern on the board to figure out what is half of a million?" I asked.

"I know how to write it," Lizette said. Lizette wrote *500,000* on the board, and we all read it together. Ernest verified the answer on the calculator.

"Could you prove this is correct the way you proved that five hundred was half of one thousand?" I asked Drew.

"Sure," he said. Drew came to the board and wrote:

$$
\begin{array}{r}
500,000 \\
+\,500,000 \\
\hline
1,000,000
\end{array}
$$

I continued reading the story. Hugh Thomas followed the swamp path to Papa-Daddy and Elder Abbajon's houseboat. The children listened closely as I read about ghosts and pirates' treasure. The students' anticipation rose when I read: "The boy hummed and quickened his step. Something was stalking him, closing in fast."

"What do you think was stalking him?" I asked.

"A snake?" Kristy guessed.

"A raccoon!" Lizette said confidently.

"You seem very sure of yourself," I said, half joking.

"There was a picture of a raccoon on the cover of the book," Lizette said.

"Sure enough," I responded. "A raccoon named Mosley stopped Hugh Thomas and demanded a toll. The boy offered him half of his catch."

I stopped reading and asked the class, "If Hugh Thomas had five hundred thousand fish and Mosley the raccoon took half, how much would Hugh Thomas have? Talk to the people at your table to figure it out." When the children's voices died down, I asked for their ideas.

"Half of five hundred thousand is fifty thousand," Ernest said.

"I think it's three hundred thousand, because three is in the middle of one hundred thousand and five hundred thousand," Barbara said.

"You can't get one-half of five hundred thousand because five is an odd number and you can't split it evenly," Justine said.

"What's half of five?" I asked.

"Two and a half," Anton answered.

"Sometimes mathematicians write two and a half as two point five," I explained. "I'm going to record some numbers on the board again and see if you can figure out half of five hundred thousand by looking at a pattern."

To begin the pattern, I wrote 5 and recorded half of it as *2.5*. I then wrote *50*, and the students readily offered twenty-five as the answer. I continued with 500, 5,000, 50,000, and finally 500,000, each time asking how much was half and recording the answer. While some students seemed to have a sense of half of each quantity, others figured by following the emerging number pattern.

5	*2.5*
50	*25*
500	*250*
5,000	*2,500*
50,000	*25,000*
500,000	*250,000*

I returned to the book. Mosley wouldn't settle for only half of Hugh Thomas's catch; he demanded it all. Hugh Thomas suggested a contest. Mosley agreed to a jump-rope (actually, a jump-snake) contest. If Mosley jumped more times, he would get all of Hugh Thomas's catch; if Hugh Thomas jumped more times, then he would give the raccoon only half of the catch. Mosley jumped 5,552 times before missing, but Hugh Thomas won by making 5,553 jumps.

"Do you think it's likely that they jumped that many times?" I asked.

"No!" the children responded.

I then said, "Maybe five thousand couldn't be the number of times a person jumps rope, but it could be . . ." I left the last part of my sentence for the students to complete.

"The number of pounds an elephant weighs!" Simone answered.

"The amount of money in are savings account!" Elliott added.

I finished reading the book, and then I turned back to the part where the two swampers are telling the story about the turkey and the lantern.

"Remember when the swampers said that the turkey weighed five hundred pounds?" I asked. The students nodded.

"Five hundred couldn't be the number of pounds a turkey weighs, but it could be . . . ," I said, again leaving the sentence unfinished for the students.

"It could be the number of students in our school," Ben said.

I continued, "And three hundred and fifty couldn't be the number of years a lantern could stay lit, but it could be . . ." Many hands shot up this time.

"The number of days in almost a year!" Keziah said, giggling. The class laughed with her.

I then wrote on the board:

_____ could not be the number of _____,
but it could be the number of _____.

"Suggest some numbers that we could use to begin the sentence," I said.

The students offered many numbers. Their suggestions ranged from three to one million. After recording about twenty numbers on the board, I explained what they were to do.

"Pick a number, either one from the board or any other you'd like to use," I instructed. "Use the number to begin the sentence I wrote on the board, then complete the sentence and illustrate what you wrote."

"Can we do more than one number?" Colette asked.

"Yes," I said. "You should do two numbers, and then we'll put all of your work together into a class book. One of the numbers you choose should be a large number, and one of the numbers should be a small number. Then, if you'd like, you can do another page."

"What's a large number and what's a small number?" Nadine asked.

"That depends on how you think about it," I said. "A number that is small in one situation can be large in another."

"What do you mean?" Ned asked.

"If I said that I saw a person eat eight apples, that's a large number of apples for someone to eat," I explained. "But if I said that a total of eight people attended a rock concert, that would be a very small audience. In the first situation, eight is a large number; in the second, it's tiny."

The children got to work. As I walked around the room, I listened to them talk with their neighbors about the numbers they chose. Also, I asked some children questions about what they were writing.

Matthias was writing down his thoughts about one million. I asked him to read to me what he wrote. He read: "One million could not be the number of a person's age, but it could be the number of people in Mexico."

"You're right, Matthias, that a person can't be one million years old," I said. "But I once visited a Mexican city that had a population of about one million, so I know the population of the whole country of Mexico is much greater. I think you need to do some research about the population of Mexico. Where could you find that information?"

"In our social studies book," he replied, and he hurried over to the bookshelf to begin his research.

Kristy chose a number with which she was comfortable. She wrote: *50 could not be the number of stripes on the flag, but it could be the number of stars on the flag.*

Tyler was struggling with the number 9,999. He was able to identify what the number could not be (he chose a person's age), but he was stumped when it came to thinking of something that would number 9,999. Marnie, who was sitting next to him, offered some help.

"When I was in northern California, we visited the redwood trees. I think that some redwoods are about ten thousand years old," she said.

Maureen wrote: *25 could not be the number of hairs on your head, but it could be the number of books you read in a month.*

"Is it possible for someone to have twenty-five hairs on his head?" I asked.

"If you're my father," she said, without cracking a smile.

Lizette was having fun with her paper. She wrote: *1,000,000 could not be the number of socks you have, but it could be the number of socks in the WORLD. (What a disgusting odor!)* (See Figure 15–1.)

Figure 15–1: Lizette's idea about the number of socks in the world was called into question during the class discussion.

When the students finished writing, I had volunteers share their work with the rest of the class. Some of what students wrote was immediately called into question by the others, giving the students a chance to teach one another about numbers. For example, when Lizette shared her thoughts about one million being the number of socks in the world, Matthias raised his hand.

"When I was looking at our social studies book, I found out that there are over three billion people on Earth," he said. "So I don't think that there would only be one million socks in the world."

"How many pairs of socks do you think each person would have?" I asked.

"I have about six pairs," Lizette said.

"What if each person in the world had as many pairs of socks as Lizette? How many socks would that be?" I asked. "Talk with the people at your table and see what you come up with." After a minute or so, several students raised their hands. I called on Ben.

"I liked Lizette's idea, because my paper had to do with the number of people in the world, too," he said. "We think that if you have six pairs of socks, that's twelve socks. Then you would have to multiply twelve times three billion, and twelve times three equals thirty-six. So that would be thirty-six billion socks!"

When Douglas shared his idea that five hundred million could not be the number of whales in Sea World, but it could be the number of people in the United States, Artrina disagreed.

"I don't think there are that many people in the U.S.," she said.

"I know there are; I read it in a book," Douglas countered.

Figure 15–2: Keziah illustrated some of the thirty children she felt could be in a class.

30 could not be the number of kids or people in a school but it could be the number of kids in a class

I tabled the disagreement by writing Douglas's idea on the board under the title "Under Investigation."

Simone's writing led to an entirely new investigation. She read from her paper: "Sixty couldn't be the number of people in the world, but it could be the weight of a fourth grader."

"Get out the scale," Grant responded.

One good lesson often leads to another, and in this case, the students led the way. (See Figure 15–2 for another student's paper.)

On the Day You Were Born

On the Day You Were Born, by Debra Frasier (1991), celebrates life by listing forces in the natural world, "each ready to greet you the very first moment of the very first day you arrived." Colorful wood-block prints accompany a gentle text that describes migrating animals, the spinning Earth, the pulling gravity, the flaming Sun, the rising tide, and more—each of which was doing something "on the day you were born." At the end of the book, a paragraph describes each natural wonder in simple scientific terms. The lesson based on this book has students explore the number of days that have passed since they were born.

MATERIALS

$1\frac{1}{2}$-by-2-inch sticky notes, 1 per student

Introducing the Investigation

"Do you think we have any birthday twins in our class?" Maryann Wickett asked her fourth-grade class.

"What's a birthday twin?" Jodie asked.

"Birthday twins are two people who share a birthday," Maryann responded.

"Do they have to be the same age?" Heather asked.

"No," Maryann replied. "You could be my birthday twin if we both have the same birthday. Raise your hand if you think there are any birthday twins in our class." Most of the students raised their hands.

"How could we find out if we have any birthday twins?" Maryann asked.

"Everyone would have to tell when their birthday is," Evan said.

"Listen as I explain how we'll collect your birthday information," Maryann responded. "Each of you should write your birth date and your name on one of these sticky notes." Maryann held up a pad of $1\frac{1}{2}$-by-2-inch notes.

"Do we write down the month we were born in and the number of the day?" Jolene asked.

"That's right," Maryann replied. "For example, I'll write my name and May second. Then I'll stick my note on the board." The students quickly posted their information. Soon the board was filled with thirty yellow sticky notes.

"Raise your hand if you have an idea about how to organize our birthday information on the board," Maryann asked.

"Put them in order," Chelsea suggested.

"Explain more about what you mean," Maryann said.

"Put the Januarys together, then the Februarys, and all the way up to December, so we can see if there are any birthday twins," Chelsea explained. Maryann hesitated, and Chelsea gave further instructions.

"Just write the months down the side of the board," she explained. "Then you put the Januarys in one row, and the Februarys in another, like that."

Maryann quickly rearranged the sticky notes following Chelsea's directions.

"What do you notice about our birthday graph?" Maryann asked.

"Tirina and I are birthday twins!" Sandra exclaimed. Tirina and Sandra were excited to discover that they shared the same birthday. Some students seemed a little disappointed that there was only one pair of birthday twins in the class.

"What else do you notice?" Maryann continued.

"January is the mode. It has the most birthdays," Yvonne said.

"March and June only have one," Toby said. "They have the least."

"December, October, July, April, and February have two," Maya said.

"There are thirty birthdays in all," Alex said.

"January has three more than May, August, September, and November," Alan said.

"January has five more birthdays than March or June," Jodie added.

"February could fit in January three times," Jorge said.

"What questions could we raise after examining the information on the birthday graph? What might you wonder about?" Maryann asked.

"I wonder how it would change if the absent people put their birthdays on the graph," Justine said.

"If Mrs. Martin's class made a birthday graph, would it look the same as ours?" Freddie asked.

There were no more volunteers, but Maryann waited a moment and posed the question again. "What else might we ask or investigate?"

"If we did a graph of the whole school's birthdays, I wonder what the most popular month would be," Oliver said.

"Does the graph tell us who the oldest person in the class is?" Kyle asked.

"No!" others responded.

Maryann then showed the children *On the Day You Were Born* and explained that she was going to read it aloud. "I'm going to ask you to solve a mathematical problem when I've finished reading the book," she told the class.

The references to the natural world prompted some students to ask questions. For example, when Maryann read, "On the day you were born gravity's strong pull held you to the Earth with a promise that you would never float away . . . ," Alan raised his hand.

"What's gravity?" he asked.

"Can someone explain what gravity is?" Maryann inquired.

"It's like a magnet," Jodie explained. "The Earth is like a magnet that pulls us to it."

After Maryann read, "On the day you were born the Moon pulled on the ocean below, and, wave by wave, a rising tide washed the beaches clean for your footprints . . . ," Maya had a question.

"I don't get it. How does the moon pull?" she asked.

Jolene raised her hand to answer. "That's how we get high tides and low tides," she said.

"There are explanations about your questions at the end of the book," Maryann said. "We can read them after I've finished the story."

After finishing the book, Maryann showed the children the section in the back titled "More About the World Around You." She read two parts of the section—"Pulling Gravity" and "Rising Tide"—and told the children they could read other parts on their own if they were interested.

Maryann then raised a question. "How long does it take Earth to make one complete turn?" she asked. Many hands went up.

"It takes twenty-four hours for the Earth to turn around. That's a day," Oliver said. Others nodded their agreement.

"How many days do you think have passed since you were born?" Maryann asked the class. The students were quiet, and Maryann asked another question.

"What would you need to know to figure out how many days old you are?"

"I know! I know!" Chelsea exclaimed. "We need to know how many years old we are, then how many days in a year."

"Well, you each know how many years old you are," Maryann said. "Chelsea said you would also need to know how many days there are in a year. How many days are there?"

The responses that Maryann heard startled her. Students suggested 150, 362, 336, 225, 364, and 365. After listening to many guesses, she wrote $365\frac{1}{4}$ on the board.

"How can you have a quarter of a day?" Joseph asked.

"That's why we have leap years," Stacy explained. "When there have been enough quarters, then they add another day."

"The number of quarters they have to have for an extra day is four," Alan said.

"Every four years we add an extra day," Maya clarified.

Maryann then listed the months and, with the help of the students, recorded the number of days in each. Again, she was surprised that some children had no idea.

"Can someone describe how you remember the number of days in each month?" Maryann asked.

"I know the 'Thirty Days Has September' poem," Heather said. "My grandma taught me."

"Say it for us," Maryann urged. Heather did so, and a few children chanted quietly along with her.

"Would someone be willing to write down that poem for others who haven't learned it?" Maryann asked. Alan volunteered.

"I know another way," Oliver said. He made a fist and explained. "You count knuckles and spaces. You say January and point to a knuckle, then February to a space, then March on a knuckle." Oliver demonstrated for the class. July landed on the last knuckle, and he explained how you start over again. "August goes on the same knuckle as January. The knuckles all have thirty-one days, and the others have thirty, but you just have to remember about February."

Maryann then gave directions. "Use this information to figure out how many days old you are," she said. "You may work by yourself or with a partner." The students began to work.

Observing the Students

Maryann circulated as the students began to work. "You get a calculator and I'll get the paper," Alex said to Elvis as the two boys excitedly got started.

"Let's figure out your age and then my age," Kyle suggested to Toby.

"Do you think Mrs. Wickett could be a million days old?" Jamie whispered to Chelsea.

Heather overheard and chimed in, "I doubt it!"

Rick and Alan were exchanging ideas. "You have to multiply by three hundred sixty-five," suggested Rick, reaching for a calculator.

"But that's not exactly all," Alan said. "My birthday is June Eighth, so I think I have to add more days." This was September 21.

"Oh, man, me, too!" Rick moaned. "How are we going to figure that out?"

"Hm, well, let's look at the months and days on the board. We could add thirty-one for July, thirty-one for August . . . but I'm not sure what we do with September," Alan replied.

A moment later Alan exclaimed, "Wait, I know! We add twenty-one for the twenty-one days in September and twenty-two for June."

"Add it all up?" Rick questioned. "How come only twenty-two in June? It says there are thirty days."

"Well, I subtracted eight from thirty because my birthday is June Eighth," Alan said.

Rick didn't seem completely sure about Alan's reasoning, but he watched Alan do his calculation. Then Alan offered to help Rick figure out his, and Rick seemed to appreciate the help.

A Class Discussion

When all the students were finished, Maryann gathered them on the rug to share their results. Alex and Elvis were excited and wanted to share first.

"I am three thousand five hundred sixty-nine days old," Alex began. "Elvis is three thousand three hundred and twenty-eight. I'm older."

"Yeah, by two hundred forty-one days," Elvis said.

"I used the calculator and did math addition," Alex added.

Jodie reported next and gave a detailed explanation. "I added three sixty-five nine times because there are three hundred sixty-five days in a year and I'm nine years old, and that came to three thousand two hundred eighty-five," she reported. "Then I added twenty-one days in April because my birthday is April twenty-first. Then I added all the days in May, June, July, and August. I added twenty-one days for September, because today is September twenty-first. That came to a hundred sixty-five extra days. Then I added three thousand two hundred eighty-five plus one sixty-five, and I'm three thousand four hundred and fifty days old." (See Figure 16–1.)

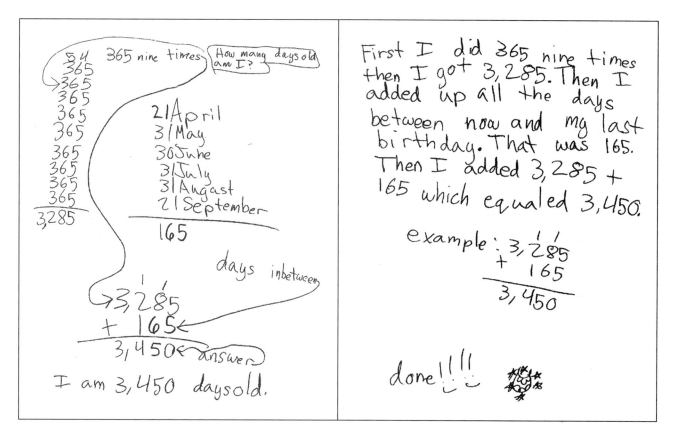

Figure 16–1: Jodie showed with words and numbers how she reached her answer.

Jodie's confidence made her reasoning persuasive, and it wasn't until later that Maryann realized that Jodie shouldn't have added twenty-one days for April, but instead the nine days that were left in the month from April 21 until April 30. "Sometimes it's hard to play close attention to all the details when I'm concentrating on keeping the class organized," Maryann said. "I talked with Jodie later, and she realized her error."

Manuel also gave a detailed explanation. "I'm nine years old," he said, "so I did three hundred sixty-five times nine and got three thousand two hundred eighty-five, and that told me how many days old I was on my birthday. But that was on August twelfth, so I counted and there were nineteen more days in August. And then I added on twenty more days in September to get thirty-nine. But Oliver showed me that I had the date wrong and it's September twenty-first, so I added on one more and changed the thirty-nine to forty. So I'm three thousand three hundred twenty-five days old." (See Figure 16–2.)

"That was good!" Toby said, impressed with Manuel's presentation.

Stacy volunteered next. "I started like Manuel did," she said. "I multiplied nine times three hundred sixty-five and that's three thousand two hundred eighty-five. And then I added on three hundred eighteen more because it's been three hundred eighteen days since my birthday." (See Figure 16–3.)

"How did you figure that out?" Maryann asked.

"I counted forty-seven more days until my next birthday, and I figured out that three hundred eighteen plus forty-seven makes three hundred sixty-five, which is the whole year. So I added three hundred eighteen to the three thousand two hundred eighty-five and got three thousand six hundred three."

"Mine was a lot easier to figure," Kyle said. "My birthday is on September twelfth. That was only nine days ago. So I did three hundred sixty-five times nine and added nine. I'm three thousand two hundred ninety-four days old."

Figure 16–2: Manual explained what each number meant in his equation.

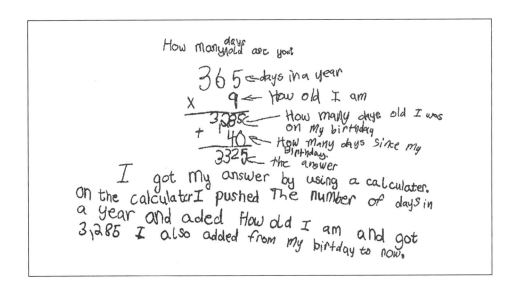

Figure 16–3: Stacy used the number of days until her next birthday to figure out how many days old she was.

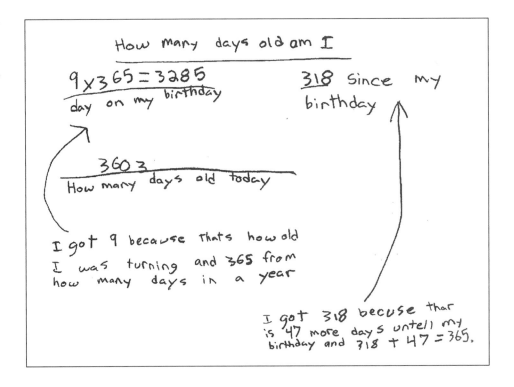

Maryann noticed that none of the students incorporated into their calculations what they had briefly discussed about leap years. "The idea of leap years was new to many of the students, and they seemed to have a good deal to think about for the problem without this information. I decided not to push them to include it," she commented.

A Follow-up Activity

The following day, Maryann explained to the children that she was interested in what they thought about this activity. "Write a letter to me telling three things," she said as she listed three prompts on the board:

1. *What did you like about the birthday investigation?*

2. *What did you learn?*

3. *Write about something from this activity that you wonder about.*

Kyle wrote: *I learned how to find how many days old I was. It was totally fun. And we learned some math. It was like a present. But it was difficult. I still think it is fun.*

Alan wrote: *I learned about how many days are in a year. I wonder how you have all your information and you can put it all together to get your answer. I wonder how it works.*

Stacy wrote: *I wonder if we added everones number in are class up how much it would be I guss 100,000.*

Joseph wrote: *I like it because it was complcated. I Wonder: If ther is enyone else that has the Same Birthday as me.*

Jodie wrote: *I liked using calculators; it improved my math skills and I learned other peoples birthdays . . . I learned how many days I've been alive. I wonder . . . I wonder how many hours I've been alive. (Don't make us figure it out!! Please!!)*

Reflecting on the experience, Maryann reported, "This lesson was successful on two accounts. It was an opportunity for children to see the usefulness of multiplication. Also, I've been working hard to build the class into a community of learners who cooperate and support one another, and the activity helped encourage this."

The $1.00 Word
Riddle Book

Marilyn Burns's *The $1.00 Word Riddle Book* (1990) presents a system for figuring the value of a word by adding up the values of its letters—the letter A is worth one cent, the letter B is worth two cents, C is worth three cents, and so on up to Z (twenty-six cents). The answers to the riddles in the book are all words that are worth one dollar. Some of the riddles are presented with written clues, for example: "What's the opposite of minimize?" (Answer: maximize.) Other riddles are presented with drawings that have captions with missing one-dollar words. As an extension, students are challenged to find the thirty-eight one-dollar words in a story about Robin Hood (a one-dollar name!). The book serves as a springboard for providing students useful practice with addition as they first figure the values of their names and then search for one-dollar words.

MATERIALS

chart paper, 1 sheet
removable white correction tape

Day 1

Marilyn began the lesson by introducing the fifth graders to *The $1.00 Word Riddle Book*. She showed them the cover of the book, which shows a girl blowing a whistle to manage performing circus elephants.

"I like riddles," Michael said. Others agreed.

Marilyn opened the book and read the first page, which explains that this isn't an ordinary riddle book and that the answers to all of the riddles are one-dollar words. None of the students knew what made a word a one-dollar word.

Marilyn then read the next page of the book, which explains that for these riddles, the letter *a* is worth one cent, the letter *b* is worth two cents, *c* is worth three cents, and so on, with *z* being worth twenty-six cents. Marilyn wrote these values on the board, modeling the two different standard notations for representing cents as well as the notation of using ellipses to indicate that information is missing:

$$a = 1¢ \text{ or } \$.01$$
$$b = 2¢ \text{ or } \$.02$$
$$c = 3¢ \text{ or } \$.03$$
$$\cdots$$
$$\cdots$$
$$\cdots$$
$$z = 26¢ \text{ or } \$.26$$

"How much do you think the letter *l* is worth?" Marilyn asked to check the students' understanding. She observed most of the students using their fingers to figure out that *l* is a twelve-cent letter. Marilyn recorded on the board:

$$l = 12¢ \text{ or } \$.12$$

"And the letter *y*?" Marilyn asked.

"Twenty-five cents," the students answered in unison.

"And what about the letter *o*?" she asked. "Check with your partner before raising your hand." Marilyn specifically chose these three letters because the students would use their values in a moment to verify the value of a word. When most of the students had raised their hands, she asked them to say the value of *o* together in a whisper voice.

"Fifteen cents," they whispered. Marilyn recorded the values for *y* and *o* on the board:

$$y = 25¢ \text{ or } \$.25$$
$$o = 15¢ \text{ or } \$.15$$

Marilyn then continued reading that the word *riddle* is worth $.52 and the word *zoology* is worth $1.15. She wrote on the board:

$$riddle = 52¢ \text{ or } \$.52$$
$$zoology = 115¢ \text{ or } \$1.15$$

"You typically don't see values over one dollar written with the cents sign," Marilyn said, pointing to the word *zoology*. "That's because when you have more than one hundred cents, you have at least one dollar, and the second notation uses a decimal point to separate the dollars from the cents." The students seemed fine with this explanation.

Marilyn then said, "Work with your partner and check that the value of *zoology* is correct. The values of all of the letters except for the letter *g* are on the board." Marilyn circulated as the students worked. After a few minutes, the students agreed that the value was correct.

Then Marilyn continued reading. The top of the next page begins, "Maybe your name is worth $1.00. That's how Henrietta got to be on the cover of the book." Marilyn again showed them the cover illustration of Henrietta.

Marilyn then gave directions. "Now, working by yourself," she said, "figure out the value of your first name. Then check with your partner, each of you figuring out the value of your partner's name. If you still have time before everyone is finished, then check to be sure that *Henrietta* is really worth one dollar." Marilyn wrote *Henrietta* on the board.

"Can we use a calculator?" Arthur wanted to know.

Marilyn responded, "No, don't use a calculator for this. I think that the addition isn't too hard to do for these problems, and adding on your own will give you practice." The students accepted this decision. While calculators are available to all of the students in their table supplies, Marilyn is clear when she does and doesn't want students to use them. In this instance, the addition practice provided by this activity is useful for the students.

Marilyn circulated as the students worked. They were curious about the values of their names and Marilyn observed them tackling the task in different ways. Some used their fingers to count and figure out the value of each letter in their names, writing the values down and then adding them. Some kept running totals as they worked. Some listed all of the letters of the alphabet and wrote the value of each next to it. Elissa was one of these students, but she stopped her list after the letter *s*. "I don't need the rest," she explained.

Marilyn interrupted the class when she saw that all of the students had figured out the values of their names. (Some had also had time to verify that *Henrietta* was a one-dollar name.) "Who thinks that your name is worth the least?" Marilyn asked.

"I know that *Cara* is worth less than mine," Mara said. "We're only one letter different, and *c* costs much less than *m*."

"How much is your name, Cara?" Marilyn asked.

"Twenty-three cents," Cara responded.

"Does anyone have a name that is worth less than twenty-three cents?" Marilyn asked. No one raised a hand.

"Who do you think has the most expensive name in the class?" Marilyn asked. The students looked around the room, considering each other's names. "Does anyone have a name that is more than one dollar?" Marilyn added. Charlotte raised her hand.

"My name is a dollar and two cents," Charlotte said. No one had a name that cost more. "Is anyone's name worth exactly one dollar?" Marilyn asked.

Travon said, "I checked *Henrietta* and it's one dollar." Several others agreed.

"My name is fifty cents," Marco said, "and that's half a dollar."

"Mine, too," Hiro added.

"But we don't have any one-dollar names in our class?" Marilyn asked.

"I think that one-dollar names are hard to find," Kaisha said.

"Why do you think that?" Marilyn asked.

Kaisha responded, "Well, it's like when you go to the store. Things don't add up exactly to one dollar, not usually."

Marilyn then returned to the book and read to the class the sentence on the book's cover, "Whenever Henrietta whistled, trembling costumed elephants merrily performed." She wrote the sentence on the board and then told the students, "In this sentence, each word is worth exactly one dollar."

"No way!" Hassan exclaimed.

"Let's check," Marilyn said.

Travon said, "But I already checked *Henrietta,* so let's check the others." Marilyn agreed and assigned each table group one of the words and, because there were only six groups and seven words, she left the last word for everyone to check. After a few minutes, they agreed that all of the words were indeed worth one dollar each.

Marilyn then read from the bottom of page 5 in the book, telling the class that several hundred one-dollar words have been found by addition-loving kids across the United States. She gave them the assignment of searching for one-dollar words. "To help you get started, I'll give you some riddles. The answer to each is a one-dollar word." Marilyn read the riddles on the back cover of the book: "Which day of the week is worth one dollar? What Halloween word is worth one dollar? Which United States coin is worth one dollar, though it's really worth less? Which one of Snow White's dwarfs has a one-dollar name?" Marilyn abbreviated these on the board and added a few others:

a day of the week
a Halloween word
a U.S. coin
one of Snow White's dwarfs
a Thanksgiving word
a number that's less than 100 and more than 20
what you can wear on your hands to keep them warm

"You can find one-dollar words by using these riddles as clues, or you can search on your own for other words," Marilyn said.

"Can we test the names of the other people in our family?" Alexandra wanted to know.

"That would be fine," Marilyn responded.

"Can we use names of cities or rivers?" Raul asked.

"Yes," Marilyn said.

There were no other questions and the students worked on the assignment for the rest of the period. Marilyn suggested that they continue their search at home that evening. "Explain what one-dollar words are to your parents and see if they can help," Marilyn said. This assignment is useful for helping parents see that addition practice can come in a less traditional way.

Day 2

Marilyn planned to share more of the book, so before class, she used nonstick correction tape to cover the answers to the riddles, which all appear upside down at the bottom of the pages. Also, she posted a sheet of chart paper to begin a class list of the one-dollar words the students had found.

To begin the lesson, Marilyn listed the answers to the riddles she had posted the day before—*Wednesday, pumpkin, quarter, Grumpy, turkey, thirty,* and *mittens.* Then Gissele reported that she found out that her sister, Kristin, had a one-dollar name.

"So does my mother," James said. "Her name is Suzanne." Marilyn added *Kristin* and *Suzanne* to the chart.

Andy reported, "I tried words that had letters from the end of the alphabet. I only found one—*excellent.*" Others said that they also tried that strategy, and reported finding *swimmer* and *writing.* Marilyn added these to the list.

Ebony said that she tried long words. "*Chimpanzee* works," she said.

"Hey, I found that one, too," Arthur said.

Natanya said, "I tried cities, like Raul said, and I found *Portland.*" Marilyn wrote these on the list.

"My mom had an idea," Keely said. "She figured out that since S costs nineteen cents, she could use it if she found an eighty-one-cent word." Keely then added, "My mom is a real word person. She does crossword puzzles all the time."

"Why does her idea work?" Marilyn asked.

"Because eighty-one plus nineteen is a hundred, and that makes a dollar," Keely explained.

"Is that right?" Marilyn asked the class, writing $81 + 19 = 100$ on the board. She gave the students a few moments to think and then asked, "Who can explain?"

George said, "Eighty-one plus ten is ninety-one, and nine more makes one hundred."

Mara explained, "You can take one off the eighty-one so it's eighty, and then put it on the nineteen to make twenty. Then it's easy. Eighty plus twenty is a hundred."

De'anna explained using the standard algorithm. She said, "You write them one on top of the other. Then you do nine plus one is ten, and you put down the zero and carry the one. Then eight and one is nine and one more is ten, so it works." Marilyn recorded the problem vertically on the board as De'anna explained:

$$
\begin{array}{r}
1 \\
81 \\
+19 \\
\hline
100
\end{array}
$$

Marilyn then turned back to Keely. "Did you and your mom find any words using that strategy?"

Keely answered, "We found two. Well, really she found them. First she thought of *vacuum* because it had the V and the two Us, and it was worth eighty-one cents, so *vacuums* works." Marilyn wrote that on the list. "And then she thought of *wizard*, and the S makes it work." Marilyn added *wizards* to the list.

While some had found several words, others weren't successful. "We'll keep the list up," Marilyn said, "and when you find words, just add them. But before you put a word on the list, be sure that someone else has checked and agrees that it's really worth one dollar."

Marilyn then introduced the students to the visual riddles in the book. She showed them the illustration on page 6 with the caption below: "A _____ putting _____ into _____." The illustration shows a turkey putting shovels into mailboxes, and the students quickly verified that *turkey*, *shovels*, and *mailboxes* were one-dollar words. *Turkey* was already on the list, and Marilyn added *shovels* and *mailboxes*. (See Figure 17–1.)

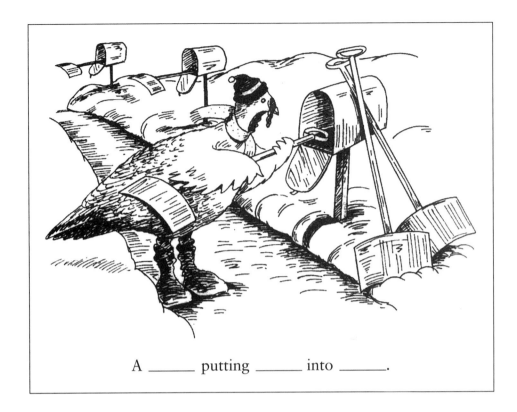

A _____ putting _____ into _____.

"I didn't think there were so many," Cara said.

"There are hundreds of them," Marilyn answered. The students seemed impressed.

Marilyn then showed them the illustration on the facing page with a caption of one line for just one word. The illustration shows two growling dogs behind a locked chain-link fence. The students thought and thought, but the riddle stumped them. They became frustrated and Marilyn finally told the answer—*watchdogs.*

"We should have gotten that!" Scott exclaimed.

"Well, there are lots of other riddles to try, both ones like these with drawings and some with words, like regular riddles," Marilyn said. "The answers to the riddles appear upside down at the bottom of each page, and I've put correction tape over them. I'll leave the book out for you to look at during choice time. Please don't remove the correction tape yet. I'll take it off after everyone who wants to has had a chance to look at the book."

Marilyn then explained the challenge at the end of the book. "A story titled 'Robin Hood and the Hot-Blooded Hawkers' is at the end of the book," she said. "*Robin Hood* is a one-dollar name if you add up the values of the letters in both *Robin* and *Hood.* And *Hot-Blooded* and *Hawkers* are also each worth one dollar, and that's the name of Robin Hood's rock band." Marilyn read the first sentence of the story, "An astounding piece of historical information was recently revealed— rock music was around as far back as in the days of Robin Hood."

"Hey, is that really true?" Hassan asked.

"No," Marilyn said, "this is just a story."

"Does he still steal from the rich?" Gabriel wanted to know.

"Let me read the story to you," Marilyn said. She read the story, revealing Robin Hood's idea to form a rock group that would charge the rich for concerts and give the money to the poor. But the music wasn't very popular, since rock music had never been played before, and the band wasn't very good. But the plan worked anyway. The band played in front of the houses of rich people and stopped playing only when the people paid them enough. The students were amused by the story. Marilyn then told them, "There are thirty-eight one-dollar words in the story. If you're interested, see if you can find some of them."

The students continued searching for one-dollar words over the next few weeks. Some were more interested and diligent than others, but they all were pleased to see the class list grow.

One Riddle, One Answer

One Riddle, One Answer, written by Lauren Thompson (2001), is the tale of a Persian princess named Aziza who loves numbers and riddles. When it is time for her to marry, she goes to her father, the sultan, and makes a proposition: she will pose a riddle, and whoever can answer it will be the one she will be happiest to marry. The sultan agrees. One by one, suitors try and fail to solve Aziza's riddle. Finally, a farmer name Ahmed figures the answer and wins Aziza's hand in marriage. After hearing the story, students first try to solve Aziza's riddle themselves, then they write their own number riddles for their peers to solve.

MATERIALS

Day 1

Introducing Number Riddles

"Who can explain what a riddle is?" Danielle Gilligan asked her fifth graders.

"It's like a mystery you have to figure out," Jill said.

"It has clues that help you solve it," Ramon added.

"They're fun to solve, 'cause you don't know the answer right away!" exclaimed Amanda.

"I have a book that I'd like to read to you today," Danielle said. "It's a book about a riddle. I'm going to read the story and stop at a certain point so that you can try to figure out the answer to the riddle."

The students were excited. The room grew quiet as Danielle showed the cover of the book with an illustration of the main character, Aziza, wearing what looks to be a traditional Persian outfit.

"This story is from ancient Persia," Danielle began. "The country of Iran is now where Persia used to be. In those days, a sultan ruled the land. This is his daughter." Danielle pointed to the picture on the book's cover.

Danielle started reading *One Riddle, One Answer* to her class. As she read, her students learned about Aziza, the sultan's daughter, who loved numbers and riddles. They listened attentively, hearing how the sultan's advisors all wanted their sons to get a chance to become Aziza's husband, once it was time for her to marry. Danielle stopped reading at the part in the story where Aziza proposes that she write a number riddle. In the story, the princess tells her father that she would prefer to marry the person clever enough to answer her riddle. The sultan agrees.

"I'm going to show you the riddle that Aziza wrote," Danielle told her class. "I've written it on a piece of chart paper. We'll read the riddle together, then I want you to think about the clues silently first. You can use scratch paper to jot down your thoughts. Then, whisper your ideas about the answer to a partner."

Danielle posted the chart paper on which she'd written Aziza's riddle:

> *Placed above, it makes greater things small.*
> *Placed beside, it makes small things greater.*
> *In matters that count, it always comes first.*
> *Where others increase, it keeps all things the same.*
> *What is it?*

After directing the class to read the riddle together in a choral voice, Danielle gave students a minute or so to think and take notes. Then she circulated the room, listening to students' guesses. Some thought the answer was one. A few thought that zero would work. Many students were stumped, having no idea what number would work.

Danielle took students' predictions, then continued reading until she came to the part in the story where the scholar guesses that the sun is the answer to Aziza's riddle. She stopped at this point and addressed the class.

"The scholar's guess is true for the first line in the riddle ('Placed above, it makes greater things small')," she said, pointing to the copy of the riddle on the chart. "But does that answer work for each of the other clues?"

"No," Anna responded. "It doesn't make sense for any of the others. Like, the sun doesn't come first when you count."

"That's right," Danielle confirmed. "An answer to a riddle must fit all the clues, not just some of them."

Danielle continued to read. Each time a suitor in the story guessed an answer to Aziza's riddle, Danielle stopped and checked with the students to see if the answer fit all the clues. When Ahmed, the farmer in the story, guessed that the answer to the riddle was the number one, Danielle again checked with the students to see if it worked with all the clues, and it did.

"But zero works too!" Amanda cried.

"Yeah!" Joe and Elise chimed in.

Danielle was taken aback. She later confided that she hadn't thought about another possible answer. "Explain what you mean," she challenged the three students.

"Well, placed above a number, it works," Amanda explained. "Like, if you put zero above five when you multiply, it makes five smaller. And it works for any number you multiply it by."

"You mean like this?" Danielle asked, recording Amanda's idea on the board:

$$
\begin{array}{r} 0 \\ \times 5 \\ \hline 0 \end{array}
\qquad\qquad
\begin{array}{r} 0 \\ \times 2 \\ \hline 0 \end{array}
$$

Amanda nodded her head in agreement. Then she continued with her argument. "Placed beside other numbers, it makes them greater, just like in Aziza's riddle."

"Come up and show us," Danielle urged. Amanda walked up to the board and wrote:

$$10 \qquad 20 \qquad 50$$

"When you put zero beside these numbers, it makes them bigger," she said. "Zero next to one makes it ten; zero next to two makes it twenty." Joe and Elise nodded their heads, smiling.

"And when you count, zero comes before one on the number line!" she exclaimed.

"Yeah, and on the thermometer, zero comes before the number one," Joe added.

Elise piped in, "And for the last clue, zero keeps all things the same when you add zero to it, like zero plus one is one or zero plus ten is ten. Zero keeps the number the same."

"Wow!" Danielle exclaimed. "I'm impressed with your reasoning. I hadn't thought about zero as an answer."

"I disagree," Kyle challenged. "When you count, you don't start with zero, you start with one."

"But if you're counting down the days till Christmas, on Christmas there's zero days left!" Amanda countered.

Wisely, Danielle didn't interfere. Getting students to argue passionately about their ideas in math class is a goal that is often difficult to achieve. Giving students interesting problems to solve, like Aziza's riddle, can motivate them to develop and exchange ideas.

When the short debate was over, Danielle acknowledged that there could be more than one correct answer to the riddle. Then she finished reading the story, including a section at the back of the book where the author explains how the number one works for each clue.

Brainstorming Clues for a Riddle

"Aziza's riddle helped us think about number riddles," Danielle said, starting the next part of the lesson. "Now let's try to write a number riddle together. First you have to think of a number to write about. Then you have to write some clues. I want you to practice by brainstorming some possible clues for the number ten."

Danielle gave the students about five minutes to work in groups. When conversations started to die down, she called the class together. Following are some of the clues the students came up with:

Count your fingers on both of your hands.
If you cut me in half and multiply me by 7, you get 35.
If you multiply a number by the mystery number, you'll always end in zero.
The age of a fourth grader.
Twenty divided by two.

After each student reported a clue, Danielle recorded it on the board. Then she gave the students feedback on their clues.

"When you write a riddle, the first thing you do is brainstorm a list of possible clues, just like we did for the number ten," she said. "Remember, try to make your clues tricky. It's OK if answering one of the clues gives away the secret number. But try to be tricky with your clues, like Aziza was with her riddle."

Writing Riddles for Homework

When the class was finished brainstorming clues for the number ten, Danielle assigned some homework.

"Now you have some experience with number riddles," she told the class. "You've listened to one that Aziza wrote. And together, we practiced brainstorming clues for the number ten. Since we're beginning a unit on fractions next week, I want you to practice writing a riddle for the number one-half." Danielle then distributed a half-sheet for each student on which were written the directions for writing the riddle. She read from the homework sheet:

"*One Riddle, One Answer.* Aziza's riddle was made up of clues for the number one. For homework, it's your turn to be a clever number riddle maker. Write one riddle sentence for the number one-half. On the back of this paper, use pictures, words, and numbers to explain how the sentence works for one-half."

Day 2

Sharing Homework

When the students returned to school the next day, Danielle directed them to share their clues, or sentences, about one-half with their neighbors. Then she called for the students' attention and asked for volunteers to share. Listening to students' ideas about one-half gave Danielle some important information about their existing understanding of fractions. In her class, there was a range of knowledge about one-half. Some students revealed some very sophisticated thinking, while others exposed misconceptions. Keaton shared first.

"If you have a glass of water, the water hits the middle," he read, showing a picture he drew of a glass half filled with water.

"Two people and one brownie," Brittany read. "What do they do to make the brownie equal? Answer? They cut it in half and they get an equal amount."

"If you have one inch, and you subtract the half, it is going to be . . . ?" Jean asked.

Nicholas's clue revealed his knowledge of operations with fractions, drawing "oohs" and "ahhs" from his peers.

"This number is between zero and one and if you multiply this number by two you get one." On the back of his paper, he explained why $\frac{1}{2} \times 2 = 1$: *If you multiply it by 2 you get 1 because $\frac{1}{2} + \frac{1}{2} = 1$.* (See Figure 18–1.)

Amanda had written a five-clue riddle for one-half. She read: "It's less than a whole. Greater than one-eighth. It's an even amount. Between one and one-forth. It's a number that can make one share."

Here are some other clues that students wrote and shared:

I am half of 7, subtract 3.
The fraction you're guessing is greater than $\frac{1}{4}$ and less than 1.
If you double $\frac{1}{4}$ you get this number.
It is the biggest fraction out of the following: $\frac{1}{16}, \frac{1}{24}, \frac{1}{8}, \frac{1}{4}, \frac{1}{2}$. (See Figure 18–2.)
If there is a cake with 18 pieces, and nine people ate 1 piece each. So there are 9 pieces left. $\frac{9}{18}$ is equal to your answer. (See Figure 18–3.)

McKenna's clue drew some disagreement from students. "Divide any number in half and you get me," he read.

Hands flew in the air. Danielle knew that McKenna could handle his classmates' scrutiny. She had worked hard to create a respectful classroom environment.

"I don't agree," Tania said. "If you divide ten in half, the answer's five, not one-half."

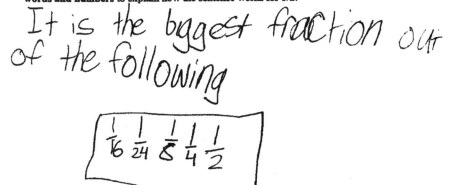

Figure 18–1: Nicholas's clue for one-half involved multiplication.

One Riddle, One Answer

Aziza's riddle was made up of clues for the number 1. For homework, it's your turn to be a clever number riddle maker.

Write **one riddle sentence** for the number **1/2**. On the back of this paper **use pictures, words and numbers** to explain how the sentence works for 1/2.

This number is between 0 and 1 and if you multiply this number by 2 you get 1

Figure 18–2: Tara posed a multiple-choice question for her clue for one-half.

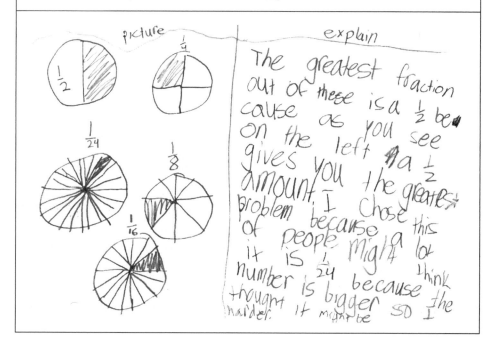

One Riddle, One Answer

Aziza's riddle was made up of clues for the number 1. For homework, it's your turn to be a clever number riddle maker.

Write **one riddle sentence** for the number **1/2**. On the back of this paper **use pictures, words and numbers** to explain how the sentence works for 1/2.

It is the biggest fraction out of the following

$$\frac{1}{16} \quad \frac{1}{24} \quad \frac{1}{8} \quad \frac{1}{4} \quad \frac{1}{2}$$

picture

$\frac{1}{2}$ $\frac{1}{4}$

$\frac{1}{24}$ $\frac{1}{8}$

$\frac{1}{16}$

explain

The greatest fraction out of these is a $\frac{1}{2}$ cause as you see on the left a $\frac{1}{2}$ gives you the greatest amount. I chose this problem because a lot of people might think it is $\frac{1}{24}$ number is bigger so I thought harder it might be

One Riddle, One Answer

Aziza's riddle was made up of clues for the number 1. For homework, it's your turn to be a clever number riddle maker.

Write **one riddle sentence** for the number **1/2**. On the back of this paper **use pictures, words and numbers** to explain how the sentence works for 1/2.

If there is a cake with 18 pieces, and nine pepeole ate 1 peice each, So there are 9 peices left. $\frac{9}{18}$ is equil to your anser.

McKenna defended his idea. "When you divide something in half, you divide it by the number two," he explained. "Like eight divided by two is four, which is half of eight, so four is like the half. Eighteen divided by two is nine; seven divided by two is three and a half; all the answers are halves of the number you start with."

Some students began to understand McKenna's logic, but were still confused by his clue.

"Writing clues is tricky," Danielle acknowledged. "So you have to be really clear when you write them, so the reader can understand."

Amanda went next. Her clue revealed a common misconception about division with fractions. "When you divide by me, you get twice as little as you did before," she read.

Danielle put her index finger to her lips and thought for a second. Then she asked Amanda for an example. Amanda read from the back of her homework paper.

"Six divided by one-half equals three," she read. "Three is half as little as six."

Danielle recorded Amanda's example on the board:

$$6 \div \tfrac{1}{2} = 3$$

"This is very tricky," Danielle told the class. "Amanda's problem is something that's really difficult to understand, even for adults!"

The students listened attentively as Danielle gave a counterexample to challenge Amanda's misconception. Danielle later told me that she didn't want to spend too much time explaining about division of fractions, because explaining doesn't necessarily lead to understanding. Operating on fractions, especially with division, is a complex idea that requires time and lots of experience; that would come later.

"Suppose," Danielle began, "that we had a different but similar problem, one that we're familiar with. Let's say the problem was six divided by two." Danielle recorded the equation on the board:

$$6 \div 2 =$$

"What's six divided by two?" she asked the class.

"Three!" students responded.

"So six divided by one-half can't be three as well," Danielle said. "The problem six divided by two is asking how many twos there are in six. How many twos are there in six?"

"There are three groups of two that can go into six," Amanda said, now realizing she'd made a mistake somewhere. "So with my problem, six divided by one-half, the problem is asking how many halves go into six?"

"That's correct," Danielle responded. "If you have six inches of licorice, for example, and you want to divide it into half-inch pieces, how many half-inch pieces would you have?"

Danielle gave students just a few seconds to think. She realized that some students were not following and were stumped, and she wanted to return to the riddle lesson as soon as possible.

"Twelve!" Chloe shouted. "You just add halves until you get to twelve."

"So six divided by one-half is twelve?" Amanda asked, a little surprised.

"Yes," Danielle confirmed. "When you divide a whole number by a fraction, the answer gets bigger, not smaller, as with whole numbers. So Amanda, you had a great idea that made us think a lot."

Realizing she'd reached the edge of most students' understanding, Danielle moved on.

"Let's get to the next part of our lesson with riddles," she said. "Now that you've had some experience with writing clues for the numbers ten and one-half, you're going to each choose a number, brainstorm clues for that number, and then write a riddle."

"How many clues does the riddle have to have?" Lisette asked.

"Well, Aziza's had four clues, so try to write a riddle with at least four," Danielle responded.

Writing and Sharing Riddles

Danielle directed students to work quietly at first as they each chose a number and brainstormed clues. Soon, however, the class began to hum with conversations as students shared their ideas with one another. As Danielle circulated, she listened to students' riddles, encouraged them to think of subtle clues rather than obvious ones, and made sure everyone stayed on task. After about thirty minutes, she pulled the class back together.

"Let's bring it back," Danielle directed, ringing a little bell to get the students' attention.

"Let's have some volunteers read their riddles. After they read their clues, we'll try to guess the answer."

Following are some of the riddles that students shared (See Figures 18–4 through 18–7.):

You'll never guess me, for I am between
4 and 3
you think I'm a whole but it turns out
I'm not
I'm an improper number and uneven as can be
and remember I'm between 4 and 3.
I am 3 plus an eighth of one whole
And between 4 and 3.

The line, "I'm an improper number and uneven as can be" was mathematically inaccurate. The answer the student was seeking, $\frac{25}{8}$, can be described as an "improper fraction," not an "improper number." And the word "uneven" isn't a word we use to describe numbers; we use "odd" for the opposite of "even," but neither even nor odd are used to describe fractions or mixed numbers, but only whole numbers. After having this conversation with the student, I let the poem stand with an eye toward poetic license.

It comes with the odd family, but spells out even.
It is less than the equation 15 − (35 ÷ 7).
But greater than the 1 × 2 × 3.
This number has 5 letters but rymes with a 6 letter word, but

Figure 18–4: Amanda wrote a riddle for $3\frac{1}{8}$.

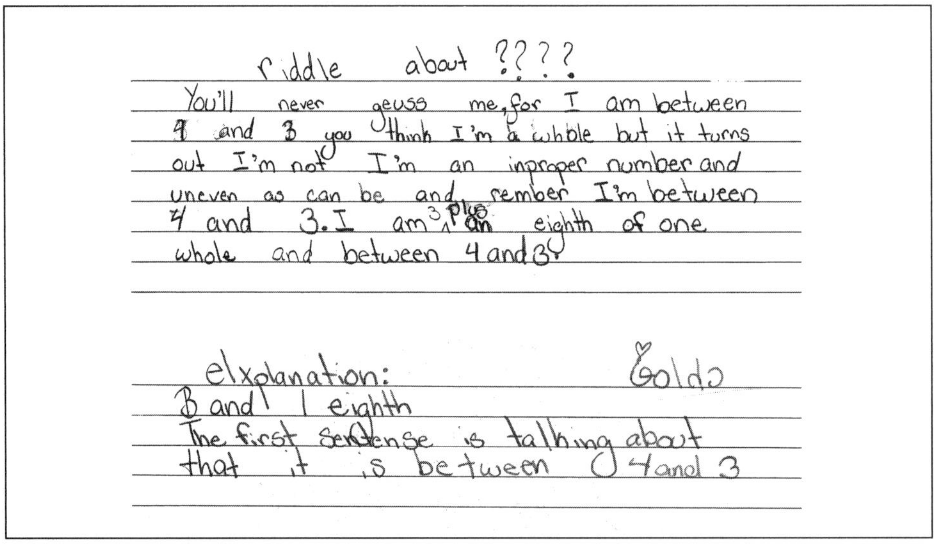
riddle about ????
You'll never geuss me, for I am between
4 and 3 you think I'm a whole but it turns
out I'm not I'm an inproper number and
uneven as can be and rember I'm between
4 and 3. I am 3 plus an eighth of one
whole and between 4 and 3

elxplanation: Golda
3 and 1 eighth
The first sentense is talking about
that it is between 4 and 3

It comes with the odd family, but spells out even. It is less than the equation 15-635-7) But greater than the 1x2x3. This number has 5 letters, but rymes with a 6 letter word, but both words have even in them, but rymes with another word that has even. What number am .I.

Figure 18–5: Adam created a riddle for the number seven.

both words have even in them but rymes with another word
that has even [in it].
What number am I.

I'm a number multple of four or two.
I am a two diget number
I'm even
When count by two or four you say this number.
I'm in the twentys.

This number is smaller than 1 and is bigger than $\frac{1}{2}$.
It is not $\frac{3}{4}$, but it is equal to $\frac{3}{4}$.
It is $\frac{2}{8} \times 3$ and $\frac{1}{4}$ bigger than $\frac{2}{4}$.

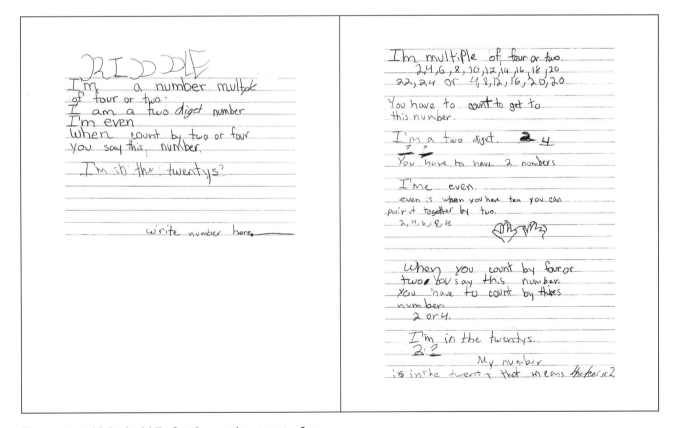

RIDDLE

I'm a number multpk of four or two.
I am a two diget number
I'm even
When count by two or four you say this number.

I'm in the twentys?

write number here.

I'm multiple of four or two.
2,4,6,8,10,12,14,16,18,20
22,24 or 4,8,12,16,20,20

You have to count to get to this number.

I'm a two diget. 2 4
You have to have 2 numbers

I'me even.
even is when you have ten you can pair it together by two.
2,4,6,8,10

When you count by four or two you say this number.
You have to count by thres number
2 or 4.

I'm in the twentys.
My number is in the twent that means the four or 2

Figure 18–6: Vivian's riddle for the number twenty-four.

Figure 18–7: Nick's riddle for six-eighths.

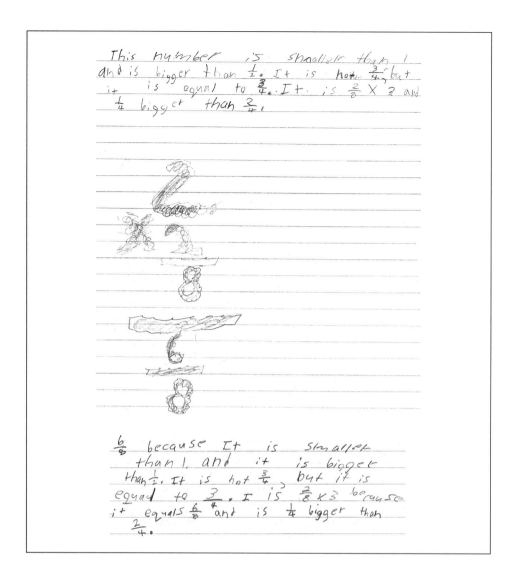

This number is smaller than 1 and is bigger than ½. It is not ¾, but it is equal to ¾. It is ²⁄₈ X 3 and ¼ bigger than ²⁄₄.

⁶⁄₈ because It is smaller than 1. and it is bigger than ½. It is not ¾, but it is equal to ¾. I is ²⁄₈ x3 because it equals ⁶⁄₈ and is ¼ bigger than ²⁄₄.

Danielle was delighted with the riddles that her students wrote. After math class was over, I asked her what she thought was most valuable about the lesson.

"There were many valuable things about this lesson," she said. "Reading the story was very motivating to my students. They love guessing games, and Aziza's riddle was challenging and got them excited about writing their own riddles. Most importantly, I realized that writing riddles helped the students develop their number sense; that is, the riddles required them to think about the characteristics of numbers and operations. It was also a good way to assess their understanding of fractions!"

A Remainder of One

In *A Remainder of One,* by Elinor J. Pinczes (2002), a troop of twenty-five bug soldiers line up to march past their queen. The bugs first line up in two groups, leaving soldier Joe alone at the end of the line. The queen "likes things tidy" and is unhappy with a single bug at the end, so Joe has to stand aside and watch the troop march without him. Over the next few days, the bug soldiers line up with three and then four in each line, again leaving out Joe. Finally, the bugs line up with five in each row, "perfect at last—and that's counting Joe." The story leads to an activity in which students use division to solve a number riddle, write their own riddles, and solve those written by their classmates.

MATERIALS

optional: color tiles, 25 per student

I read *A Remainder of One* to my class of fifth and sixth graders. They listened intently and were interested in predicting the rhymes in the book. After reading the first several pages, I deliberately began leaving sentences unfinished so that the students could guess the rhyming words. For example, I read: "All twenty-five soldiers marched past the bug crowd, nervously hoping they'd make their queen . . ."

"Proud!" the students chorused.

When I finished reading the part where the twenty-five bugs line up in four rows of six, again leaving "oddball Joe" as a remainder, I posed a question.

"How could the twenty-five bugs line up so that poor Joe isn't left as the remaining bug?" I asked. Many hands went up. I called on several students to give their ideas.

"They could line up in five rows of five," Naomi said. "That's five times five without a remainder."

"I think they should line up in one big line," Dean suggested. "That would be twenty-five times one and no remainder."

"If I were those bugs, I wouldn't listen to that old queen!" Tamar exclaimed. Everyone laughed.

When I finished reading the book, I asked the class for comments.

"Lots of words in the story rhyme," Elias said.

"It's kind of like division and multiplication," Quinn said.

"Explain what you mean," I said.

"Well, the bugs are kind of dividing themselves up into rows, and sometimes there's a remainder, like in a division problem, and sometimes there isn't, like at the end of the story," she explained. "And we used multiplication when we were guessing what would happen next, like five times five equals twenty-five."

I then said, "What I'd like to do now is have someone else read the story aloud so that I can record on the board what happens mathematically, kind of how Quinn explained." Volunteers raised their hands, and I called on Sterling since he was the person of the day, responsible for helping the teacher. As Sterling read, I recorded division sentences on the board to describe the events in the story. I wrote:

$$25 \div 2 = 12 \ R1$$
$$25 \div 3 = 8 \ R1$$
$$25 \div 4 = 6 \ R1$$
$$25 \div 5 = 5 \ R0$$

"Raise your hand if you can explain the first sentence I wrote," I then said. I waited until almost everyone had raised his or her hand. Then I called on Katherine.

"Twenty-five is the number of bugs, and they divided themselves into two rows," she explained. "That would make twelve bugs in each row with one left over as a remainder."

"Katherine's explanation makes sense to me," I said. "Talk in your groups to make sure you all understand what Katherine said. And then discuss the other sentences I wrote on the board to make sure you understand them and can tell how they are related to the story." I gave the students a few minutes to talk among themselves. I circulated and listened, satisfying myself that they understood how the division sentences related to the story. Then I called them back to attention.

"I now have a riddle for you to solve that relates to the story and the division statements," I began. "Remember that in the story, twenty-five bugs lined up in different ways. In my riddle, I'm thinking of another number of bugs, and I'll give you clues to help you guess it. My number is between one and twenty-five." I posted a sheet of chart paper on which I had written seven clues:

1. *When you divide my number by 1, the remainder is 0.*

2. *When you divide my number by 2, the remainder is 0.*

3. *When you divide my number by 3, the remainder is 1.*

4. *When you divide my number by 4, the remainder is 2.*

5. *When you divide my number by 5, the remainder is 0.*

6. *When you divide my number by 6, the remainder is 4.*

7. *When you divide my number by 7, the remainder is 3.*

After the students read the clues, I asked them to discuss the clues with the people at their tables. After about a minute, I called for their attention.

"What do you know so far?" I asked. "I'm not interested in an answer yet, but in the information you've gathered by looking at the clues."

"Well, the first clue really didn't help us, because if you divide any number by one you get a remainder of zero," Isaac said.

"Are you sure?" I asked.

"I think," Isaac replied.

"Let's try twenty-four," I said. "What's twenty-four divided by one?"

"Twenty-four!" the students chorused.

"Remainder?" I asked.

"Zero!" they replied.

"Later you can investigate Isaac's general statement to see if it's always true," I said.

"We know that your number is an even number because there's a remainder of zero when you divide it by two," Cecilia said. "When you divide an even number by two, there's no remainder. When you divide an odd number by two, you'll get a remainder," she explained.

"What else do you know?" I probed.

"Your number isn't divisible by three," Jacob said. "We know that because your clue says that when you divide your secret number by three, there's a remainder of one."

"Your number is divisible by five," Nima said. "There's no remainder when you divide it by five."

"Work in your groups to solve my remainder riddle," I told them. "When you're satisfied that you have the answer, each of you should write a remainder riddle of your own for any number between one and twenty-five. Your riddle should have seven clues, just like mine. Use my clues from the chart as a model. Copy them and just put in the correct numbers for the remainders for your secret number."

"Do we write our secret number on the back of our paper?" Shane asked.

"That's a good idea," I replied. "When you're finished, exchange papers with a friend and see if you can solve each other's riddles."

The students dove into solving my remainder riddle. Most groups wrote the numbers from 1 to 25 on their papers and eliminated numbers as they read my clues. Some also wrote division problems to check their numbers, while others figured mentally. Soon, the classroom was buzzing.

"It's ten!" several students shouted out, unable to contain themselves. As soon as they discovered the answer, students began writing riddles of their own. I circulated to give help as needed.

Sterling was having trouble writing the clues for his riddle. He had chosen the number twenty as his secret number, but he had no idea about what to do next.

"What's twenty divided by one?" I asked him. He said that he didn't know how to divide very well. Mathematics was difficult for Sterling, and he lacked confidence. He wasn't sure he could represent division symbolically, and he was hesitant to try.

"If you had twenty cookies and only one person, how many cookies would that person get?" I asked. He still didn't know. I showed Sterling how to write $20 \div 1$ and asked him to get twenty color tiles to work with.

"You can use the tiles to show twenty divided by one by putting all twenty tiles in one pile," I instructed. "How many are there in the pile?"

"Twenty," he responded.

"Any remaining?" I asked.

"No," he said.

"So that means that twenty divided by one equals twenty with a remainder of zero," I said. I recorded this on Sterling's paper.

"Let's do twenty divided by two," I then said. "Divide the tiles into two equal piles." Sterling formed two groups quickly, using both hands to move two tiles simultaneously.

"How many are there in each pile?" I asked.

"Ten," Sterling responded. He was sure about this without having to count.

"How many remaining?" I asked.

"None," Sterling answered.

"Can you write the division sentence that describes what we just did?" I asked.

"I'm not sure," Sterling said.

"Do it the way I did for putting the tiles into one pile, but write twenty divided by two instead, since they're in two piles," I instructed.

"Like this?" Sterling said tentatively, and he correctly recorded $20 \div 2 = 10$.

"There aren't any remaining," I said, "and?"

"Oh, I know," Sterling interrupted and added $R = 0$ to the sentence. I was going to tell Sterling that he didn't really have to write the remainder when it was zero, but I decided instead to keep him focused on recording division sentences in a systematic and consistent way. Also, by recording $R = 0$, Sterling would understand how to write the clues for a remainder riddle.

"Let's divide the tiles into three groups," I said. Sterling did this, counted the tiles in each group, and successfully recorded $20 \div 3 = 6 \ R2$. I watched him do twenty divided by four, and then left him to continue. Sterling was able to complete the division sentences and write the clues for his remainder riddle. (See Figure 19–1.)

While Sterling still needed concrete materials to make sense of division, others found the riddles easy to write and wanted a challenge right away.

"Can our secret number be larger than twenty-five?" Naomi asked.

"Choose a secret number between one and twenty-five first, so that we'll have easier riddles to solve," I said. "Then you can choose a larger number for a second riddle."

When all of the students had finished writing their riddles and some had started second ones, I asked for their attention.

"Raise your hand if you have any suggestions for solving a remainder riddle," I said.

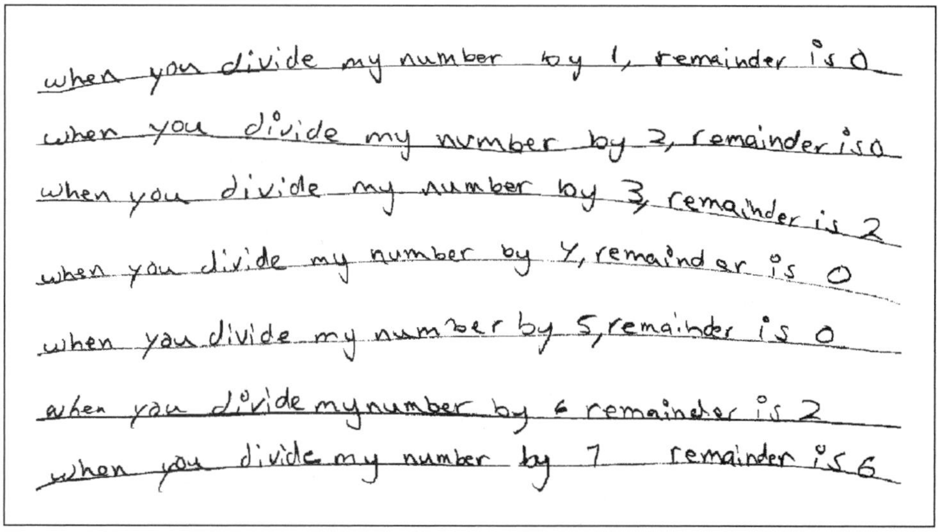

when you divide my number by 1, remainder is 0
when you divide my number by 2, remainder is 0
when you divide my number by 3 remainder is 2
when you divide my number by 4, remainder is 0
when you divide my number by 5, remainder is 0
when you divide my number by 6 remainder is 2
when you divide my number by 7 remainder is 6

Figure 19–1: After using color tiles to help make sense of the numbers, Sterling wrote a remainder riddle for the number twenty.

"It helps if you write the numbers from one to twenty-five on your paper so you can cross out ones that don't fit the clue," Brooke suggested.

"I had to try each number one at a time starting from one," Cesar said. "I read each clue and tried it out on each number. When a number didn't fit the clue, I crossed it out."

"After I read clue number two, I could eliminate either all the odd numbers or all the even numbers," Quinn said. "That got rid of half the numbers."

"It helped me to write out the division problem on another paper and solve it to see what kind of remainder there would be," Meryl said. "It was neat. I used what we learned in division to solve the riddle." (Figure 19–2 shows Meryl's riddle.)

"Now that you've had some experience solving a remainder riddle and also writing one, I want you to solve a friend's riddle," I instructed.

Students paired up to exchange riddles. All were engaged, jotting down numbers on their papers and reading clues. After they solved each other's riddles, they sought out other students to exchange with.

Isaac was one of the students who wanted a challenge and wrote a remainder riddle for a larger number. He chose sixty-three as his secret number:

1. *When you divide my number by 1, the remainder is 0.*

2. *When you divide my number by 2, the remainder is 1.*

3. *When you divide my number by 3, the remainder is 0.*

Figure 19–2: Meryl wrote a remainder riddle for the number eighteen.

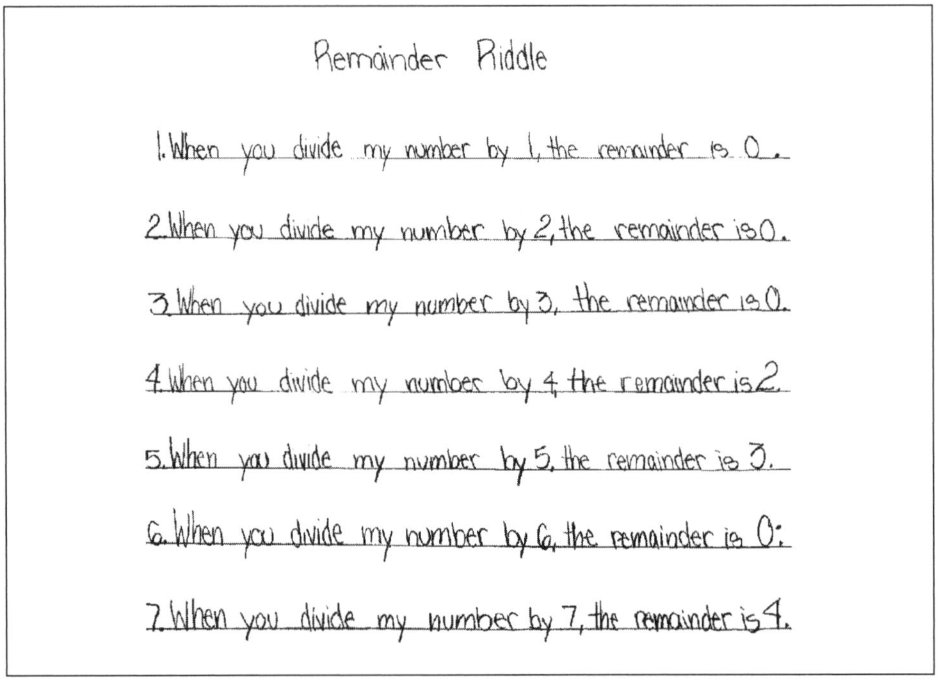

Remainder Riddle

1. When you divide my number by 1, the remainder is 0.

2. When you divide my number by 2, the remainder is 0.

3. When you divide my number by 3, the remainder is 0.

4. When you divide my number by 4 the remainder is 2.

5. When you divide my number by 5, the remainder is 3.

6. When you divide my number by 6, the remainder is 0.

7. When you divide my number by 7, the remainder is 4.

4. *When you divide my number by 4, the remainder is 3.*

5. *When you divide my number by 5, the remainder is 1.*

6. *When you divide my number by 6, the remainder is 3.*

7. *When you divide my number by 7, the remainder is 0.*

"Why do we have to write seven clues for our riddles?" Isaac asked me.

"That's a good question," I said. "I want to be sure that there are enough clues so that the riddle has only one possible answer."

"What do you mean?" Isaac said.

I answered, "Well, suppose I just gave three clues: When you divide by one, the remainder is zero; when you divide by two, the remainder is zero; when you divide by three, the remainder is zero."

"That's not hard," Isaac said. "It has to be even, and you have to be able to divide it by three, so it's six."

"I agree that six fits my clues, but it could also be twelve or eighteen," I said.

Isaac thought about that for a moment. "Oh yeah," he said. "So I need another clue."

"For some numbers, three clues might be enough," I added. "But for others, you need more. If you do all seven clues, then I'm sure a riddle for any number up to one hundred will have only one answer."

Shane was trying to solve Isaac's riddle and was having trouble. I gave him a 1–100 chart so that he could cross out numbers as he eliminated them. Shane began to notice some patterns that helped him.

"Hey," he exclaimed. "I can eliminate half the numbers when I cross out the even ones!" It took Shane a while, but he finally solved Isaac's riddle.

From my discussion with Isaac and watching Shane struggle, I realized that there was a lot more about the mathematics of divisibility to investigate with these students. However, I wanted the students to have a good deal of experience with these riddles first. Their experience would give them a chance to make discoveries that could help them then construct ideas about divisibility. In the meantime, the activity gave them practice with basic division facts and helped a few students understand the concept of division.

Sam Johnson and the Blue Ribbon Quilt

In *Sam Johnson and the Blue Ribbon Quilt*, by Lisa Campbell Ernst (1992), the women of Rosedale won't allow Sam to join their quilting club, so he forms the Rosedale Men's Quilting Club. Both clubs sew quilts for the county fair contest, and when both quilts fall in the mud, Sam devises a way to save the day—the two groups sew together the undamaged pieces of both quilts into one large patterned quilt, which wins first prize. After reading the book and looking at the various quilt patterns, students explore ideas in geometry as they work together to make paper quilts and write quilt riddles.

MATERIALS

6-inch squares of white construction paper, 1 per student

3-inch squares of dark construction paper, 2 per student

3-inch squares of light construction paper, 2 per student

"I have a book I want to share with you today," I told my fifth- and sixth-grade students. "Just by looking at the cover, what do you think the book is about?" The cover shows a bearded man perched on a fence with a dog at his side, looking over a valley.

"A farm," Stan said.

"An old man," Jeffrey added. "Maybe it's about the old man's life."

"It's about a blue ribbon quilt," Muriel said, referring to the title.

"Maybe it's about a man who makes a quilt from blue ribbons he gets at the fair."

I started reading the story and stopped after the first few pages, just after Sam's wife arrived home and Sam told her that he'd like to join her quilting club.

"Who knows what a quilting club is?" I asked the class.

"They must make quilts," Jasmine answered.

"Yes," I answered. "People work together to make one quilt. Do you know what a quilt is?"

"It's like a big blanket with different colors, made out of patches," explained Giorgio.

"It has two layers. It's a blanket made out of little pieces of rags," Ashton said.

I continued reading the book until I reached the point when the women in the Rosedale Women's Quilting Club laugh at Sam when he asks to join.

"How do you feel about men sewing?" I asked the class.

"It seems kind of weird," Stan said.

"I don't know," Jasmine responded. "I read a book once that was about a tailor, and I think most tailors are men and they sew."

"I think it's OK for men to sew," Jaime said. "Why not?"

I returned to reading. The students enjoyed the story and especially liked that the men and women competed against one another to make quilts for the contest at the fair. They were impressed with the quilt that the men and women put together at the end to solve their problem.

When I finished reading the book, I asked the class for comments.

"I noticed that around each page there was a neat border," Xavier said.

I turned to the last page in the book and read the information about the border patterns: "The border designs in this book are actual quilt patterns, each relating to the content of its particular picture." I showed the class the opening page of the book and told them that this border was called Open Book. Then I turned to page 20.

"What do you suppose this border is called?" I asked.

Many hands shot up in the air. "Spools of Thread!" several students called out, referring to the neatly placed spools that bordered the illustration.

"That's right," I said. "What else can you say about the story?"

"Well, usually it's women who are protesting for equal rights, and in this book it's men who are," Mimi observed.

"What do you think the author's message is?" I asked.

"I think the author is trying to tell us that cooperation is a good thing," said Ashton.

"I think the message is that men and women are equal and that people should work together," Sonja said.

I then gave the class directions about what to do. "In the story, the men and women of Rosedale worked together to make quilt patches and then put the patches together to make a quilt," I said. "I'd like to show you a way to make a paper quilt patch and then put four quilt patches together to make a larger quilt pattern."

I held up the paper squares I had prepared. "Each of you needs a 6-by-6-inch square of white construction paper," I said. "You also need some 3-by-3-inch squares—two squares each of two different colors."

I gave further directions. "What you're going to do is fold each colored square on the diagonal and cut it in half to make triangles," I explained as I demonstrated folding and cutting one triangle. "All the triangles will be congruent. That means that they'll be the same size and shape and would match exactly if I placed one triangle on top of another." I knew that some of the students needed to have the idea of congruence explained, while to others my explanation was merely a reminder.

"If I cut all four little squares in half, how many triangles will I get?" I asked.

"Eight," several students answered.

"Once you cut your triangles, you need to fit them inside the white square like a puzzle. You can't overlap the triangles," I instructed. "Who would like to try doing this for the class?"

The students watched as Julian demonstrated one way to make a quilt pattern with the eight triangles. He carefully placed the triangles into the white square.

"Raise your hand if you can imagine another way to fit the triangles into the white square," I said. Many hands went up. I didn't have any other students demonstrate. Instead, I gave them directions for continuing with the activity.

"You'll work in groups of two, three, or four," I directed, "and explore making patterns with the triangles. Make several quilt patch designs without gluing them down. When you find a design that all of you like, then each of you should make the same design by gluing down triangles on a 6-by-6-inch white square. Each group should make a total of four patches that look exactly the same." Some of the students reached for squares to get started, but I stopped them to give the rest of the directions.

"When your patches are complete," I said, "put them together into a larger square design. Each group will make a quilt like this one I made, and then we'll compare the different patterns you made." I held up the sample quilt patch I had made.

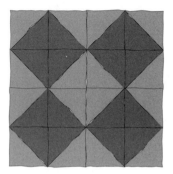

These students had been studying geometry for several weeks. They had explored the ideas of congruency and symmetry and had learned the names and characteristics of different polygons. Two students were new to the class, however, and hadn't had the same experiences as the rest of the students. For them, this activity was an introduction to geometric ideas and vocabulary.

As I watched the students work, I noticed that some students found it easy to flip and rotate their triangles to fit on the white square. Other students, however, found the task difficult and struggled to arrange the triangles so that they covered the white square completely without overlaps.

As the students completed their individual patches, they began to discuss and explore different ways to combine and tape together their patches into one large quilt. After about an hour, we had posted all of the quilts on the board in the front of the room.

The Next Day

"Yesterday you made your quilts," I said to the class and pointed to the quilts posted on the board. "Today we're going to look at our quilts as mathematicians." I posted the quilt I had made (see above).

"Can anyone make an observation about my quilt patch that has to do with geometry?" I asked.

"It has parallel lines," Ashton offered. "There are four sets of parallel lines." Ashton came up and pointed with his finger to show what he noticed.

"There are five shapes that look like jewelry," Jasmine observed. "They're diamonds."

"If you rotated those diamonds, what geometric shape would you have?" I asked.

"Squares!" several students answered.

"I see lots of quadrilaterals," Jaime said.

"What is the definition of a quadrilateral?" I asked.

"It has four sides, four angles, and it's a closed shape," Jaime answered.

"What else do you notice about my quilt?" I probed.

"It has a line of symmetry," Stan answered. "Can I come up?"

"Yes," I responded.

"If you fold it in half this way," he said, showing a line down the center of my quilt, "it's symmetrical, like a butterfly."

"What else?" I asked the class after Stan had sat down.

"One side of the quilt is the same as the other side," Mimi observed. "If you picked up one side and put it on top of the other side, they'd match perfectly. They're congruent."

As each student made an observation, I recorded the information on the board next to my quilt design. When we were finished, I had written:

parallel lines
shapes that look like jewelry
squares
quadrilaterals
symmetrical
congruent

I then began a discussion about riddles.

"Who can describe what a riddle is?" I asked. Many hands shot up.

"It's like a secret that you give clues to," Julian said. "An animal riddle would be like this: It's a king and it has a mane and only the females hunt for food. Oh, and they're carnivorous!"

"A lion!" several students guessed.

"That's an example of an animal riddle," I said. "You're going to work in your group to write quilt riddles using geometric clues about your quilts. When you're all finished writing your riddles, we'll read them and try to match them with the quilts."

"Before you write your riddles, I'm going to give each group a piece of paper," I continued. "I want you to look at your quilt and write down all the things you notice about it. Use as many geometry words as you can to describe your quilt. When you're finished, use your notes to help you write the clues for your quilt riddle. Also, think of a name for your quilt."

As I circulated, I noticed that everyone was busy writing down observations and rotating the designs, trying to identify as many geometric properties in the quilts as possible. The students worked together to find appropriate names for their quilts. For many, finding

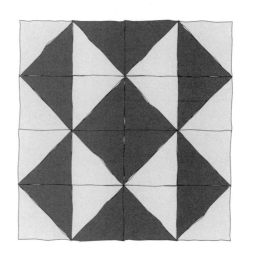

the hour Glass

It has 2 lines of symmetry
1 from the middle of the sides to the oposite.

2 It has 2 bowties that are Blue and yellow.

3 It has a Big blue Square in the middle

It has 14 large triangles
4 made from the Small blue and yellow triangles.

Figure 20–1: Muriel, Suzannah, and Lindsey found everyday objects and geometric shapes in their quilt pattern.

a name for their patch was a good start for writing their clues. (See Figure 20–1.)

Jasmine and Sonja were discussing their patch while I was observing.

"These are equilateral triangles," Sonja said.

"No, they're not," Jasmine argued. "Equilateral triangles have sides that are all the same size."

"Well, I know our patch is not symmetrical, because when you fold it in half, the two sides don't match," Sonja said.

I didn't intervene, but listened to their arguments and made mental notes about what they knew about their quilt. Over the year, I add to my information about what students do and don't understand from the many opportunities I have to observe them. From my mental notes, I often jot down information on sticky notes and put them in a student's folder. This sort of information helps me when I'm sharing student progress with parents. It also serves as a guide for conversations I need to have with students about certain mathematical ideas.

In their riddles, the children described objects such as faces, houses, school colors, and windmills. At the same time, they included geometric vocabulary such as *symmetrical, triangle, trapezoid, congruent, hexagon,* and *parallelogram.*

When the students finished their quilt riddles, they posted the riddles and quilts at the front of the room. I asked them not to post their riddles next to their quilts so that we would have the challenge of matching riddles and quilts. I numbered the quilts to make it easier to identify them.

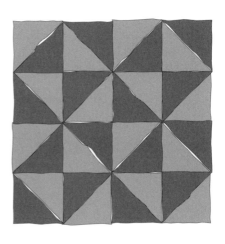

Figure 20–2: José and Jaime named their pattern The Cross (La Crus). Translation: There are five little squares and four blue windmills and four purple windmills. There's an X. Two corners have the same color.

"You're going to take turns reading your riddles to the class," I said. "Please let each group read all of the clues before guessing."

Julian and Judd went first. They had written the following clues:

1. *It has five shapes of diamonds.*
2. *There are four blue windmills.*
3. *There are for purple windmills.*
4. *There are 6 squares with at least 8 triangles.*
5. *It has 2 lines of symmetry on the diaganal. It's name is "Triangle Checkerboard."*

After several tries, the other students guessed the correct quilt.

Jane and Megan went next. They read: "It has a horizontal line of symmetry. It has a vertical line of symmetry. It has a big blue diamond. It has six triangles. It has four small triangles. It's name is Triangles and Squares."

The riddle game gave the students the chance to link written descriptions and geometric vocabulary with geometric designs. After a few riddles, the students got better at guessing. Sometimes the name of the quilt gave it away, and sometimes the clues assisted the students. (See Figure 20–2.)

Marie suggested that we post the quilts in the office with the riddles on a separate piece of chart paper. We did, and the quilt riddles served as a math activity for visitors, students, teachers, and even the school principal!

Two Ways to Count to Ten

Two Ways to Count to Ten: A Liberian Folktale, is retold by Ruby Dee (1990). In the story, the leopard, king of the jungle, decides that it's time to find a successor who will eventually become king. He invites animals from far and wide and says, "[I] shall seek the cleverest among you, for your king must be wise." He says that the new prince will be the animal that can throw up a spear and count to ten before it hits the ground. Many animals try and fail. Finally, an antelope throws up the spear and counts to ten by twos, winning the contest. After reading this story, students investigate finding the factors of numbers.

MATERIALS

Day 1

One morning, I began class by showing my fifth graders *Two Ways to Count to Ten*. "This is a folktale from Liberia, a country in West Africa," I said.

As I read the story, the students waited with anticipation as each animal tried to count to ten before the spear hit the ground. Some chanted along with me as each animal announced, "I will be king, I can do this thing!"

When I read that the antelope tossed the spear up into the air and called out only five words, some of the students immediately figured out what the antelope said. I heard several whisper, "Two, four, six, eight, ten."

After reading the story, I posed a question for the class. "In the story, the antelope counted to ten by twos," I said. "Are there other ways to count to ten?"

Hands shot up, and several students had ideas. "Count by ones." "Just start with ten and you're there." "You go five, ten, and it works." I wrote on the board:

1, 2, 5, 10

"You can count by threes, too," Elias said. "You go three, six, nine, plus one."

"How is Elias's way different from the other ways you counted to ten?" I asked the class.

"You don't land exactly on ten using the same steps," Brittany said.

"How about one, two, three, and skip to ten," Abbott suggested.

"That's the same as Elias's," Nima said. "They're not even steps."

I then explained to the class, "When we count to ten by one, two, or five, we follow a pattern. Once you know the pattern, you're able to predict what the next number will be. If I counted 'three, six, nine,' as Elias did, then it would be logical to predict that twelve would come next. I'm interested in investigating ways to count to numbers in predictable patterns."

"So mine isn't right?" Abbott asked.

"The problem with your suggestion is that we could use your method to get to any number," I responded. "It could be one, two, three, skip some, and then twenty-three, or sixty-five, or seven thousand four hundred and thirty-one." Some of the students giggled; Abbott nodded.

"Today we'll investigate how to count to numbers using what Nima called 'even steps,'" I continued. "For ten, we have four ways of counting, by ones, twos, fives, and ten. How many ways are there for counting to twelve?" I wrote *12* on the board.

"Talk about this with the person next to you," I directed. After about a minute, at least one student from each group had a hand in the air. I called on Quinn.

"You can count to twelve by ones, twos, threes, fours, sixes, and twelve," she reported. I wrote next to the 12 on the board:

1, 2, 3, 4, 6, 12

I called on students to demonstrate the numbers to verify that we would reach twelve for each with even steps.

"So we have ways to count to ten and twelve," I said. "Now we are going to find all the ways to count to the numbers from one to forty-nine."

I pointed to three large charts I had taped to the board. I had ruled each chart into three columns and labeled the columns: Number, Ways to Count, and Number of Ways. On the first chart I had listed the numbers from 1 to 17 in the first column. On the other charts, I had listed 18 to 34 and 35 to 49. (I listed only the numbers to 49 because later in the lesson, I was going to ask students to find the factors for fifty.) I ruled lines across the charts under each number.

I went to the number 10 on the first chart and in the Ways to Count column, I wrote *1, 2, 5, 10*. In the Number of Ways column, I wrote *4*. Then, next to the number 12, I wrote *1, 2, 3, 4, 6, 12* in the Ways to Count column and *6* in the Number of Ways column.

Number	Ways to Count	Number of Ways		Number	Ways to Count	Number of Ways		Number	Ways to Count	Number of Ways
1				18				35		
2				19				36		
3				20				37		
4				21				38		
5				22				39		
6				23				40		
7				24				41		
8				25				42		
9				26				43		
10	1,2,5,10	4		27				44		
11				28				45		
12	1,2,3,4,6,12	6		29				46		
13				30				47		
14				31				48		
15				32				49		
16				33						
17				34						

"Who can explain what I recorded?" I asked. I waited until about half of the students had raised their hands and then called on Donna.

"You wrote the starting numbers for counting in the second column and then counted up how many there are," Donna explained succinctly.

"That's right," I said. Then I explained how the students were to investigate numbers.

"You'll work in pairs," I said, "and each pair will investigate as many numbers as you have time to do. You and your partner should find all the ways to count to whatever numbers you choose and record your findings on a sheet of paper."

"When we find all the ways to count to a number, do we record the ways on the chart?" Naomi asked.

"No," I replied, "record just on a sheet of paper. After everyone has figured the ways to count to these numbers, I'll fill in this chart with your ideas."

"Do we have to do the numbers in order?" Eartha asked.

"No," I answered. "Choose ones you're curious about or interested in. Do a variety—some large and some small."

There were no more questions, so I had the students pair up. As I observed the students work, I noticed that they were using different strategies for finding ways to count to their numbers. Some used calculators, some were skip-counting, some were multiplying, and others were using division.

A few students were using a strategy based on part of the multiplication unit we had started a few weeks earlier. In one of the multiplication activities, the students had used $\frac{1}{2}$-inch-squared paper to create rectangular arrays for the numbers from one to thirty-six. For example, for the number twelve, they had cut out three rectangles— a 3-by-4, a 2-by-6, and a 1-by-12. I had introduced the word *factor* to describe the numbers used in multiplication to arrive at an answer, or product, and had connected the idea of factors to the dimensions of the rectangular arrays.

After about fifteen minutes, I asked for the students' attention. "I know you can still do more," I said, "but I'm interested in taking a moment to hear about the different strategies you're using to find the ways to count to a number."

"We were looking at the chart we made for the rectangles," Brittany said.

"How did the array chart help you?" I asked.

"Well, the arrays for twenty-four are one-by-twenty-four, two-by-twelve, three-by-eight, and four-by-six," Brittany replied. "So I knew you could count by one, twenty-four, two, twelve, three, eight, four, and six."

"Ooooh, that's neat," Jacob said.

"What's neat?" I asked him.

"How she used the rectangle chart to figure," he responded and looked at the chart to locate one of the numbers he had been working on.

"Yes, the chart of arrays shows that one, two, three, four, six, eight, and twelve are all factors of twenty-four," I said to reinforce the use of the word *factor* and connect it to this activity. I used this term as often as possible during the activity to help the children become familiar with it in the context of what they were doing and thinking about.

Isaac reported next. "Like for twenty, I started with one and I know that one times any number equals that number, so one times twenty equals twenty," he said. "Then I went in order. Like two times what makes twenty? Then three, then four, and I kept going like that."

Eartha had a different method. "I used a multiplication chart to see how to count up to a number," she explained.

"I used a calculator," Jacob said. "I did thirty-six, and first I tried two. I pushed two, then plus, then I kept pushing the equals sign to see if I would land on thirty-six. I tried that for each number."

"I used division to help me find all the ways," Nima said.

"Can you explain how you used division?" I asked.

"I took nine," she said. "I thought about what you could divide nine by and not have a remainder. I did nine divided by one equals nine and nine divided by three equals three."

"Did anyone use a different method?" I asked.

"With forty-four, you can keep adding on to find the ways," Brooke said. "I did four plus four equals eight, eight plus four equals twelve, then twelve plus four equals sixteen. I kept adding on to see if I could get to forty-four counting by fours. It worked."

"Any other ways?" I asked the class.

"Well, forty-six divided by two is twenty-three, so I know I could count by twos to forty-six," Jacob said. "And since twenty-three is half of forty-six, I can count by twenty-three. You go twenty-three, forty-six."

"We were investigating the number thirty-eight," Bethia said. "Half of thirty is fifteen, half of eight is four, and fifteen plus four is nineteen. So you can divide thirty-eight by nineteen. So I know I can count by nineteen and I can count by one."

"And I know that I can count by twos because thirty-eight is an even number," her partner, Elias, said.

"From listening to your ideas, I see you have many different strategies for finding the ways to count to a number," I said. "Go back to work, and also think about how you can make sure you have found all the factors or ways to count to your number." The students worked for the rest of math class. I collected their papers and told them that we would continue our investigation the next day.

Day 2

"I looked over your papers," I said to begin class. "Now I'm going to give them back to you so you can report what you've discovered."

After handing back their papers, I asked who worked on the number one. Several pairs reported that one has only one factor—itself. I walked over to the Ways to Count chart and wrote a *1* under Ways to Count and a *1* under Number of Ways.

I continued to call out each number up to forty-nine, recording on the charts the factors for each number and the number of ways to get that number. Filling in the charts in front of everyone was helpful. If several pairs did the same number, they checked to be sure they agreed. When we got to a number that no one had chosen, we investigated it together as a class.

When I had filled in the charts up to the number 36, I stopped to ask a question. "Let's look at the charts so far," I said. "What do you notice? Discuss this with your group, and jot down some of your ideas." After a few minutes, I asked for the students' attention and repeated my question.

"There are prime numbers up there," Isaac said. I had introduced the idea of prime numbers when the students had cut out the rectangular arrays. The prime numbers each had only one rectangle—1-by-13, 1-by-23, and so on.

"Tell us what a prime number is," I said.

"It's a number that has only one and itself as factors," he responded. I wrote Isaac's statement about prime numbers on the board.

"Help me list all the prime numbers from one to forty-nine," I said to the class. I knew that for some students this would be easy, while others would have difficulty. Having the students respond in unison allowed those who were unsure to listen to the others. I recorded on the board:

2, 3, 5, 7, 11, 13, 17, 19, 23, 29, 31, 37

Then the going got hard because our chart of rectangular arrays went only to 36. Finally, I added *41*, *43*, and *47* to the list.

"What do you notice about the possible ways to count for prime numbers?" I asked.

"There are only two ways to count to prime numbers," Bethia said. I recorded her idea.

"That's because prime numbers have only two factors," I said. "What else do you notice about the chart?"

"All the prime numbers are odd except for two," Cesar said.

"Every number has one and itself as factors," Nima said.

"Every even number has two as a factor," Nathan said.

I recorded their ideas as they presented them. Then I asked, "What do you notice about the square numbers? What numbers are square numbers?"

"If you look at the rectangular arrays, the square numbers are the ones with cut out squares," Brittany said. "Like a three-by-three square and a four-by-four square."

As students called out the square numbers—1, 4, 9, 16, 25, 36—I drew squares around each of them on the charts and then listed them on the board.

"What would the next square number be?" I asked. "Talk to your partner about this."

In a moment, more than half of the students had raised their hands. "Let's say together what the next square is," I said.

"Forty-nine," the students said in unison. I added *49* to the list on the board.

"It's seven times seven," Eartha added. "We did that number."

"What do you notice about the square numbers?" I asked.

"Square numbers have an odd number of factors," Isaac said. The others checked and seemed surprised by this and impressed that Isaac had noticed it. I recorded Isaac's idea.

"What else do you notice about the chart?" I probed.

"I notice something!" Quinn exclaimed. "If a number ends in zero or five, one of its factors is five." I recorded her statement and instructed the students to check the chart to see if that was true. They agreed it was.

"I have one!" Jacob exclaimed. "Every odd number has only odd factors."

I recorded Jacob's idea and then had the class check to see if Jacob's conjecture was true. I pointed to each odd number to be sure that all of its factors were odd numbers. Jacob smiled when we confirmed that he was correct.

"All even numbers have some factors the same as the number that is half of that number," Elias said. "Like twenty-four. Half is twelve. The factors for twelve are one, two, three, four, and six, and twenty-four has those same factors."

"Elias's observation shows us how some numbers are connected," I said, recording his idea.

No other students had ideas to share, so I continued filling in the chart up to 49. Then I introduced another problem for them to solve.

"I think that your ideas are useful to help you figure out how to find the ways to count to a number," I said. "Try the number fifty. Find the factors of fifty and explain how you know each number is a factor. Also, try to explain how you know you have found all the factors."

The students worked for about twenty minutes finding the factors for fifty. When most were finished, I asked for volunteers to share.

Nathan wrote: *1 is a factor becaues 1 × 50 = 50. 2 is a factor becaues it gos in to any even number. 5 is a factor becaues 5 × 10 = 50. 10 is a factor becaues it gos into any number that are in ten's place. 25 is a factor becaues if you have two qurtors that would add up to 50¢ 50 is a factor becaues every number has it self as a factor.* (See Figure 21–1.)

Donna wrote: *First of all, one has to be a factor, because 1 and itself are always factors of a number. 50 is an even number so 2 is*

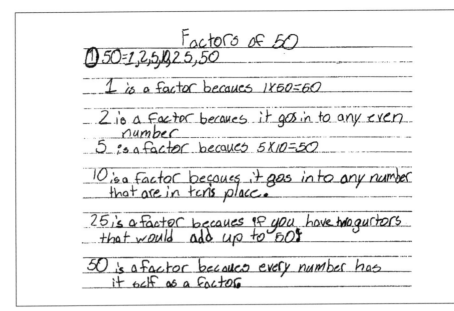

also a factor. 5 is a factor because 50 ends in 0 and 5 × 10 = 50. I just said why 10 is a factor. 50 is an even number and $\frac{1}{2}$ of it is 25. Then of course, there's 50. When I was explaining 1 I told you why 50 must also be a factor. The number itself is always its highest factor, so that was as far as I could go.

Shane explained how he knew he had all of the factors for fifty: Once you get half way [25] no number can fit in it. That's how I kwon [know] how to find them all.

"Can you explain your thinking a little more, Shane?" I asked.

"Well, one, two, five, and ten and twenty-five are factors of fifty," he explained. "I know that twenty-five is halfway to fifty and there are no more factors of fifty past twenty-five except for fifty itself."

Throughout the week, the students worked on an extension of the activity by investigating the numbers from fifty-one to one hundred. We continued to discuss how we were sure we had found all the ways to count to each number. We also made predictions about which numbers between one and one hundred would have the most factors. Figure 21–2 shows how Angelo found the factors of fifty.

Presenting the Problem to a Fourth-Grade Class

Shelley Ferguson's fourth graders had been studying about multiplication and had also built rectangular arrays for the numbers from one to thirty-six. The students had represented the arrays on a class chart using graph paper.

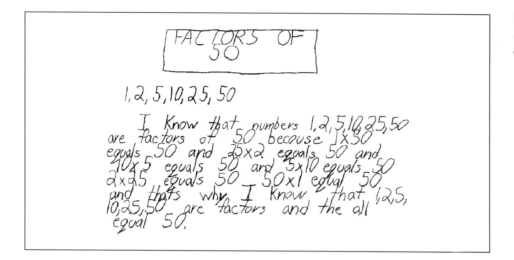

After reading aloud *Two Ways to Count to Ten*, Shelley posed a problem. "The antelope had to count to ten," she began, "but suppose the antelope had to count to twenty-four? How many ways are there to count to twenty-four?"

Shelley tried to help her students make a connection between skip-counting and the rectangular arrays they had made. "Look at the rectangular arrays," Shelley said, "and see if the arrays can help you count to a number."

The students worked on this problem in a variety of ways. Some used calculators, some skip-counted by twos, threes, eights, and twelves, and some used square tiles to make different rectangular arrays.

When the students figured out the ways to count to twenty-four, Shelley posed a similar problem. "What are the ways to count to thirty-six?" she asked. "How can you find all the ways? How will you know when you've found them all?"

Shelley asked her students to explain their reasoning by writing a letter to the antelope (or another animal) to suggest ways to count to thirty-six.

Cassidy wrote: *Dear Lion, I think you should count by 12's to 36 because it's quick. I do not think you should count by 18's or 36's because someone could acoue [accuse] you of cheating.*

Figure 21–3 shows how Jocelyn tackled the problem.

Presenting the Problem to a Sixth-Grade Class

Suzanne McGrath's sixth graders had just completed a unit on factors and multiples when she read *Two Ways to Count to Ten*. Her sixth graders listened attentively to the story and investigated the factors for each number from one to one hundred.

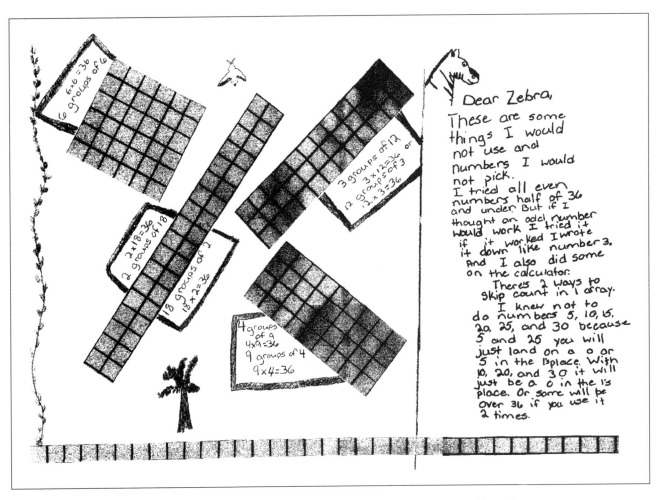

The handwritten letter in the figure reads:

Dear Zebra,
These are some things I would not use and numbers I would not pick.
I tried all even numbers half of 36 and under But if I thought an odd number would work I tried it if it worked I wrote it down like number 3. And I also did some on the calculator.
There's 2 ways to skip count in 1 array.
I knew not to do numbers 5, 10, 15, 20, 25, and 30 because 5 and 25 you will just land on a 0 or 5 in the 1's place. With 10, 20, and 30 it will just be a 0 in the 1's place. Or some will be over 36 if you use it 2 times.

The array labels read:

6×6=36
6 groups of 6

2 2×18=36
2 groups of 18
18 groups of 2
18×2=36

3 groups of 12
3×12=36 or
12 groups of 3
12×3=36

4 groups of 9
4×9=36
9 groups of 4
9×4=36

Figure 21–3: Jocelyn used rectangular arrays to find and explain the ways to count to thirty-six.

The following week, Suzanne began a unit on geometry. When they were studying angles, one of Suzanne's students asked, "Why do circles have three hundred and sixty degrees?"

"I don't know," Suzanne replied, "but I think I know where we can look for the answer."

Suzanne brought to class the book *Circles: Fun Ideas for Getting A-Round in Math,* by Katherine Sheldrick Ross (1993). This book explores the history of different geometric shapes—circles, spheres, cylinders, cones, and others. The book also offers interesting activities for children ages 8 to 14.

Suzanne turned to page 37 and read to her class about why circles have 360 degrees. Her students were fascinated to learn that the ancient Babylonians based their number system on 60 and that they were the ones who decided to divide a circle into 360 equal parts. They chose 360 because it's divisible by so many whole numbers.

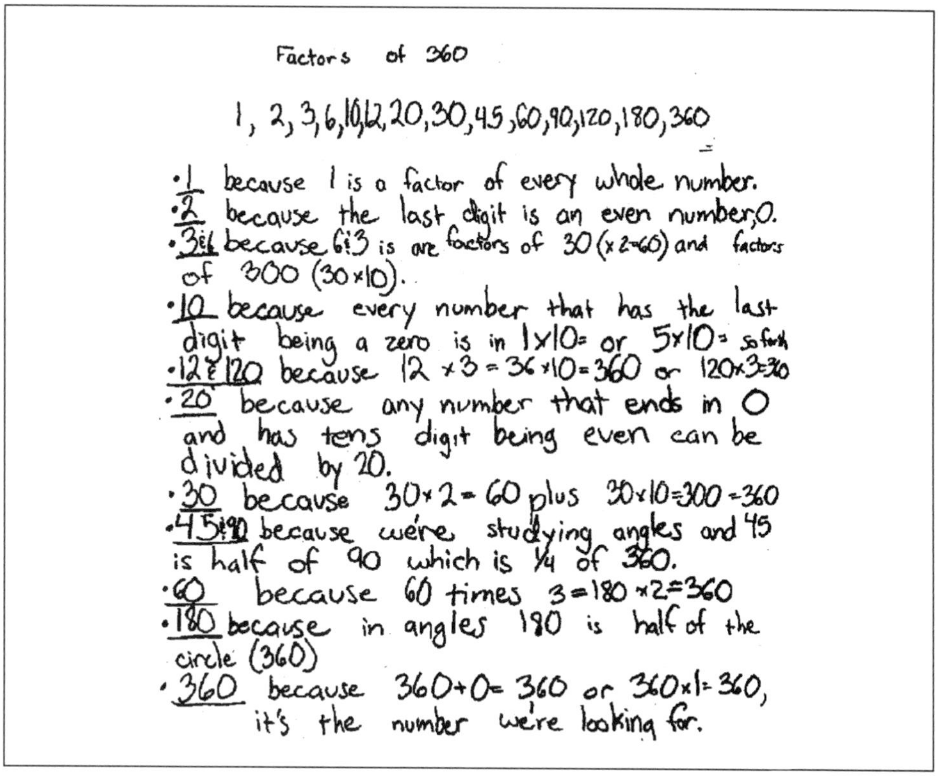

Figure 21–4: Lesley explained how she found all the factors for 360.

Factors of 360

1, 2, 3, 6, 10, 12, 20, 30, 45, 60, 90, 120, 180, 360

- 1 because 1 is a factor of every whole number.
- 2 because the last digit is an even number, 0.
- 3 & 6 because 6 & 3 are factors of 30 (x2=60) and factors of 300 (30×10).
- 10 because every number that has the last digit being a zero is in 1×10= or 5×10= so forth
- 12 & 120 because 12 × 3 = 36 ×10=360 or 120×3=360
- 20 because any number that ends in 0 and has tens digit being even can be divided by 20.
- 30 because 30×2= 60 plus 30×10=300 =360
- 45 & 90 because we're studying angles and 45 is half of 90 which is ¼ of 360.
- 60 because 60 times 3 =180 ×2=360
- 180 because in angles 180 is half of the circle (360)
- 360 because 360+0= 360 or 360×1= 360, it's the number we're looking for.

Figure 21–4: Lesley explained how she found all the factors for 360.

"How many numbers divide evenly into three hundred sixty?" Suzanne asked. Suzanne reported that this problem was a perfect extension for *Two Ways to Count to Ten*. She added that it was also a nice way to connect one topic of mathematics with another. (See Figure 21–4.)

The Warlord's Puzzle

The Warlord's Puzzle, written by Virginia Walton Pilegard (2000), is a story of the origin of the tangram puzzle. A fierce warlord in China receives a ceramic tile as a gift from an artist. The artist accidentally breaks the tile into seven pieces, and the warlord decides to punish him. To escape the warlord's wrath, the artist cleverly proposes that a contest be held. Whoever is talented enough to put the tiles back together will be asked to live in the warlord's palace . . . and the artist's life will be saved. To the relief of the artist, the puzzle is solved by a little peasant boy who figures out how to put the tangrams back together into a perfect square. After hearing the story, students use their own set of tangrams and explore making different polygons.

MATERIALS

1 plastic set (or overhead set) of tangrams

6-inch squares of construction paper, 1 per student

scissors, 1 pair per student

Tangram record sheet, 1 per student (see Blackline Masters)

Tangram instructions, 1 per student (see Blackline Masters)

Introducing the Activity

The thirty-four fourth graders in Robin Gordon's class sat quietly at their desks, waiting for me to give the signal to gather on the rug at the front of the room. The students each had a set of their own tangrams in envelopes on their tabletops. They'd made the tangrams the day before from 6-inch squares of colored construction paper, following the directions Robin had given them.

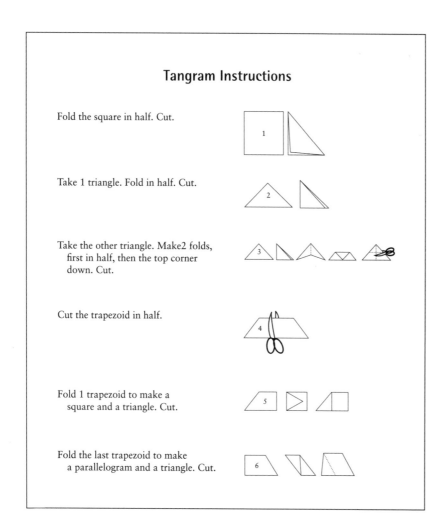

Tangram Instructions

Fold the square in half. Cut.

Take 1 triangle. Fold in half. Cut.

Take the other triangle. Make 2 folds, first in half, then the top corner down. Cut.

Cut the trapezoid in half.

Fold 1 trapezoid to make a square and a triangle. Cut.

Fold the last trapezoid to make a parallelogram and a triangle. Cut.

Once on the rug, the students listened carefully as I asked a question that was intended to tap their prior knowledge about tangrams and give them an opportunity to make some predictions.

"Raise your hand if you have an idea of where tangrams originated," I said.

Students guessed China, Russia, Japan, and Asia.

"Those are good guesses as to where tangrams originated. Does anyone have an idea about how they came to be?"

"I think they were used to write stories—I mean, make pictures to go with stories," Jalen said.

"I think they came from clay," Janelle guessed.

"Asia makes a lot of origami," Daniel commented. "And tangrams are like origami."

After hearing students' predictions, I began reading *The Warlord's Puzzle*. The students recognized the picture of the tangram puzzle in the story immediately. They sat quietly, taking in the colorful illustrations that depicted the ancient kingdom of the T'ang dynasty: its palaces, mountains, and rivers and the Buddhist monks, artists, warlords, and peasants.

I stopped a few times to make sure that students understood the meanings of the words *jade, monk,* and *mend*. When geometry words were introduced, such as *parallelogram, square,* and *triangle,* I pointed to the shapes in the book. Robin's class had just begun a unit on geometry, and this seemed a perfect introduction to geometric shapes.

When I finished reading the story, I dismissed the students back to their seats, directing them to get out their sets of tangrams and be ready to look up and listen to me on the count of five.

"One, two, three, four, five . . . eyes up here, please," I said. Standing beside the overhead projector, I picked up the two small triangles from my plastic set of tangrams and held them in the air, directing the students to hold up their two small triangles. I prompted the class to say the name of the shape together. I placed the two small plastic triangles on the overhead projector and then placed the medium-sized triangle next to them.

"Take a look at the small triangles and the medium-sized triangle," I said to the class. "How are they alike and how are they different?"

After a few moments, many hands were in the air. I called on Enrique.

"The small and big one are the same, are *triangulos* [Spanish for 'triangles']—triangles, I mean," he said.

"How?" I probed. "Tell how the triangles are the same shape."

"Well, they have three sides and two of the sides are the same . . . ," he began.

I waited a few seconds to give him time to think, then helped him out.

"The same length?" I asked. He nodded in agreement. Enrique's first language was Spanish, and like many English language learners, he sometimes needed assistance as he built his vocabulary.

"When two sides of a triangle are the same length, mathematicians call it an isosceles triangle," I noted, writing the new vocabulary word on the board, then sketching a triangle next to it.

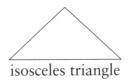

isosceles triangle

"How are the triangles different?" I asked.

"They are the same shape, but not the same size," Nina observed.

"That's correct," I said. "Mathematicians call them similar shapes because they're the same shape but not the same size, like Nina and Enrique said." I quickly sketched the small and medium-sized triangles next to each other on the board and wrote the words *triangle* and *similar* under the shapes. Next I held the two large triangles in the air and directed the students to do the same with theirs.

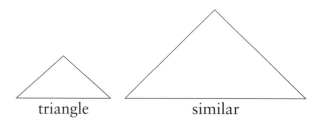

triangle   similar

"These two triangles, like the two small triangles, are exactly the same size and shape. What would a mathematician call shapes that are the same size and shape?" I asked. After a few moments, there were no hands in the air, so I introduced the word *congruent* and wrote it on the board along with the words *same size, same shape.* Finally, I placed the square and the parallelogram on the overhead projector.

"How are these the same and how are they different?" I asked. "Talk with your partner sitting next to you." The room erupted in conversations. Partner talk can be a very effective way to give everyone a chance to voice his or her ideas in math class. I gave the students about a minute to talk, then asked for their attention.

David went first. "One is a square and the other shape is a diamond if you twist it around."

"So if you take the square and rotate it, it looks like a diamond?" I asked, rotating the square on the overhead. I wrote the word *rotate* on the board.

"They both have parallel lines," Henry added.

I wrote the word *parallel* on the board, quickly sketching both the square and the parallelogram next to the word.

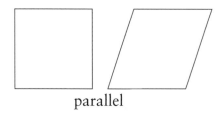

parallel

"Actually, both of these shapes are parallelograms because each has two pairs of parallel lines," I noted, using my fingers to designate the parallel lines and drawing arrows from the pairs of lines to the word *parallelogram*. "Who can tell us in your own words what we mean by *parallel lines*?"

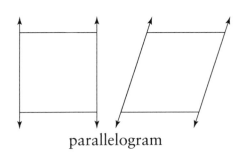

parallelogram

After waiting for a few seconds, I called on Andrea.

"They're never going to touch each other," she explained.

"That's right," I confirmed. "Parallel lines go on next to each other and will never touch or intersect." I purposely inserted correct mathematical vocabulary along with Andrea's wording and wrote the new vocabulary word (*intersect*) on the board. In addition, I quickly drew a trapezoid as a counterexample and showed how it had one pair of parallel lines but that the other pair of lines would eventually intersect.

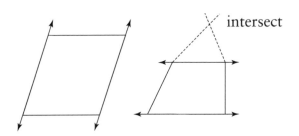

intersect

With the intention of helping them apply what they had just learned, I asked the students to take a quick look around the room, challenging them to find parallel lines in their immediate environment. As they did so, I circulated, listening in on students' conversations as they identified several parallel lines in the room: on the ceiling, the door, the board, their desks, and so on.

Once students had identified all the tangram shapes and we had discussed some key vocabulary words, I asked the students to explore making things with their tangram pieces. This free exploration time is essential when introducing a new math material. Students need time to get acquainted with manipulatives and learn how to use them.

Modeling How to Draw Tangram Shapes

After giving the class a couple of minutes to explore, I called for the students' attention and asked them to put all of their tangrams to the side, except for the two small triangles.

"Using the two small triangles, I want you to make a square on your desktop," I directed.

After giving the class just a couple of seconds to complete this rather easy task, I called on a volunteer to come up and make the square on the overhead projector using my plastic tangrams. Next, I modeled how to make a drawing of the shape by first sketching the outline of the square, then using dotted lines to show the two triangles inside the square.

"It's important to watch me," I warned, "because in a few minutes you'll be making shapes with your tangrams and drawing the shapes on a record sheet."

After I finished modeling how to draw the square on the board, I told the students to make a different shape using the two small triangles. The class responded enthusiastically to my direction and soon there were several students with their hands wiggling in the air, ready to share the triangle and parallelogram they'd made. After a few students showed the new shapes they'd made on the overhead projector, I modeled how to draw the triangle and parallelogram made from the two small triangles.

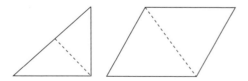

"Now I want you to use the two small triangles and the medium-sized triangle and make a shape on your desktop," I told the class.

"But this time, you'll practice drawing the shape on a record sheet."

As students were making their shapes, I distributed record sheets for their tangram drawings. When they were ready to draw their shapes, I told them to find the box in which the drawing should go and reminded them to first make an outline of the shape and then use dotted lines to designate the smaller shapes inside the main shape.

Tangram Record Sheet

	3 Smallest Triangles	5 Small Pieces	All 7 Pieces
Square			
Triangle			
Rectangle			
Parallelogram			

Making Shapes with Three, Five, and Seven Tangram Pieces

At this point in the lesson, students had been introduced to some new geometry vocabulary words, had learned how to make some basic shapes using two and three tangram pieces, and had learned how to draw the tangram shapes. Now the class was ready to explore making different shapes using either three, five, or all seven tangram pieces.

As I circulated the room observing the students at work, I noticed that they were sliding, flipping, and turning the tangram pieces, fitting them together to make shapes. These actions help students develop their spatial sense, which is important in learning mathematics. Some students have a natural spatial sense; others are easily confused by spatial information. While some of the fourth graders in Robin Gordon's class found making shapes from tangrams easy, others moaned and groaned and initially experienced some frustration. I recognized this and made a comment.

"I notice that some of you are using all seven tangram pieces to make shapes," I said, addressing the entire class. "It might be easier if you start out with three or five tangram pieces. Also, is it OK to make mistakes while you're trying to make a shape?"

"Yes!" the students chorused.

"That's right; making mistakes is how you learn," I told them. "Mathematicians sometimes work on problems for years before they find a solution, so try to stick with it and experiment with your tangram pieces. Making shapes isn't as easy as it looks!"

During the lesson, everyone in the class was able to make at least a few shapes, including a couple of students who were identified as having severe learning disabilities. Although some students needed a little extra help, the task was accessible to everyone and posed a challenge to all as well.

Summarizing the Activity

I gave the class about twenty minutes to work before stopping the students to summarize the lesson. My plan was to have volunteers come up to the overhead projector and use my plastic tangrams to build one of the shapes they'd discovered. I knew that it would be unrealistic to expect all the students to be completely attentive if they still had their tangram pieces in front of them. So I decided to allow the class to continue working quietly while volunteers shared. This ended up working just fine and allowed everyone to remain engaged. (See Figures 22–1 through 22–3 for three students' work on this activity.)

As each volunteer came up to build his or her shape on the overhead projector, I encouraged the student to describe the shape using correct mathematical vocabulary. Cesar was first to share. He used two small triangles to make a parallelogram.

"This is a parallelogram because it has four lines that are parallel," he began. "These two are parallel and these two are also," he continued, pointing to the lines with his index finger.

One reason for summing up a lesson is to revisit concepts and skills learned, so I was happy to see that Cesar remembered about parallel lines.

Figure 22–1: Henry
recorded five different
solutions.

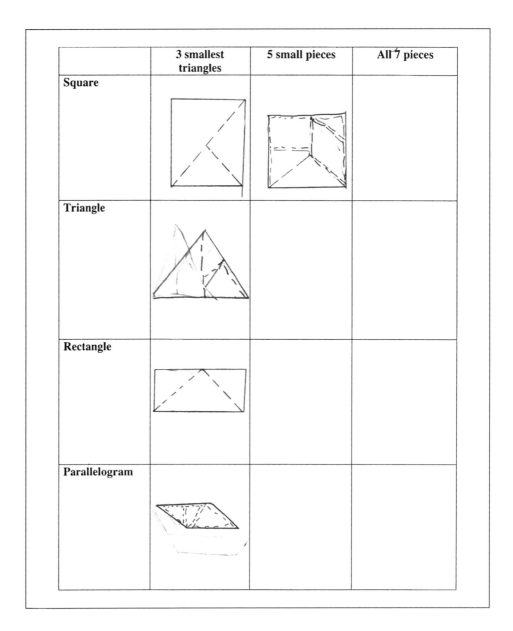

	3 smallest triangles	5 small pieces	All 7 pieces
Square			
Triangle			
Rectangle			
Parallelogram			

Brandon came up next and made the same shape as Cesar. He realized this, and it was a nice opportunity for the class to revisit the word *congruent*. Denise volunteered next and got stuck trying to make a shape using five pieces.

"It looks different up here on the projector than it looks on my paper," she noted.

"It's really hard to look at something on paper and build it, isn't it?" I acknowledged.

After a few more students shared shapes they'd made, Aldiv came up to the overhead and, after struggling for a minute or so, re-created the square using all seven tangram pieces. The class cheered for him.

"It's just like in the story!" several students commented. Making this connection to *The Warlord's Puzzle* was a perfect way to end the lesson!

	3 smallest triangles	5 small pieces	All 7 pieces
Square	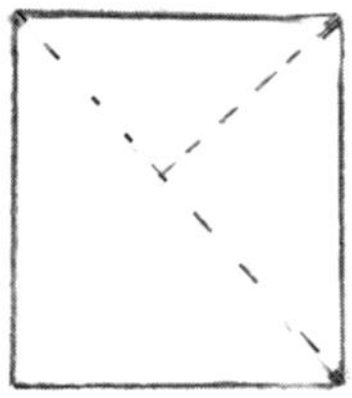		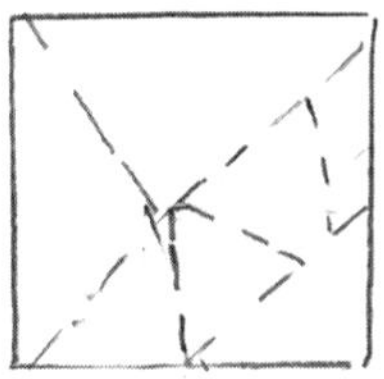
Triangle	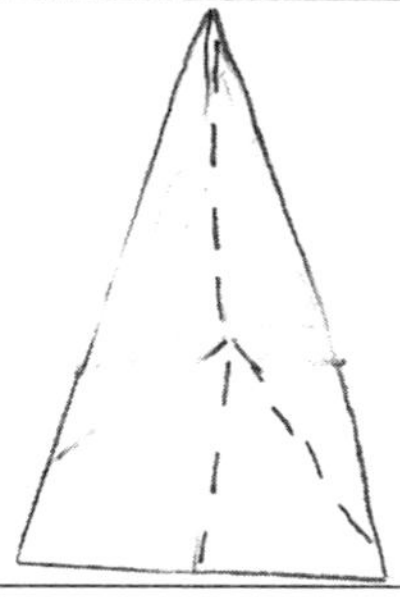		
Rectangle			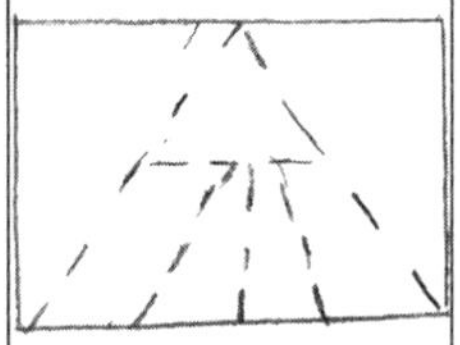
Parallelogram	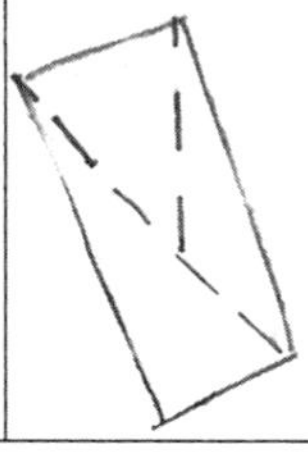		

Figure 22–2: Enrique found six different solutions using the tangrams.

Figure 22–3: Although Rain made several different shapes using her tangrams, it was difficult for her to record them on paper.

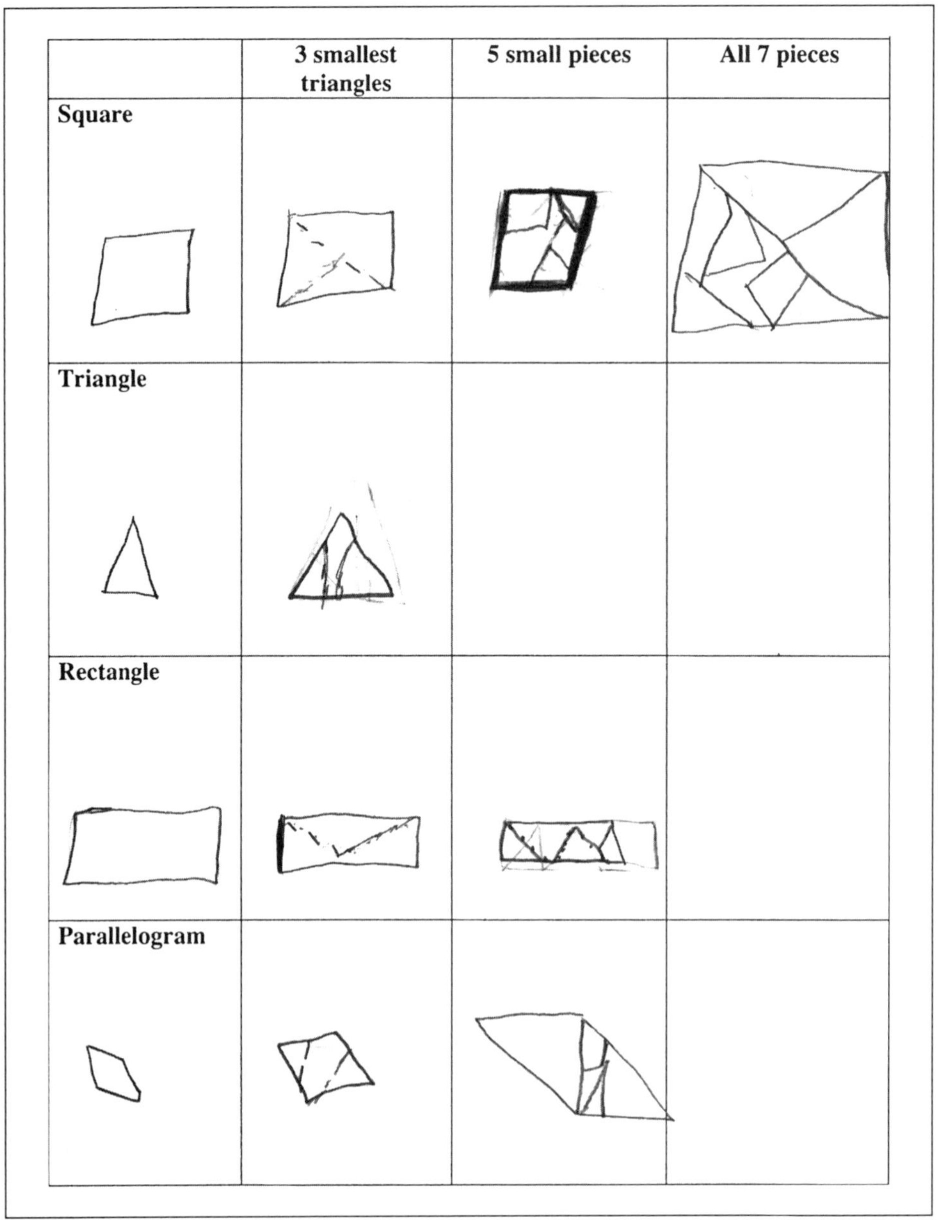

	3 smallest triangles	5 small pieces	All 7 pieces
Square			
Triangle			
Rectangle			
Parallelogram			

Math and Literature, Grades 4–6

Blackline Masters

Roll Two Dice Record Sheet
Letter Frequency Record Sheet
Tangram Instructions
Tangram Record Sheet

Roll Two Dice Record Sheet

2	3	4	5	6	7	8	9	10	11	12

Finish Line

Letter Frequency Record Sheet

a
b
c
d
e
f
g
h
i
j
k
l
m
n
o
p
q
r
s
t
u
v
w
x
y
z

Tangram Instructions

Fold the square in half. Cut.

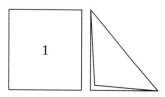

Take 1 triangle. Fold in half. Cut.

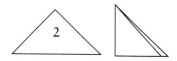

Take the other triangle. Make 2 folds, first in half, then the top corner down. Cut.

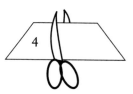

Cut the trapezoid in half.

Fold 1 trapezoid to make a square and a triangle. Cut.

Fold the last trapezoid to make a parallelogram and a triangle. Cut.

From *Math and Literature, Grades 4–6* by Rusty Bresser. © 2004 Math Solutions Publications.

Tangram Record Sheet

	3 Smallest Triangles	5 Small Pieces	All 7 Pieces
Square			
Triangle			
Rectangle			
Parallelogram			

From *Math and Literature, Grades 4–6* by Rusty Bresser. © 2004 Math Solutions Publications.

References

Anno, Mitsumasa. 1999. *Anno's Magic Seeds*. New York: Puffin.

Barry, David. 1994. *The Rajah's Rice: A Mathematical Folktale from India*. Illus. Donna Perrone. New York: W. H. Freeman.

Birch, David. 1993. *The King's Chessboard*. Illus. Devis Grebu. New York: Scott Foresman.

Briggs, Raymond. 1997. *Jim and the Beanstalk*. New York: Puffin.

Burns, Marilyn. 1990. *The $1.00 Word Riddle Book*. Illus. Martha Weston. Sausalito, CA: Math Solutions Publications.

Clement, Rod. 1994. *Counting on Frank*. Boston: Houghton Mifflin.

Dahl, Roald. 2002. *Esio Trot*. Illus. Quentin Blake. New York: Puffin.

Dee, Ruby. 1990. *Two Ways to Count to Ten: A Liberian Folktale*. Illus. Susan Meddaugh. New York: Henry Holt.

Ernst, Lisa Campbell. 1992. *Sam Johnson and the Blue Ribbon Quilt*. New York: HarperTrophy.

Frasier, Debra. 1991. *On the Day You Were Born*. New York: Harcourt.

Giganti, Paul Jr. 1999. *Each Orange Had 8 Slices: A Counting Book*. Illus. Donald Crews. New York: HarperTrophy.

Hopkins, Lee Bennett. 2001. *Marvelous Math: A Book of Poems*. Illus. Karen Barbour. New York: Aladdin.

McKissack, Patricia C. 1996. *A Million Fish . . . More or Less*. Illus. Dena Schutzer. New York: Dragonfly.

Meddaugh, Susan. 1998. *Martha Blah Blah*. Reprint. New York: Houghton Mifflin.

Pilegard, Virginia Walton. 2000. *The Warlord's Puzzle*. Illus. Nicolas Debon. Gretna, LA: Pelican.

Pinczes, Elinor J. 2002. *A Remainder of One*. Illus. Bonnie MacKain. New York: Houghton Mifflin.

Pittman, Helena Clare. 1996. *A Grain of Rice*. Reprint. New York: Bantam Doubleday Dell Books for Young Readers.

Ross, Katherine Sheldrick. 1993. *Circles: Fun Ideas for Getting A-Round in Math*. Illus. Bill Slavin. Reading, MA: Addison-Wesley.

Schwartz, Amy. 1991. *Annabelle Swift, Kindergartner*. Reprint. New York: Orchard.

Scieszka, Jon, and Lane Smith. 1995. *Math Curse*. New York: Viking Children's.

Shannon, George. 2000. *Stories to Solve: Folktales from Around the World*. Illus. Peter Sís. New York: HarperCollins.

Tahan, Malba. 1993. *The Man Who Counted: A Collection of Mathematical Adventures*. Trans. Leslie Clark and Alastair Reid. Illus. Patricia Reid Baquero. New York: W. W. Norton.

Thompson, Lauren. 2001. *One Riddle, One Answer*. Illus. Linda S. Wingerter. New York: Scholastic.

Tompert, Ann. 1997. *Grandfather Tang's Story*. Reprint. Illus. Robert Andrew Parker. New York: Dragonfly.

Van Allsburg, Chris. 1981. *Jumanji*. New York: Houghton Mifflin.

Wells, Robert E. 1993. *Is a Blue Whale the Biggest Thing There Is?* Morton Grone, IL: Albert Whitman.

Index